# Supervision of Art Psychotherapy

*Supervision of Art Psychotherapy* will be an inspiration for advanced practitioners and students in training. It is the first book to formulate a unique theoretical base to current practice in art psychotherapy supervision. A central theme is the nature of the image in supervision, defining its difference from other forms of supervision in the mental health professions. Clinical practice is brought to life through vivid vignettes from diverse settings with a variety of client groups.

- Part I establishes a theoretical base, introducing innovations in practice and addressing complex clinical issues in child and adult work. Topics include the narrative of imagery in supervision, enchantment, ambivalence, a topographical approach, engagement in supervision, and working with the network in art psychotherapy with children.
- Part II focuses on supervision in groups addressing training, difference and peer group image consultation, as well as supervision of experienced practitioners.
- Part III explores theory related to purposes and challenges in supervision and research.

A vital contribution to the literature in the context of continuing professional development, this volume establishes the image as central in the supervision of art psychotherapists. It brings the experience of the artist in the psychotherapist into the frame, provoking questions about the meaning of images and image making in supervision.

**Joy Schaverien** is a Jungian Analyst in private practice, Visiting Professor in Art Psychotherapy at the University of Sheffield, a Professional Member of the Society of Analytical Psychology in London, and a Training Therapist and Supervisor for the British Association of Psychotherapists.

**Caroline Case** is an Analytical Art Therapist working in private practice with children and adults. She is also a Child and Adolescent Psychotherapist working in a child and family mental health service in the NHS in Bristol.

# Supervision in the Arts Therapies
## Series Editor: Joy Schaverien

'This splendid series breaks new ground in its depth, breadth and scope, guided by Joy Schaverien's recognition that the time is right for a comprehensive, multi-faceted study of supervision in the arts psychotherapies. With each volume, the reader is invited to imagine, explore, and reflect on the expressive qualities of a particular art form in clinical supervision, turning special attention to art, music, dance, drama, and sandplay through contributions by leading experts from different parts of the world. These five volumes will make a lasting contribution as essential reading for supervisors and supervisees across the psychotherapies. The series also contributes towards a deeper understanding of the mentor–student relationship and the healing power of the arts.'

**Joan Chodorow, Jungian Analyst and former President of the American Dance Therapy Association**

'This new series of *Supervision in the Arts Therapies* is both timely and necessary. Now that all the arts therapies are established as state registered professions in their own right, there is a lack of resources that can support both the more advanced practitioner and the student. The writers of these individual titles are leaders in their respective fields both as researchers and practitioners. These publications make very important and innovative steps, and should be read by everyone in related fields of work.'

**Dr Sue Jennings, Consultant Dramatherapist and Supervisor**

'Each volume will not only communicate across the arts therapies but also to colleagues in other psychotherapies and health professions, to our mutual benefit.'

**Diane Waller, Professor of Art Psychotherapy, Goldsmiths College University of London, President of the British Association of Art Therapists**

This innovative series comprises five edited volumes, each focusing on one of the arts therapies – art, music, drama, dance or sandplay – and reflects on the dynamic nature of the presentation of that art form in supervision. The series reveals similarities and differences encountered in the theory and practice of supervision in each modality and within a range of contexts, and with diverse client groups.

*Supervision in the Arts Therapies* makes a timely contribution to the literature and will be essential reading for experienced practitioners and students of the arts therapies, as well as psychotherapists and other professionals engaged in supervision.

*Titles in the series*

**Supervision of Art Psychotherapy**
*Joy Schaverien and Caroline Case*

**Supervision of Music Therapy**
*Helen Odell Miller and Eleanor Richards*

**Supervision of Dramatherapy**
*Phil Jones and Ditty Dokter*

**Supervision of Dance Movement Therapy**
*Helen Payne*

**Supervision of Sandplay Therapy**
*Harriet Friedman and Rie Rogers Mitchell*

# Supervision of Art Psychotherapy

## A theoretical and practical handbook

Edited by Joy Schaverien and
Caroline Case

Routledge
Taylor & Francis Group

LONDON AND NEW YORK

First published 2007
by Routledge
27 Church Road, Hove, East Sussex BN3 2FA

Simultaneously published in the USA and Canada
by Routledge
270 Madison Avenue, New York, NY 10016

*Routledge is an imprint of the Taylor & Francis Group, an informa business*

Typeset in Times by Garfield Morgan, Swansea, West Glamorgan
Printed and bound in Great Britain by TJ International Ltd, Padstow, Cornwall
Paperback cover design by Sandra Heath
Paperback cover images by Peter Wilson from the 'Decoy' series of
woodcuts, 1994, 33×30 cm

This publication has been produced with paper manufactured to strict
environmental standards and with pulp derived from sustainable forests.

*British Library Cataloguing in Publication Data*
A catalogue record for this book is available from the British Library

*Library of Congress Cataloging-in-Publication Data*
Supervision in art psychotherapy / edited by Joy Schaverien and
Caroline Case.
        p. ; cm. – (Supervision in the arts therapies)
    Includes bibliographical references and index.
    ISBN-13: 978-0-415-40960-5 (hbk.)
    ISBN-10: 0-415-40960-8 (hbk.)
    ISBN-13: 978-0-415-40961-2 (pbk.)
    ISBN-10: 0-415-40961-6 (pbk.)
    1. Art therapy—Study and teaching—Supervision. 2. Art therapists—
Training of. I. Schaverien, Joy, date II. Case, Caroline, 1948– III. Series.
    [DNLM: 1. Art Therapy—organization & administration. 2.
Psychotherapy—organization & administration. WM 450.5.A8 S959 2007]
    RC489.A7S87 2007
    616.89'1656—dc22
                                                          2006039173

ISBN: 978-0-415-40960-5 (hbk)
ISBN: 978-0-415-40961-2 (pbk)

# Contents

# Contributors

**Chris Brown** is an art therapist working in Adult Mental Health in the NHS. He was formerly a part time lecturer at the University of Hertfordshire on the MA Art Therapy and now teaches on the MA Art Psychotherapy at Goldsmiths College, University of London. He is also a supervisor in private practice and a member of the Tavistock Society of Psychotherapists and Allied Professionals.

**Caroline Case** is an analytical art therapist working in private practice with children and adults. She is also a child and adolescent psychotherapist (SIHR) working in a Child and Family Mental Health Service in the NHS in Bristol. She supervises art psychotherapists and other therapists working with children and adults. She has published widely on art psychotherapy, including *Working with Children in Art Therapy* (Routledge, 1990), *The Handbook of Art Therapy* (Routledge, 1992, 2nd Edition 2006) and *Art Therapy with Children: From infancy to adolescence* (Routledge, forthcoming 2007), all with Tessa Dalley, and *Imagining Animals: Art, Psychotherapy and Primitive States of Mind* (Routledge, 2005).

**Tessa Dalley** is an experienced art therapist who works in private practice and as a clinical supervisor. She is also a child and adolescent psychotherapist, working in an inpatient adolescent unit and in the Parent–Infant Project at the Anna Freud Centre. She has published a number of books on art therapy and is currently editor of the *International Journal of Art Therapy: Inscape*.

**Barrie Damarell** attended Dartington College of Arts where he became interested in sculpture. He trained as an art psychotherapist at St Albans in 1983/4. He has since worked almost exclusively with people with learning disabilities who experience additional mental health difficulties. He took the Advanced Diploma in Art Psychotherapy, and later a Masters degree in Art Psychotherapy, at Goldsmiths College, University of London. Barrie is currently an editorial board member and book review editor of the *International Journal of Art Therapy: Inscape*. He is

currently registered as a research student at Goldsmiths College exploring the significance of 'place' and 'space' on the development of the
learning disabled person's sense of self and the expression of these factors
in the studio environment and art forms made within. He is the professional lead for the arts therapies for Plymouth Teaching Primary Care
Trust, where he also manages an arts psychotherapy team in the
Learning Disability Partnership.

**Andrea Gilroy PhD** is Reader in Art Psychotherapy at Goldsmiths College,
University of London, where she teaches across a range of qualifying and
post-qualifying programmes and supervises MRes, MPhil and PhD
students. She is also involved in art therapy research and research
supervision at the University of Western Sydney, NSW, Australia. Her
publications include: *Pictures at an Exhibition: Selected Essays on Art &
Art Therapy* (Routledge, 1989) with Tessa Dalley; *Art Therapy: A Hand-
book* (Open University Press, 1992) with Diane Waller; *Art & Music:
Therapy & Research* (Routledge, 1995) with Colin Lee; *The Changing
Shape of Art Therapy: New Developments in Theory & Practice* (Jessica
Kingsley, 2000) with Gerry McNeilly; and *Art Therapy, Research and
Evidence-Based Practice* (Sage Publications, 2006).

**David Henley** is a nationally known art therapist in the USA whose
speciality is children with early onset bipolar disorder, attention deficit
disorder and the autistic spectrum disorder, particularly Asperger's
syndrome. He is Professor of Art and Art Therapy at Long Island
University at the C.W. Post Campus in Brookville, New York, where he
is a noted art critic and teaches both clinical and studio coursework. Dr
Henley is an author with scores of research publications, including his
latest book *Clayworks in Art Therapy* (Jessica Kingsley, 1999). A long-
time practicing artist, he works in poetics, graphite, clay, mixed media
and photography

**Katherine Killick** qualified as an art therapist in 1978. She worked at Hill
End Hospital in St Albans for over 15 years, where her interest in
working with regressed states of mind in adults developed. She went on
to train as an analyst with the Society of Analytical Psychology, of which
she is a Professional Member. She works in private practice near Milton
Keynes and teaches on the training programmes offered by the Society
of Analytical Psychology and the British Association of Psychotherapists. She has published a number of papers and is co-editor with Joy
Schaverien of the book *Art, Psychotherapy and Psychosis* (Routledge).

**Riitta Laine** is a Finnish art therapist. She took her diploma in Art Therapy
in 1982 at the University of Hertfordshire, England and completed it
according to the Finnish requirements in 1995. In 2005 she took a
diploma in Art Therapy Supervision and Teacher's Training Programme.

She was employed as a full time art therapist in an acute psychiatric hospital in Helsinki from 1982 to 1990 and since 1990 she has been a private practitioner and supervisor in Helsinki. She has held numerous courses and seminars in art therapy. In 1991 and 1998 she has been the chairperson of the Finnish Association for Art Therapists. She has also published some articles on art therapy. In her free time she paints.

**Julia Meyerowitz-Katz** was born in South Africa where she obtained a degree in fine art. After several years of teaching art she moved to the UK where she trained as an art therapist and worked in a range of settings, including the NHS, private practice and as a lecturer on the MA Art Therapy at the University of Hertfordshire. She currently lives in Sydney, Australia and is working as a supervisor and art therapist with adults and children in private practice and as a visiting tutor on the MA Art Therapy at the University of Western Sydney. She is currently on the editorial board of the *International Journal of Art Therapy: Inscape*. She is training to be a Jungian analyst with ANZSJA. She continues her involvement in her own art making as a potter.

**Arthur Robbins Ed.D** is: Professor of Creative Arts Therapy, Pratt Institute, Brooklyn, New York; Founding Director and Faculty of the Institute for Expressive Analysis; Faculty of the National Psychological Association for Psychoanalysis, author of six books and numerous articles; Workshop Leader and Keynote Speaker in numerous conferences internationally and nationally. Currently Dr Robbins conducts a private practice with specialisations in individual and group supervision. His text *Between Therapists: The Processing of Transference and Counter-transference* has laid the basis for his current practice in multi-layered dynamic supervision. He has been in practice for 54 years and is a pioneer in the Art Therapy Movement. He is a registered art therapist and an Honorary Life Member of the American Art Therapy Association.

**Julia Ryde** is an art therapist and Jungian analyst working in private practice with adults. She works as a part time lecturer at the University of Hertfordshire on the MA Art Therapy.

**Joy Schaverien PhD** is a Jungian analyst in private practice, Visiting Professor in Art Psychotherapy at the University of Sheffield and the Northern Programme for Art Psychotherapy (Leeds Metropolitan University). She is a Professional Member of the Society of Analytical Psychology in London and a Training Therapist and Supervisor for the British Association of Psychotherapists. She has supervised in the UK, Sweden, Denmark and Russia and is an honorary member of the Finnish Art Therapy Association. Formerly co-coordinator (with Penny Pickles) of the IAAP supervision programme in Moscow, her books include: *The Revealing Image: Analytical Art Psychotherapy in Theory and Practice*

(Routledge, 1991 and Jessica Kingsley, 1999), *Desire and the Female Therapist: Engendered Gazes in Psychotherapy and Art Therapy* (Routledge, 1995) and *The Dying Patient in Psychotherapy* (Palgrave, 2002). She is editor of *Art, Psychotherapy and Psychosis* (with Katherine Killick) and *Gender, Countertransference and the Erotic Transference* (Routledge, 2006).

**Sally Skaife** is lecturer and programme leader of the MA Art Psychotherapy at Goldsmiths College, University of London, where she has been employed since 1986. She has worked as an art therapist since 1975 in adult mental health and currently runs an art therapy group at the Medical Foundation for Victims of Torture. She is dually qualified as art therapist and group analytic psychotherapist, is past chairperson of the British Association of Art Therapists and was co-editor of *Inscape*, the journal of the British Association of Art Therapists, from 1984 to 2004. She is currently working towards a PhD on the subject of theoretical issues in group art psychotherapy. She published an edited book with Val Huet, *Art Psychotherapy Groups: Between Pictures and Words* (Routledge, 1998), and has numerous chapters in books and journal articles.

**Chris Wood PhD** works as the Director and Team Leader for the Northern Programme for Art Psychotherapy. This is in Sheffield and it provides training and research based upon the partnership between Sheffield Care Trust and Leeds Metropolitan University. She is happy to be in a position to continue to combine work in higher education with therapeutic practice in the public sector. She is interested in the uses of contemporary art and popular culture, in the relationship between mental health and politics and in the many ways in which people with long-term mental health problems manage to live well.

# Preface to the series

*Supervision of Art Psychotherapy* is the first book in the five-volume series *Supervision in the Arts Therapies*. The series was conceived after several invitations were received to contribute to courses on supervision in the different arts therapies. Collaboration with colleagues from Music, Drama, Dance Movement and Sandplay therapies has led into discussion about the similarities and differences between the roles of the different arts media in therapy and supervision. The evidence was that there was a developing body of theory in the field of supervision in the arts therapies but relatively little literature on the topic. It seemed that, despite the rapidly increasing publications on supervision in analytical psychology, psychotherapy, psychoanalysis and counselling, there was very little literature on supervision in any of the arts therapies. So it was that the idea of a series of books on *Supervision in the Arts Therapies* was conceived and, with the encouragement of Joanne Forshaw at Routledge, the series came into being.

It is hoped that this volume, along with its companion volumes in the other arts therapies, will be of interest to all arts therapists and integrative arts therapists, and those working in the fields of art, music, dance movement and drama therapy as well as sandplay therapy. However, the anticipated audience includes Jungian analysts, psychotherapists, psychoanalysts and counsellors, who often supervise arts therapists. It is also addressed to all whose clients apply the arts in psychotherapy.

**Joy Schaverien**
*September 2006*

# Preface to this book

A book on Supervision of Art Psychotherapy with chapters by international colleagues with many years of experience between them seemed a timely contribution to the literature in this expanding field.

The collaboration of the editors of this book goes back a long way. Since the early 1980s we (Caroline Case and Joy Schaverien) have worked together in a number of different settings, teaching and supervising art psychotherapists, advanced practitioners and students in Britain and abroad. We met at St Albans Art College (now the University of Hertfordshire) in 1982 when we were both teaching art therapists in training. Caroline had originally trained as a teacher, specialising in sculpture and dance, and then became an art therapist working in schools and social services. Joy first trained in Fine Art at the Slade, specialising in painting and printmaking, and then became an art therapist working mainly in adult mental health. Later we trained as a Child Psychotherapist and Jungian Analyst respectively and so have dual qualifications; as well as being members of the British Association of Art Therapists, we are registered with the British Psychoanalytic Council. Our interest in supervision goes back to the 1970s when we began supervising art therapists on placement (C.C. participated in a course of seminars for supervisors of group work at the Institute of Group Analysis in 1986). We have been involved in supervision in numerous situations, including working together in peer supervision. Those we have supervised over the years include professionals from many of the mental health professions.

Awareness of the need for this book arose out of the fact that we have frequently been asked to speak on the topic of supervision for regional groups of the British Association of Art Therapists and training courses in Britain and Scandinavia. In addition there were also invitations from Art Therapy training courses[1,2], Drama Therapy[3] and Music Therapy[4]. These occasions led to dialogue with our colleagues and the realisation that there is a developing body of theory that is very particular to the application of supervision in the arts therapies. It is hoped that this book will reflect these developments and encourage art therapists to have confidence in the practice of supervision.

**Joy Schaverien and Caroline Case**
*September 2006*

## Notes

1 Chris Wood at the University of Sheffield invited both editors of this book to contribute to a supervision course in September 1999 in Bristol.
2 Chris Wood invited C.C. to contribute to a supervision course for art psychotherapists working in CAHMS in 2005 under the auspices of the Northern Programme for Art Psychotherapy based in Sheffield.
3 The training courses on Supervision, initiated by Marina Jenkyns, were among the first of their kind for arts therapists and she invited J.S. to contribute in 1997 and 1998.
4 Helen Odell Miller asked J.S. to contribute to the Clinical Supervisor's course for the MA in the Department of Music Therapy at Anglia Polytechnic University in 2003.

# Acknowledgements

We would like to express our gratitude to our colleagues, supervisors and supervisees. The identities of those who have given us permission to discuss vignettes from supervision practice are concealed, for reasons of confidentiality, but their contribution and that of their clients and patients are central. We are indebted to them for all that we have learned in the collaborative venture that is supervision. As ever, we acknowledge the generous support of our families, especially Peter, David and Isobel. Their encouragement and understanding made the work possible.

# Introduction

*Joy Schaverien*

The focus of this book is, as its title suggests, *Supervision of Art Psychotherapy*. It is the first volume in the series *Supervision in the Arts Therapies* and we hope that, along with its companion volumes in the other arts therapies, it will appeal to a wide and professionally diverse readership. It is written for experienced practitioners and those beginning to supervise, as well as students entering supervision for the first time.

Primarily intended for art therapists and art psychotherapists, we are confident that this book will be of interest to those working in the allied fields of art, music, dance movement and drama therapy, as well as sandplay therapy. However the anticipated audience is wider than this, including analytical psychologists, psychotherapists and counsellors. This is because for many Jungian analysts imagery and art play a central role in their clinical practice. Jung himself applied the arts in analysis and he inspired many of the early art therapists (see Baynes 1940; Champernowne 1969, 1971; Stevens 1986). Moreover, psychotherapists and counsellors sometimes have clients who spontaneously use art as a means of expression. These colleagues may choose an art psychotherapist supervisor for that case. This exchange has a long history, as in the early days of the profession supervision from a practising art therapist was not always possible; they were relatively few and their geographical spread was often limited. Therefore art therapists often turned to psychotherapists, analytical psychologists and colleagues from other professions for supervision. This is less often the case now as, except in remote areas, the numbers of members of the profession have increased. Even so some art therapists choose to have supervision from other professionals. We anticipate that these supervisors too will be interested in this book.

Supervision is a way of monitoring and reflecting on clinical practice through consultation with a more experienced member of the profession. However peer supervision, which is consulting a colleague at a similar level of qualification and expertise for supervision of each other's work, is a common practice for experienced practitioners. Supervision usually takes place weekly or sometimes fortnightly and is a requirement of the registration of Continuing Professional Development in the psychotherapy professions in the UK. Trainings in supervision are now widely available whereas many of the first supervisors had to learn to supervise whilst engaged in the process. As the practice comes of age, it seems important to establish that what began as an intuitive mentoring by a more experienced colleague of one with less experience has developed into a practice with a developing body of theory. This book is intended to elucidate that theory and so to make a specific contribution to the literature in this rapidly expanding field.

The literature on supervision in analytical psychology, psychoanalysis, psychotherapy and counselling has increased dramatically in the last few years. Langs (1979, 1994) and Searles (1955, 1962) were early exponents of the need for psychoanalytic supervision. Certainly when we started supervising these were important writers for us both as supervisees and also as supervisors. We have decided to review the literature on art psychotherapy supervision in depth (see Chapter 1) but first we acknowledge a number of the titles on supervision in analytical psychology, psychotherapy and counselling. We do not plan to review this literature in depth but rather will give a brief overview of the field. The interested reader is referred to the introduction to Wiener, Mizen and Duckham (2003) for a detailed review of the literature on supervision in general.

In terms of art therapy two books give detailed discussion of supervision in art psychotherapy (Dalley *et al.* 1993; Malchiodi and Riley 1996) and both are reviewed in Chapter 1. In analytical psychology Kugler's (1995) collection of essays by established analytical psychologists (Jungian analysts) from a variety of theoretical fields gives an excellent overview of the theory of supervision in that field at that time. Shipton (1997) invited a number of art therapists to contribute to *Supervision Today: The Psychoanalytic Legacy in Supervision of Counselling and Psychotherapy – Making a Place to Think* (1997). Martindale *et al.* (1997) contains chapters by a number of psychoanalysts and of particular interest is Sedlak's chapter on working with therapists who have not had a full psychoanalytic training (see Dalley in this volume, Chapter 4). Other edited books include Driver and Martin's *Supervising Psychotherapy* and *Supervision and the Analytic Attitude* (2002, 2005), Clarkson's *Supervision* (1998), Lawton and Feltham's *Taking Supervision Forward* (2000) and Hawkins and Shohet's *Supervision in the Helping Professions* (2000).

As well as these books there are a number of articles, published in psychoanalytic and analytical psychology journals, that merit mention so that the readers can pursue these in future. Gee (1996) writes about the use of tape recordings for supervision. This practice is not widely used and yet in the past it has been a very helpful way of monitoring the supervision of psychotherapists in training. Berman (2000) discusses an intersubjective approach, which focuses on countertransference issues. He describes supervision as a 'matrix of object relations of at least three persons' each bringing their subjective reality to the situation (Berman 2000: 276). Norman and Salomonsson (2005) discuss peer group supervision and particularly draw attention to the influence of group dynamics when presenting case material in a group. Recently a qualitative investigation on countertransference in supervision was published in the *International Journal of Psychoanalysis* (Zaslavsky *et al.* 2005). Astor (2000) writes of countertransference and the use of empathy in supervision. One of the most creative views of supervision is the psychoanalytic contribution of Ogden (2005), who gives four vignettes from supervision to illustrate what he calls the experience of 'dreaming the patient'. This is a vivid image for the process of engaging in supervision. He describes as a fiction the recreation in supervision of the analyst's experience of the analysand, including conscious and unconscious impressions (Ogden 2005: 1267). He writes that: 'In the act of presenting a case in supervision, the supervisee turns facts into fictions' (Ogden 2005: 1267–1268). He proposes that it is only through this process that the patient becomes real. This is a creative approach in which both supervisor and supervisee become immersed in an imaginative approach in supervision (this is quoted by Schaverien in Chapter 3 and Killick in Chapter 12).

In *Supervising and Being Supervised* (Wiener *et al.* 2003) analytical psychologists address issues faced in supervising in different settings as well as problems encountered in training and supervising analytical colleagues or inexperienced counsellors. The problems of management are addressed in detail and Gee (2003) discusses boundaries and what, following Jung, he calls unconscious identity. Supervising the erotic transference is a sensitive issue discussed by Schaverien (2003, 2006). This topic is relevant to the supervision of art psychotherapy but rather than repeat that already published chapter we decided to publish the references for the interested reader. McGlashan's discussion of supervision in terms of the individuation of the supervisor is particularly helpful. He applies different Greek myths to illustrate different types of supervisor or different stages in supervision. We summarise these below because he considers some of the personal challenges for the supervisor to confront (McGlashan 2003: 21–22):

- There is the supervisor who is ambivalent about his authority, does not know how to own it and so is anxious, falsely modest and self-effacing.
- 'The envious supervisor who is intensely insecure about his own competence and feels threatened by the potential of his students. As a result he becomes destructively critical and disparaging of their efforts. . . .'
- The Procrustean supervisor is rigid and tries to fit his supervisees into the same mould.
- The supervisor who is 'parentally possessive and protective towards his supervisees . . . who wins vicarious triumphs through their successes'.

- The supervisor who clothes themselves in 'divine and mysterious authority, which cannot be questioned or challenged, and to protect that authority they can avoid giving direction when it is called for'.

This is a précis of McGlashan, included because it is helpful in bringing to consciousness potentially unconscious responses in the supervisor. In the end the individuating supervisor becomes conscious of these elements in him or herself and this 'opens the door to reflection, to extension of consciousness, to increasing freedom of choice and to individuation' (McGlashan 2003: 33).

The papers and books discussed reveal many situations that are common in art psychotherapy supervision as well. However the use of artwork and imagery adds another dimension. Many of the contributors to this book openly discuss challenges in the process of supervision. It becomes clear that there is no ideal supervision and that the things that apparently go wrong in supervision are just those situations from which supervisor and supervisee learn the most. Clearly when art objects feature as an element in both clinical and supervisory settings they will influence the interactions, sometimes in profound ways. Therefore the theories discussed above are helpful but are extended and developed in relation to the application of the art form. Therefore in this introduction and the literature review that follows, we will draw attention to existing debates and indicate some of the new perspectives specific to the practice of art psychotherapy supervision that will be developed in the chapters that follow.

## Who do we supervise?

Before discussing the contents of the book the issue of whom we supervise is addressed. Whereas many counsellors and psychotherapists work in private practice, art psychotherapists are employed in many diverse settings and their requirements from supervision inevitably differ accordingly. As a profession, recognised by the Health Professions Council, art therapists in Britain commonly work in the state sector. Thus, many are employed by the National Health Service or by Social Services and increasingly in education. They work in hospitals, health centres, community mental health teams with adults or children, child and family units, prisons, young offenders institutions, special schools, palliative care, facilities for the elderly mentally ill and mother and child speciality units. Others are employed by charities and some work in the private sector in hospitals or special schools. Some art therapists work in private practice and some of these have dual qualifications as counsellors, psychotherapists and analysts, as well as art therapists.

Thus, the prospective supervisor might be approached for supervision by art psychotherapists working in any of these settings. If the supervisee's client group is not the primary experience of the supervisor it is important for the supervisor to be flexible and prepared to learn about the supervisee's work setting and to understand what is required in this particular supervision. Respect for what the supervisee knows and affirmation and encouragement are important in supervision alongside the courage to challenge. Most of all, this is a situation in which all parties benefit: the therapist learns from the patient, the therapist learns from the supervisor and the supervisor of course learns from both. Casement (1985, 1990) has made very clear how much learning is to be gained from each other and from mistakes in psychotherapy.

The diversity of employment settings means that there are frequently institutional issues presented before the clinical work can be approached. Whilst anxieties generated by these have to be addressed, this may also be a defence against exposing clinical work for attention. The supervisor can feel de-skilled or unused if the focus is constantly on the institution and staff relations. Sometimes anxiety is deflected onto the institution and so, although it is important to reflect on the institutional problems the practitioner is encountering, it is essential that the client does not get lost in the institutional dynamics. Wiener (2007) gives a very honest and relevant account of her experience of some of the challenges of supervising clinicians working in institutional settings.

## The book

This book grew out of our long collaboration as colleagues, teaching and discussing our clinical work in peer supervision. When this book began to take shape we decided to invite colleagues from a variety of different backgrounds, working in diverse settings, to contribute a chapter on their own interest in supervision. Therefore the chapters in this book represent the wide diversity of the expertise and interests of the contributors. As a result, we hope the book reflects the current practice of supervision in the profession. The contributors are art psychotherapists with many years' experience of supervising in clinical, education and research settings. Some have dual qualifications as psychotherapists or analytical psychologists. Many have international reputations in specific areas of practice. Their theoretical positions may differ but the linking thread, shared by all, is a profound interest in the influence of imagery and artwork in supervision. All the contributors offer insights developed from long years involved with training art therapists as well as working in clinical practice. The book begins with a literature review (Chapter 1) and is then divided into three parts: Chapters 2–6, 7–10 and 11–13.

In Chapter 1 the literature on art therapy supervision is reviewed. The individual contributions discussed reveal the emergence of a developing set of theories, providing a background and context for the theoretical innovations that will be discussed in the chapters that follow.

In Chapter 2 Barrie Damarell gives a vivid and creative account of supervising art therapists working with learning difficulties. Drawn from his interest in sculpture he applies a 'topographical model' that he proposes is relevant to art psychotherapists practising in other fields. Discussing how we live in a three-dimensional world he challenges the convention in supervision of looking at art works flat on a table or the floor and suggests that much is to be gained from looking from a different position. This is demonstrated in vivid clinical examples.

In Chapter 3 Joy Schaverien proposes that countertransference could be understood as a form of unconscious enchantment, where the art psycho-therapist may become spellbound through the combination of client and picture. The frame of supervision is significant in restoring the symbolic attitude when, as a result of the impact of the transference, it becomes temporarily lost. The complexity of countertransferences in supervision is discussed in relation to the pictures presented. At times the pictures enchant, affecting both therapist and supervisor. Clinical examples demonstrate how this may be restored through supervision, which brings consciousness and so breaks the spell.

In Chapter 4 Tessa Dalley applies the metaphor of a jigsaw puzzle for supervision, proposing that there is an emerging picture to which all aspects of the supervision contribute. Focusing on a single case in supervision over six years, she traces the story of a 'looked after' child who was ten years old when the therapy began. As he develops and grows up the setting for therapy also changes and the supervision process tracks the therapist's responses to these changes. This is an unusual opportunity because the chapter focuses on the work of one supervising pair and so gives a sense of the changing process of long-term supervision.

In Chapter 5 David Henley discusses supervising art therapists working with children. He introduces a model for analysing cases in art therapy. This model focuses on 'assessment, intervention and outcome'. He gives three very vivid case illustrations of the use of this approach: one of a trainee, another a graduate intern and the third example is of himself as supervisee. (Like Case in Chapter 6 and Killick in Chapter 12, he uses his own experience as a supervisee to illustrate.) His discussion of these vignettes draws on the work of Lowenfeld, as well as Art Brut. His approach is inspired and influenced by the work of Edith Kramer in the USA, parti-cularly her idea of the art therapists intervening as a 'third hand' to enhance the aesthetic outcome of a piece of work, and Edward Adamson in the UK with his creation of the studio as an 'enabling space'.

In Chapter 6 Caroline Case focuses on the role of images in supervision and what she calls the 'below the surface narrative of supervision' that is the mental and felt images that are present in a session. She discusses her model of supervision and gives vivid clinical examples of the complexities of supervision as a supervisee and as a supervisor. A theme that is threaded throughout this chapter is that of idealisation. With vivid examples she takes us into discussion of the non-verbal aspects of the image presented in supervision and how imagery, whether depicted or described, gives a vital way into the work.

In Chapter 7 Riitta Laine 'contributes to the discourse on the role of images in the supervision of art therapists' through discussion of an experienced group of art psychotherapists engaged in a form of peer supervision that they call 'Image Consultation'. In 'image consultation' the response of the art therapist's peer group to viewing the client's images challenges the viewing habits and so helps to revitalise and deepen the therapist's relationship to the unconscious process in her client. She identifies some of the potential problems and benefits of the leaderless group. She draws on philosophical and aesthetic theory and evokes the meditative qualities of art therapy.

In Chapter 8 Sally Skaife describes a supervision group that took place in the context of art therapy training and in which difference became a significant issue. She explores issues of race and colour in the context of a group, which became extremely painful for all the participants. She sent a questionnaire to the participants: some were unable to respond, others had forgotten significant aspects of the group. Skaife proposes that the group became as if autistic and that this silence is a communication. She considers the paradox of silence as an emptiness that has materiality, and as an absence allows something to speak powerfully.

In Chapter 9 Arthur Robbins draws on his experience of clinical supervision and teaching to discuss supervision as an art form that takes place within a professional context. He proposes that it is not 'intellectual but a mind/body experience'. He suggests that supervision is not a suitable place to work out negative transferences, except in the case of resistances, where primitive states are being communicated. His example is a vivid one of gender issues, generated in a supervision group through discussion of sexual abuse.

In Chapter 10 Chris Brown, Julia Meyerowitz-Katz and Julia Ryde describe a student supervision group in which the student therapist's image-making fostered understanding of their clients. Drawing on the comments of the students from the group they argue that this places the aesthetic training of the art therapists centrally and enhances and deepens their clinical work. Vignettes from these supervision groups illustrate how they may become central in helping the students understand the emotional experiences of therapy and being a therapist. In common with Laine's 'image consultation groups' (Chapter 7), the therapists taking part in these groups were doing so in addition to being in individual clinical supervision.

In Chapter 11 Chris Wood writes of agency in clinical supervision and discusses why it is needed. She suggests that it sustains the capacity to think and 'not to be overwhelmed by the plight of our clients'. She develops an argument challenging some previous writing on supervision. She discusses why many British art therapists use a psychoanalytic perspective in their clinical practice in order to better understand unconscious elements of the therapeutic relationship. She usefully addresses the realities of working with poverty and deprivation in the public sector and the consequent danger of erosion of the therapist's confidence, and how this can be renewed and supported through good clinical supervision.

In Chapter 12 Katherine Killick writes about ambivalence sometimes encountered as a defence against 'the creative regression' required in order to engage in supervision. The problems she identifies relate to projected idealisation of the supervisor (see Case in Chapter 6, who also discusses idealisation). She suggests that the state to which she refers reflects some of the primitive despair that is active in the therapy and is replayed in the supervision, preventing a genuine form of relatedness. Giving an example from her own experience, she demonstrates how difficult it is to engage in supervision when the material of the therapy sessions is unthinkable and so projected into the therapist.

In Chapter 13 Andrea Gilroy writes about supervising art therapy research and discusses the importance of selecting the right supervisor. Based on a questionnaire sent to current and previous research students, she gives a sense of the importance of the supervisor's presence and understanding. Tellingly she addresses the impact on the student of the supervisor's interventions. This is of course something that is significant to consider in clinical supervision as well. This is a very lively chapter on a subject that has been little written about and will be of interest to all those supervising and those considering embarking on research.

In this introduction we have summarised the field in general and given an overview of the book. Regarding illustrations, we have realised that to ask the artist's/patient's permission to publish pictures from supervision is far more complex than to do so from therapy. It would be hard to justify such a disruption to therapy on ethical grounds. Therefore, apart from Chapters 5 and 6, pictures are described rather than shown. The chapter that follows offers a review of the literature on art therapy supervision.

## References

Astor, J. (2000) 'Some reflections on empathy and reciprocity in the use of counter-transference between supervisor and supervisee', *Journal of Analytical Psychology*, 45 (3): 367–383.

Baynes, H. G. (1940) *The Mythology of the Soul*, London: Routledge and Kegan Paul.

Berman, E. (2000) 'Psychoanalytic supervision: the intersubjective development', *International Journal of Psychoanalysis*, 81 (2): 273–290.

Casement, P. (1985) *On Learning from the Patient*, Hove: Brunner-Routledge.

Casement, P. (1990) *Further Learning from the Patient: The Analytic Space and Process*, London: Tavistock/Routledge.

Champernowne, I. (1969) 'Art therapy as an adjunct to psychotherapy', *Inscape, 1*: 1–10.

Champernowne, I. (1971) 'Art and therapy: an uneasy partnership', *Inscape, 3*: 1–14.

Clarkson, P. (1998) *Supervision: Psychoanalytic and Jungian Perspectives*, London: Whurr Publishers.

Dalley, T., Rifkind, G. and Terry, K. (1993) *Three Voices of Art Therapy: Image, Client, Therapists*, London: Routledge.

Driver, C. and Martin, E. (2002) *Supervising Psychotherapy: Psychoanalytic and Psychodynamic Perspectives*, London: Sage.

Driver, C. and Martin, E. (2005) *Supervision and the Analytic Attitude*, London: Whurr.

Gee, H. (1996) 'Developing insight through supervision: relating, then defining', *Journal of Analytical Psychology, 41* (4): 529–552.

Gee, H. (2003) 'Boundaries in supervision', in Wiener, J., Mizen, R. and Duckham, J. (eds), *Supervising and Being Supervised: A Practice in Search of Theory*, Basingstoke: Palgrave/Macmillan, pp. 151–166.

Hawkins, R. and Shohet, R. (2000) *Supervision in the Helping Professions*, Buckingham: Open University Press.

Kugler, P. (1995) *Jungian Perspectives on Clinical Supervision*, Einsiedeln, Switzerland: Daimon.

Langs, R. (1979) *The Supervisory Experience*, New York: Jason Aronson.

Langs, R. (1994) *Doing Supervision and Being Supervised*, London: Karnac Books.

Lawton, B. and Feltham, C. (2000) *Taking Supervision Forward: Enquiries and Trends in Counselling and Psychotherapy*, London: Sage.

Malchiodi, C. and Riley, S. (1996) *Handbook of Supervision and Related Issues*, Chicago, IL: Magnolia Street Publishers.

Martindale, B., Morner, M., Rodriguez, M. E. C. and Vidit, J.-P. (1997) *Supervision and its Vicissitudes*, London: Karnac Books.

McGlashan, R. (2003) 'The individuating supervisor', in J. Wiener, R. Mizen and J. Duckham (eds), *Supervising and Being Supervised*, Basingstoke: Palgrave/Macmillan, pp. 19–33.

Norman, J. and Salomonsson, B. (2005) 'Weaving thoughts: a method for presenting and commenting psychoanalytic case material in a peer group', *International Journal of Psychoanalysis, 86* (5): 1281–1298.

Ogden, T. (2005) 'On psychoanalytic supervision', *International Journal of Psychoanalysis, 86* (5): 1265–1280.

Schaverien, J. (2003) 'Supervising the erotic transference', in J. Wiener, R. Mizen and J. Duckham (eds), *Supervising and Being Supervised*, Basingstoke: Palgrave/Macmillan, pp. 167–184.

Schaverien, J. (2006) 'Supervising the erotic transference', in *Gender, Counter-transference and the Erotic Transference: Perspectives from Analytical Psychology and Psychoanalysis*, Hove: Routledge.

Searles, H. (1955) 'The informational value of the supervisor's emotional experiences', in *Collected Papers on Schizophrenia and Related Subjects*, London: Maresfield (1986 edition), pp. 157–176.

Searles, H. (1962) 'Problems of psychoanalytic supervision', in *Collected Papers on Schizophrenia and Related Subjects*, London: Maresfield (1986 edition), pp. 584–604.

Shipton, G. (ed.) (1997) *Supervision of Psychotherapy and Counselling*, Buckingham: Open University Press.

Stevens, A. (1986) *Withymead*, London: Coventure.

Wiener, J. (2007) 'The analyst's countertransference when supervising: friend or foe?', *Journal of Analytical Psychology*, 52 (1): 51–69.

Wiener, J., Mizen, R. and Duckham, J. (2003) *Supervising and Being Supervised: A Practice in Search of a Theory*, Basingstoke: Palgrave/Macmillan.

Zaslavsky, J., Tiellet Nunes, M. L. and Eizirik, C. L. (2005) 'Approaching countertransference in psychoanalytical supervision: a qualitative investigation', *International Journal of Psychoanalysis*, 86 (4): 1099–1132.

# Chapter 1

# Review of the literature on art therapy supervision

*Caroline Case*

There have been some significant articles published on supervision in art psychotherapy. As is well known, in the UK, artists practised in hospitals (as therapists) until the foundation of training programmes in the early 1970s. Art therapy then had to pioneer a place among the other clinical disciplines and gradually develop as a profession. Supervision was assimilated from social work practice, as well as psychology, and the emerging psychotherapies. There were two main reasons for this, firstly these were already available as models and, secondly, the pioneering status of the profession meant that students were supervised by many other disciplines on-site at their placements. Qualified art therapists simply were not in existence at the many varied placements that were becoming available. The richness of practice and the multitude of contexts in which art psychotherapists practice today would not have been possible without this pioneering generation who often had to explain art therapy to their supervisors and sometimes fit uncomfortably into the ways of thinking of other disciplines.

## 1970s and 1980s – placement supervision

The first articles regarding supervision emerged in the late 1970s and 1980s. The focus was on the student or trainee art therapist and their relationship with their placement supervisor. This is a very complex relationship as the student may work alongside the supervisor, observing or shadowing his or her practice. This was a relationship, that often progressed to that of colleagues. The supervisor was the interface between the student and the rest of the institution and was sometimes in the role of mentor, educator, co-therapist and assessor.

It is very difficult to address the uniqueness of the image in therapy when using a model of supervision from another discipline. Marion and Felix (1979) recognised this and illustrate their article with some vignettes of supervisor and student working alongside each other, noting how an intervention from the supervisor could be a practical one, or a verbal-emotional comprehension of a situation. They show how the student could be permitted to make mistakes and work towards their own solution. Sometimes supervisors may visit the student at another site to observe them working and this needs a sensitive presence, as it may be tempting for the supervisor to take over. It is a subtle dynamic to participate enough for all to feel relaxed with the supervisor's/assessor's presence.

## Envy and professional jealousy

Because art therapists are sometimes seen as privileged to work with images, they may encounter professional jealousy from other members of a therapeutic multi-disciplinary team. The envy or competitiveness may manifest over the art therapist's insistence on confidentiality and their non-disclosure of confidential issues. These and other aspects of the art therapist's role in the team, as well as management problems, have to be dealt with at times. The supervisee's envy of the supervisor often manifests itself in the supervisor's sense that the therapist 'knows it already'. This can produce feelings in the supervisor of having little or nothing to offer or being drawn into competition. It is helpful if the supervisor resists being drawn into competition and holds to the frame until the underlying anxiety of the supervisee can be expressed.

Marion and Felix (1979) begin to address this as well as the supervisor's awareness of their own envy of the student, who may be creative and innovative in one area, whilst needing a great deal of support in another. They suggest the need for a continuous dialogue with flexibility and cooperation, which may lead to mutual growth:

> The mentors we remember – those whose styles, attitudes and techniques we incorporated into our own work – are those who somehow made us feel like colleagues while we honed our own rough skills on their experience.
>
> (Marion and Felix 1979: 40)

Wilson, Riley and Wadeson (1984) explore the tasks for the supervision dyad at different phases of the placement. Wilson comments on the need for self-examination in the student, which must be separated from the self-examination of personal issues in therapy. She acknowledges that they can become entwined in clinical work. Supervision groups at college, running parallel to individual supervision on-site, allow students not to feel alone with what are usually shared concerns. In student supervision an assessment is being made of the students' capacity to learn from mistakes. Wilson highlights two common difficulties – the desire to be active and the difficulty of 'staying with', and the desire to know *the* meaning of a patient's artwork. This can lead to prescriptive interpretation rather than allowing the image to reveal its possible meanings through a slower reverie. Riley, discussing the middle phase of therapy, notes the parallel process between the student's casework and the supervisory relationship. Both student and the student's client may need to move out of a dependent position but may progress, stand still or regress at the same pace. The student needs to work with resistance and countertransference in therapy in order to grow and feel able to challenge the supervisor's interpretations:

> The gift of supervision is the permission for the trainee to hypothesize, experiment, and fantasise creative moves both with the therapeutic plan and the art expression.
>
> (Wilson, Riley and Wadeson 1984: 103)

The supervisory relationship often comes to an end when the placement ends and Wadeson explores this, pointing out how this therefore parallels the ending of client relationships. This is a testing time for the student and regression may take place as the re-working of old issues comes to the fore. The student may feel that no change has been made. There may have been a strong transference to the institution from both student and client. This phase of therapy needs much thought, preparation and holding in supervision. Wadeson comments on the huge emotional investment made by students in their training and how one's initial patients are 'important, meaningful and memorable'. The supervisor needs to hold the focus on the ending and explore, as fully as possible, the loss and separations involved and the students' move towards being qualified and the anxieties that this may arouse.

A well-illustrated article followed an experiment by Durkin, Perach, Ramseyer and Sontag (1989). As previous writers, they recognised that a whole rich area of images and art making could be ignored in the supervisory process with supervisors from other disciplines. They set up an experiment using art 'to understand further the dynamics of the supervisory relationship'. Wadeson (1984, 1987) had already suggested that images might be used to explore the transition to being qualified but, as far as is known, this is unique in exploring the *supervisory relationship* with art, rather than the therapist/client relationship. The paper traces two supervisory dyads that supplemented verbal supervision with two other modalities: journal writing and art making. Supervisor and supervisee therefore used artwork and journal writing to supplement verbal communication about their own relationship, exploring their thoughts and feelings about each other, as well as the whole placement experience. It was not prescribed as to how frequently the different modalities were used. The dyads proceeded slightly differently, however they had in common that both were in placement supervision and both dyads met formally once a week. They agreed to use journals and make artwork at home, as moved to do so, and after two months they incorporated all materials into supervision. They therefore discussed their developing relationship at the placement and the effect that they had on each other. This enabled them to explore conscious and previously unconscious dynamics, through the images that they made, or the feelings and impressions that they wrote down in journal form. Of note is that both supervisors were supervising for the first time. It is difficult to imagine someone with a supervisory practice being able to follow and respond to perhaps eight supervisees in this way.

The commentaries are interesting for highlighting the dynamics of a relationship, which in some ways is like therapy and in other ways very different. The supervisors explored feelings towards their own past supervisors: their wish to 'get it right'; feelings of envy and sibling rivalry; the effect on other staff relationships of having a student; and the shifts in the relationship as the supervisee progressed through the training. The supervisees explored the countertransference with clients: the illusion that they were 'fine'; envy of supervisors' qualities; the wishes that emerged around ending supervision and the relationship with the institution; fear of becoming a professional; dependence versus autonomy; and depression/regression were also highlighted. The first dyad called the artwork 'visual dialogues', which permitted

> rich imagery for on-going conversations about the concepts of projection, transference and counter-transference, owning roles in conflicts and accepting individual limitations.
>
> (Durkin *et al.* 1989: 40)

One gain was the setting up of a model for self-reflection and the facilitation of a non-judgemental atmosphere, in that both people were learning from each other. One feels that the newness of the participants to their respective roles helped this experiment to work. It was clearly very exposing at times and one supervisor found it useful to take material to her supervision group for supervisors. The article does not state whether any of the participants were in therapy, as one would expect these training relationships to be discussed in that context.

After reading this thought-provoking article I was left with reservations, particularly with regard to the exposing nature of some of the personal feelings in a supervisory context. I was left wondering who would sort them out when they became entangled with material that might be discussed in therapy. However it was an interesting experiment and does raise questions about journal keeping/artwork and how it might be used in training, as well as the relationship between therapy and supervision. In this book Brown, Meyerowitz-Katz and Ryde (2003, Chapter 10), Henley (Chapter 5), Robbins (Chapter 9) and Skaife (Chapter 8) all explore aspects of supervision in college and training.

## 1990s – therapy and supervision: the image and fantasy

Case and Dalley (1992, 2006 2nd edn) give a basic introduction to supervision issues, introducing them for the student and new practitioner and presenting a case for ongoing supervision as an ordinary part of the working week. They stress that new light can be thrown on the working practice of the very experienced through supervision, providing objective insights and new understandings. Expanding on their previous work, in this book Case (Chapter 6) explores the different states of mind and imagery that are helpful to the supervision process, illustrated by clinical work with children; and Dalley (Chapter 4) discusses the complex network around work with children and young people and the need for containment.

One of the only full length, in depth, discussions of supervision is by Dalley, Rifkind and Terry (1993). In *Three Voices of Art Therapy* they give a lavishly illustrated case study of art therapy from the respective viewpoints of client, therapist and, what they call, the supervisory voice. Although she was not the supervisor of the case Dalley observes the process, described by the other two, and offers a supervisory overview. This gives a very vivid discussion of the art process in art therapy. It also reveals the role of the supervisor as an objective person, reflecting on the pictures, as well as the process in which the therapist and client are engaged.

Malchiodi and Riley's (1996) *Handbook of Supervision and Related Issues* reflects their dual qualifications as a counsellor and a family therapist respectively. This informs much of the suggested practice in the book. They have an 'aesthetic-pragmatic' approach to therapy:

> The therapeutic encounter contains the creative elements of artistic and imaginative solutions to difficulties while simultaneously attending to the practical solutions that give support and comfort to the client.
>
> (Malchiodi and Riley: 4)

The handbook focuses on art therapy students and placements, taking an educational approach rather than a psychotherapeutic one. They are critical of the emphasis on countertransference in the British literature of the time, citing ethical, legal, professional identity, documentation and welfare issues as also needing to be given attention. The emphasis on legal issues reflects the differing contexts of practice in the USA and UK and concerns about malpractice lawsuits. They cover thoughts about the development of professional identity in supervision, quoting Friedman and Kaslow (1986); working with the difficult supervisee, quoting Kadushin in Edwards (1993); and the possibility for integrating the art process in supervision. Some of these topics are expanded and developed in this book; the difficulties of engaging supervisees are discussed by Killick (Chapter 12), and the art process in supervision by Brown, Meyerowitz-Katz and Ryde (Chapter 10).

Malchiodi and Riley have a useful chapter on peer supervision that highlights the need for structure, inclusion of all members, maintenance of a common focus and the necessity for objective feedback, which they point out can be difficult if there are friendships in the group. Decisions need to be made as to whether the peer group is a leaderless group or there is a designated leader each week. (Exploration of the image in a peer group setting is discussed by Laine, Chapter 7, in this book.) This supervision handbook was pioneering in its day, having chapters on practical issues such as how to make notes on a session, the use of video and making a plan for a training course for supervisors, but has been largely superseded by developments in the profession, particularly in the last six years.

## Keeping personal therapy and supervision separate

Keeping personal therapy and supervision separate is a topic that is addressed by several writers in this book. As a supervisor, it can be tempting, at times, to be drawn into the personal problems of the supervisee but it is very important to maintain a boundary in one's own mind about this. This tension, between therapy and supervision, is explored by Edwards (1993, 1997), who takes a historical perspective, exploring the psychoanalytic legacy on supervision today. Edwards (1997) refers to the early divide in psychoanalytic training as to whether supervision should be concerned with the teaching of technique and theory, or the exploration of emotional and unconscious responses to the client. These two approaches were taken up by the Viennese and Hungarian schools of psychoanalysis respectively, the former arguing for a separate analyst and supervisor, and the latter for the analyst to also be that analysand's supervisor.

One of the questions with which Edwards (1997) is concerned is the extent to which 'supervision ought to be concerned with helping the therapist or trainee learn about their own feelings, as opposed to learning about therapeutic techniques and strategies' (p. 11). This could be re-framed as a question of whether supervision is primarily for the protection and well-being of the client or for the continuing development and support of the therapist. To some extent this is a false divide, as it is in the interests of both for the therapist to have a space set apart, within which to reflect on the work and relationship with their patients. A containing space for the therapist reduces anxiety and allows a new perspective on the work, which may lead to a new approach. Exploring the countertransference/transference dynamic will increase self-awareness and self-reflection. In supervision there is frequently an educative element, particularly during training, but also afterwards. It helps with reflecting on professional development and the gaining of insight in cases where the therapist feels stuck.

One of the complex dynamics in supervision, as we have seen, is the unequal nature of the relationship and that there are powerful transferences.

This was made visible in the images made in the experiment described by Durkin, Perach, Ramseyer and Sontag (1989). In training, the supervisor may function as a door-keeper, guarding entry to the profession. After training the supervisor may be in several different roles to the therapist, including a managerial or administrative one. Even when this is not the case the therapist may see their supervisor as a role model or mentor and want them to think well of them. This could affect the decision as to what material to bring to supervision.

The model most commonly used in art psychotherapy training today is to have a separate analyst, psychotherapist or art psychotherapist as therapist, and a supervisor at each successive placement, as well as a college supervision group. The work of both therapist and supervisor is to aid the personal growth of the trainee. Michael and Enid Balint (1964) were influenced by the Hungarian approach to bring aspects of therapy and supervision to their group work with social workers to help them understand their clients. There is an aspect of this dual role present at times in every supervision: the supervisor will be faced with the intertwining of personal and professional issues in the presentation of case-material, or in the countertransference. The supervisee is sometimes aware that some of their own material has surfaced with a particular patient, but it may be unconscious and picked up by the supervisor, who then has to decide whether to discuss this in supervision or to suggest to the supervisee that it may be helpful to take it to therapy.

Edwards (1993) argues that supervision has 'a vital role to play' in training, in bringing together the different forms of learning about self, client and the making of images, in the context of a psychotherapeutic relationship. He discusses the demands of training on students' emotional and intellectual resources and how 'nervous anticipation and excitement' experienced by students at the beginning of training can be transformed into 'waves of anxiety, confusion, uncertainty, vulnerability and helplessness' (p. 214).

He considers the in-college supervision group, the purpose of which is to 'assist students with their learning while on placement'. This includes a focus on the students' relationship with their placement supervisor as well as 'issues, feelings and images arising from the placement situation'. These first experiences of supervision are important in establishing a mode of support for the student's work as a therapist. Edwards warns of the dangers of newly qualified therapists finding defensive or destructive coping strategies, in order to survive difficult situations, and points out how they may be prey to fantasies of 'not being good enough'. Establishing supervision as an ordinary part of the working week is essential for the protection of client and therapist. Edwards sees several tasks for the college based supervision group: reducing anxiety, improving the service to the client, playing with new ideas and approaches, examining prejudice and helping

the student to develop a professional identity through increasingly independent thinking. It is necessary to create an atmosphere of 'warmth, safety
and trust' so that the students can articulate painful or exposing questions,
overcoming the fear of appearing 'foolish, ignorant or worse'. Once they
feel safe, students will begin to bring up their difficulties with establishing
or maintaining the therapeutic relationship with their client, as well as the
difficult feelings that arise when clients do not make images.

In supervision the student brings the therapeutic relationship to be
examined and aspects of it will be seen in supervision through what has been
described as 'reflection process' (Searles 1955), 'parallel process' (Ekstein
and Wallerstein 1972) or 'paralleling' (Wilmot and Shohet 1985). All of these
describe the feelings/dynamics of the therapeutic session that are sometimes
re-played between therapist and supervisor. Edwards, referring to Mollon
(1989), discusses the kind of thinking in supervision that aids the supervisees'
capacity to think about the processes inherent to therapy. This is not
necessarily straightforward problem solving but rather the creation of states
of mind more like reflection, dreaming, free-associating or playing. Edwards
encourages students to make images to bring to supervision, as a way of
reflecting on their experiences with clients. This brings to consciousness
issues of which the student may have been unaware.

Edwards gives a vivid clinical example, which demonstrates the pressures
that can be brought to bear on the student and the use of mental imagery,
in the therapist's mind, to understand powerful projections. Here, as in his
later paper (Edwards 1997), he questions where this work should happen
and whether it should be in one relationship. He cites Balint and Balint
(1964) and Woodmansey (1987), who suggest that one relationship, combining therapy and supervision, might better enable students to learn about
feelings. Pedder (1986) suggests that trainees need a separate therapist and
supervisor, although he also sees the two processes of therapy and supervision as a continuum. The role of supervision is further taken up by Wood
(Chapter 11) in relation to training and later to clinical practice, and by
Gilroy (Chapter 13) in relation to research supervision.

It is not until Henzell's (1997) and Maclagan's (1997) papers that writers
about art psychotherapy begin to focus on the different nature of supervision when the patient's image is bought to supervision. It therefore has a
concrete as well as imaginal presence in the room between the therapist and
supervisor. Henzell discusses situations where image making may augment
conversations in therapy suggesting that:

> Therapy occurs within an 'inscription' which survives the moment in
> which it was created, rather than being retained only in the memory of
> the participants. In this way an image made in the session is 'part of the
> very tissue of the session'.
>
> (Henzell 1997: 71)

It could be added that images can look, feel and have a different presence in the different contexts of therapy and supervision. For instance paintings will be dry, not wet. Other communications will also be present, for instance the way that a supervisee brings images to supervision will be meaningful; for example how they present the painting to the supervisor, how they might protect a clay object, or be careless of it.

The papers of both Henzell and Maclagan are informed by Jungian analytical psychology, which influenced the development of early art therapy in Britain. They draw on Hillman (1975) who considers the image to be central in thinking about the way in which the psyche manifests (itself). The approach of Henzell and Maclagan is to form a contrast to the 'linguistic' models of Freudian and Lacanian psychoanalysis. Their point of view seems to neglect modern psychoanalytic thinkers more concerned with the inter-subjective relationship and reverie in the mind of analyst and analysand (Ogden, 2002). However, they begin to explore the physicality of the made image and the way that it can take on a third presence in the room. The image between therapist and patient, and now between therapist and supervisor, brings an aspect of the patient into the room, embodying 'meaning, intention and subjectivity'. It is also a presence with which the supervisory dyad can engage. The image can be an instigator of the creation of shared meaning in an external form. Like other works of art the very presence of the image brings forth a response from the viewer, an externalised form of inner life of the patient resonating with each on-looker. Henzell argues that there is a significant difference working in the presence of images, from working with a verbal recording of a session. Drawing on the work of Schaverien (1992) he discusses her concepts of diagrammatic and embodied imagery and the way in which certain imagery can present rather than describe its concerns in a form that is not reducible to language.

Henzell and Maclagan both argue against the reductive nature of a psychoanalytic approach to interpretation, Henzell feeling it leads to the subordination of images to the word and particular psychodynamic con-structs. Maclagan, similarly sees psychoanalysis as restrictive, describing its 'confined context', perhaps unaware of the freedom to play within a struc-ture, but also both fighting the cause of the image in what seems like an unequal battle in a situation where the word is powerful and can dominate the way in which knowledge and forms of knowing are communicated. Possibly, in trying to give to the image the importance that it deserves they argue rather defensively, thereby neglecting the importance of psycho-analytic theory in the understanding of relationships and the client's inner world. (Wood discusses these papers more fully in Chapter 11.)

Maclagan argues a case for re-instating 'fantasy', that is, fantasising freely about the image as opposed to the Kleinian use of 'phantasy' for deeper unconscious processes. He is thinking about fantasy, day-dreaming and play as an ordinary accompaniment to our everyday consciousness, suggesting that this is fundamental to psychic life rather than just fanciful escapism. Drawing on the work of Hillman (1975), fantasy images are seen as: 'the privileged mode of access to knowledge of the soul'. He feels that supervision should follow this therapy approach, working freely with the fantasy of the supervisory dyad, just as the therapist–patient dyad does in the therapy session.

Unfortunately, neither writer includes material from supervision with images to illustrate their much-needed discourse on the unique nature of art psychotherapy supervision. They make a spirited attack on more verbal approaches in therapy, but lack images themselves. Work with images necessarily needs words to describe it, so that language again predominates. What Maclagan describes is akin to Jung's (1937) 'active imagination', a technique for exploring fantasy. Maclagan argues against what he sees as a 'class structure of fantasy' wanting to work with all fantasy as an ally, through therapy and supervision in imaginative elaboration. (See Schaverien, Chapter 3, and Killick, Chapter 12, for Jungian approaches in this book.)

He quotes Hillman (1978) who suggests that a dream for instance cannot be interpretatively translated into other referents but only be 'interpretatively re-imagined'. His case supports the need to work with the multiple potential meanings in made imagery in therapy, rather than searching for *the* meaning. This may have a particular use in group supervision, where play with the image presented may free a stuck situation and permit the image and therapy to breathe. In supervision, fantasising can have a role in playing out what could have been said, or might be said, as well as allowing into the frame those thoughts and feelings that are on the edge of awareness. However play can also lead away from painful material in a form of denial or alternatively it may become a fascination with itself. Schur (1998) describes group art therapy supervision where the image of the patient is discussed without any background material, using the image as a primary source. (Laine, in Chapter 7 in this book, discusses image consultation, where a group of art psychotherapists meet regularly to work, with close attention, with what images evoke.)


## Notions of difference

In a series of papers, Calisch (1989, 1994a, 1994b, 1996, 1998) has, among other supervision issues, addressed cross-cultural dynamics in the supervision of art therapy trainees. Like Catteneo (1994) she argues the importance of therapeutic competence in treating the culturally diverse 'other', but this could also be applied to thinking about other forms that difference may take, such as gender, class or disability.

Calisch explores the supervisor's cultural frame of reference and how there may be world-view conflicts between the three parties of supervisor, the art therapist-supervisee and client. Each member of the triad brings their own attitudes, aesthetics, knowledge and skills, as well as personal characteristics, modes of relating and concerns that will reflect or express cultural influences. She makes an important point that how and what is expressed in therapy, the art expression itself and its subsequent meaning, are 'interwoven with cultural attitudes and are not universal' (1998). In her work there is an exploration of the dimensions of difference, in terms of the difference of any member of the triad from the general population, from their own cultural group or from either of the other parties in supervision. She cites the following possible difficulties and issues that may arise, in a similar way that they may in therapy: client anger and resistance, therapist defensiveness, therapist over-identification, supervisee resistance, poor therapist development, supervisor countertransference and supervisor patronisation.

A helpful concept to becoming more aware of these issues is the 'World View Congruence Model' (Sue 1981; Myers 1991; Calisch 1996, 1998). World view is defined as the way individuals perceive their relationship to the world in learned ways, i.e. relationship to nature, animals, God, objects, the universe, institutions, etc. Various authors have discussed how inter-personal conflicts are often a result of conflicts on eight world-view dimensions (world view incongruence).

Their diagram aids awareness of difference by bringing these alternative views to our attention so that they are on the agenda in supervision. We may not have the same view as another but we need to know when they are different for any member of the triad so that we can acknowledge them and avoid painful misunderstandings that may lead to distrust and suspicion. Calisch gives a review of current literature on cross-cultural issues in supervision. (Skaife, Chapter 8 in this volume, explores the notion of difference, while working as a supervisor in group and individual supervision.)

Gender and sexual orientation, in supervision, are discussed by Schaverien (2003, 2006). She draws attention to how both may influence the supervisory dyad reflecting elements of the therapeutic one. She proposes that, particularly when supervising the erotic elements of the transference and countertransference dynamic, gender and sexual orientation of client, therapist and supervisor may influence the interaction. The chapter is not about art psychotherapy specifically but if such material is active in therapy it is likely that it will affect the imagery that emerges in therapy and in supervision.

Rees (1998) gives a lively overview of supervision for the practising clinician in contrast to focusing on training issues. She examines why we need supervision, quoting Bordin (1983) who identified eight functions: mastery of specific skills, enlarging understanding of the client, enlarging understanding of process issues, increasing awareness of self and impact on process, overcoming personal and intellectual obstacles to learning, deepening understanding of concept and theory, providing a stimulus to research and the maintenance of a standard of service. I would add to this the model of supervisor/therapist relationship in which each might learn from the other, which can become a counterpoint to the therapist/client relationship. It is in this relationship that the supervisor can reflect on their own countertransference and so use the present situation between his or herself and the supervisee to understand the therapeutic relationship, as enacted in the parallel process that will be mirrored between them. Rees writes from her experience of supervision stating why she thinks it works, even though research in this area as to efficacy is limited: 'It has allowed me to work with clients I would otherwise have given up on; it has given me permission not to work with certain other clients' (p. 225). She quotes Hawkins and Shohet's (1989) notion of a 'good enough supervisor (after Winnicott) who can enable the therapist to survive the negative attacks of the client, through the strength of being held in the supervisory relationship'.

Rees reviews current models of supervision giving two particularly helpful methods of conceptualising the processes underlying supervision. The first is Proctor (1994) who identifies four threads that interweave in supervision: *formative* – relating to the welfare of the client; *restorative* – the professional development of the supervisee; *normative* – ethical, professional and organisational aspects of the work; and *creative* – a space to play and explore previously unconceived possibilities.

An alternative model is that of Page and Woskett (1994) who have a cyclical model that includes: the *contract*, which underpins the supervisory process, providing shape and form; the *focus*, which permits issues to be dealt with realistically and systematically; the *space*, which is the conceptual heart of the relationship where the supervisee experiences being held in her work; the *bridge*, which is the method by which insights from the supervision itself are reintroduced as keys to learning about the therapeutic relationship; and the *review*, which is the method by which both parties assess the direction and development of the supervisory process. Rees notes that little has been written about client artwork in supervision and that only 32% of art therapists, responding to her survey, used image making to explore their own feelings and responses as part of the supervisory process (Rees 1996).

Rees ends her chapter with a discussion of some phenomena relevant to work with learning difficulties that have arisen in her own supervision. She suggests that supervision is a way of being ever-vigilant of the values-base we are operating from, particularly when working with people with learning difficulties, where experiences of devaluation and negation are endemic. One issue, which is hard for therapists to confront, is that they may unconsciously deny the extent of disability, finding it difficult to tackle with clients. This may be because of an urge to protect themselves and the client from the distress that might be involved. Rees suggests that it is a great relief for all when this can be openly spoken about. Similarly the therapist's guilt at their own 'wholeness' is sometimes defended against, by the claim that no-one is normal, which can deny severe disability. Rees writes about the experience of many clients with disability who may have been derided, humiliated, infantilised, ignored, abused and wished dead. Work of this nature may produce powerful countertransference in the therapist of dis-empowerment, feeling deskilled, of anger or a suffocating boredom. This needs careful monitoring in supervision to prevent enactment on the part of the therapist with a sometimes apparently passive client. Rees insightfully suggests that the experience of having been wished dead can act powerfully in the countertransference to prevent creative engagement, by loss of a sense of life-force. Similar issues are addressed in this book: Killick (Chapter 12) writes about working with 'unconscious despair' in supervision; and Damarell (Chapter 2) explores the way that we view images in supervision, through learnt ritual. With clinical examples from work with learning disabled clients, he challenges our usual perspective in several ways.

## 2000s – working with image and action in supervision

Of related interest is a chapter in Scaife (2001), which considers non-verbal approaches as mediums of communication in supervision in the health professions. This is with the intention of 'trying to access knowledge and understanding that a supervisee has about a client that is at the edge of awareness'. Although Scaife is a psychologist rather than an art psycho-therapist, several different approaches are explored, some of which will be familiar to art psychotherapists. There is the suggestion that these may be used when time is short, as a short cut to the main issue. However this raises concern because, in accessing unconscious material through creative approaches, the unexpected may happen, creating a situation that will need time for discussion in depth. To some extent, the different techniques should be used with caution, as some supervisees may feel uncomfortable; raw personal material may be accessed, and the technique may need a period for disengagement. For instance, in role-play or sculpting methods, where members of a supervision group enact different aspects of the client or the wider system. Different approaches to drawing the client, as well as the use of verbal or visual metaphor, are discussed (Amundson 1988; Inskipp and Proctor 1995; Ishiyama 1988) as a safer way of exploring difficult areas. As one might expect, visual approaches incline to the introduction of personal material from the supervisee. In some circumstances this may be relevant to the exploration of countertransference and in others it may overlap with issues better placed in therapy.

The use of diagrams, for instance family trees, especially in complex cases, such as with looked-after children, can add a necessary informative dimension to supervision. This almost inadvertently provides imagery, without precipitating the supervisee's own material. An example of this was a supervisee, in a therapist's supervision group, who was discussing a distressing case of multiple neglect and abandonment of a child where there was widespread incest in the family system. The way that the family tree had been drawn formed a skull; this bought to the awareness of the group and the supervisee, the impact of the loss of two family members on the client under discussion. This resonated with losses of the foster mother, which were preventing her from being emotionally available, with the consequence that the 'looked-after' child was acting out. The diagram/skull image enabled these links to be made and appropriate work to be planned for foster mother and foster child.

Another way is to use objects, such as stones, to represent the people who are part of a system being discussed. Williams (1995) also uses objects attached to magnets on a board. She suggests questions to elicit an understanding of the present system being discussed, and moves that might be made to change the system. Art psychotherapists may be more familiar with using clay in a similar way. Clay has the advantage that it can be moulded and manipulated to show and give a feeling response, as well as being moveable to different positions, for instance when relationships are being discussed.

Brown, Meyerowitz-Katz and Ryde (2003) were running supervision groups in a training context and decided to use the students' own image making to inform the process. Their article uses student feedback on the difference of including the making of images to gain emotional comprehension of a therapeutic session. They discuss different influences on their work, including that of Gordon (1992), citing important qualities in supervision, such as trust, honesty, humour and skilled listening, with the desire to create a supportive atmosphere to lessen anxiety as well as challenging the students' approach to their work. The authors were influenced by the work of Maclagan (1995, 1997), the image capturing emotional experience and his writing on fantasy, and the work of Schaverien (2000), the triangularity of art therapy relationships and the 'embodied image', which 'conveys a feeling state for which no other mode of expression can be substituted' (p. 59). They worked in groups with awareness of group process, the supervision task and parallel process. The image making by the students means that there is a tremendous visual impact when all images are brought back to the group circle. (Their work is further developed in this book in Chapter 10.)

In this chapter the literature regarding art therapy and art psychotherapy supervision has been reviewed. This gives a historical background and brings us up to date. A number of issues specific to the use of the artwork or imagery in supervision have been raised. Some of these will be developed as the book progresses and new theoretical developments will be introduced.

## References

Amundson, N. W. (1988) 'The use of metaphor and drawings in case conceptualisation', *Journal of Counselling and Development*, 66: 391–393.

Balint, M. and Balint E. (1964) *The Doctor, his Patient and the Illness*, London: Pitman.

Bordin, E. S. (1983) 'A working alliance based model of supervision', *The Counseling Psychologist*, 11 (1): 35–42.

Brown, C., Meyerowitz-Katz, J. and Ryde, J. (2003) 'Thinking with image making in supervision', *Inscape*, 8 (2): 71–78.

Calisch, A. (1989) 'Eclectic blending of theory in the supervision of art psychotherapists', *The Arts in Psychotherapy*, 16: 37–43.

Calisch, A. (1994a) 'The metatherapy of supervision using art with transference/counter-transference phenomena', *The Clinical Supervisor*, 12: 119–127.

Calsich, A. (1994b) 'The use of imagery in teaching, learning, and supervision', *Canadian Journal of Art Therapy*, 8: 30–35.

Calisch, A. (1996) 'Multiculturalism and art therapy: looking back and seeing beyond', *Canadian Art Therapy Journal*, 10 (2): 63–68.

Calisch, A. (1998) 'Multicultural perspectives in art therapy supervision', in A. Hiscox and A. Calisch (eds), *Tapestry of Cultural Issues in Art Therapy*, London: Jessica Kingsley, pp. 201–218.

Case, C. and Dalley, T. (1992, 2006 2nd edn) *The Handbook of Art Therapy*, London: Routledge.

Catteneo, M. (1994) 'Addressing culture and values in the training of art therapists', *Journal of the American Art Therapy Association*, 11 (3): 184–187.

Dalley, T., Rifkind, G. and Terry, K. (1993) *Three Voices of Art Therapy: Image, Client, Therapist*, London: Routledge.

Durkin, J., Perach, D., Ramseyer, J. and Sontag, E. (1989) 'A model for art therapy supervision enhanced through art making and journal writing', in H. Wadeson (ed.), *Advances in Art therapy*, New York: John Wiley and Sons, pp. 390–432.

Edwards, D. (1993) 'Learning about feelings: the role of supervision in art therapy training', *The Arts in Psychotherapy*, 20: 213–222.

Edwards, D. (1997) 'Supervision today: the psychoanalytic legacy', in G. Shipton (ed.), *Supervision of Psychotherapy and Counselling*, Buckingham: Open University Press, pp. 11–23.

Ekstein, R. and Wallerstein, R. S. (1972) *The Teaching and Learning of Psychotherapy*, New York: International Universities Press.

Friedman, D. and Kaslow, N. J. (1986) 'The development of professional identity in psychoanalysis: six stages in the supervision process', in F. W. Kaslow (ed.), *Supervision and Training: Models, Dilemmas and Challenges*, New York: Haworth Press, pp. 29–50.

Gordon, R. (1992) 'Supervision', Paper presented at conference on *The Practice of*

*Supervision: Some Contributions*, London: British Association of Psychotherapists.

Hawkins, P. and Shohet, R. (1989) *Supervision in the Helping Professions*, Milton Keynes, UK: Open University Press.

Henzell, J. (1997) 'The image's supervision', in G. Shipton (ed.), *Supervision of Psychotherapy and Counselling*, Buckingham: Open University Press, pp. 71–79.

Hillman, J. (1975) *Re-Visioning Psychology*, New York: Harper Colophon Books.

Hillman, J. (1978) 'Further notes on images', *Spring*: 152–183.

Inskipp, F. and Proctor, B. (1995) *The Art, Craft and Tasks of Counselling Supervision Part 2: Becoming a Supervisor*, Twickenham: Cascade Publications.

Ishiyama, F. I. (1988) 'A model of visual case processing using metaphors and drawings', *Counsellor Education and Supervision*, 28: 153–161.

Jung, C. (1937) *Analytical Psychology*, London: Ark.

Maclagan, D. (1995) 'Fantasy and the aesthetic: have they become the uninvited guests at art therapy's feast?', *The Arts in Psychotherapy*, 22 (3): 217–221.

Maclagan, D. (1997) 'Fantasy, play and the image in supervision', in G. Shipton (ed.), *Supervision of Psychotherapy and Counselling*, Buckingham: Open University Press, pp. 61–70.

Malchiodi, C. and Riley, S. (1996) *Handbook of Supervision and Related Issues*, Chicago, IL: Magnolia Street Publishers.

Marion, P. and Felix, M. (1979) 'The relationship of art therapy interns and supervisors', *Art Psychotherapy*, 6: 37–40.

Mollon, P. (1989) 'Anxiety, supervision and a space for thinking: some narcissistic perils for clinical psychologists in learning psychotherapy', *British Journal of Medical Psychology* 62, 113–122.

Myers, L. J. (1991) 'Expanding the psychology of knowledge optimally: the importance of cultural differences', in R. L. Jones (ed.), *Black Psychology* (3rd edn), Berkeley, CA: Cobb and Henry.

Ogden, T. (2002) *Conversations at the Frontier of Dreaming*, London: Karnac.

Page, S. and Woskett, V. (1994) *Supervising the Counsellor*, London: Routledge.

Pedder, J. (1986) 'Reflections on the theory and practice of supervision', *Psychoanalytic Psychotherapy*, 2 (1): 1–12.

Proctor, B. (1994) 'Supervision-competence, confidence and accountability', *British Journal of Guidance and Counselling*, 22 (3): 309–318.

Rees, M. (1996) 'The supervision of art therapists', Unpublished MA thesis, University of Bristol.

Rees, M. (1998) 'Clinical supervision in art therapy: is it really "super!"?', in M. Rees (ed.), *Drawing on Difference: Art therapy with People Who Have Learning Difficulties*, London: Routledge, pp. 222–243.

Scaife, J. (2001) *Supervision in the Mental Health Professions: A Practitioner's Guide*, Hove: Brunner-Routledge.

Schaverien, J. (1992) *The Revealing Image: Analytical Art Psychotherapy in Theory and Practice*, London: Routledge.

Schaverien, J. (2000) 'The triangular relationship and the aesthetic countertransference in analytical art therapy', in A. Gilroy and G. McNeilly (eds), *The Changing Shape of Art Therapy: New Developments in Theory and Practice*, London: Jessica Kingsley, pp. 55–83.

Schaverien, J. (2003) 'Supervising the erotic transference', in J. Wiener, R. Mizen and J. Duckham (eds), *Supervising and Being Supervised*, Basingstoke: Palgrave/ Macmillan, pp. 167–184.

Schaverien, J. (2006) 'Supervising the erotic transference', *Gender, Countertransference and the Erotic Transference: Perspectives from Analytical Psychology and Psychoanalysis*, Hove: Routledge, pp. 56–70.

Schur, Y. (1998) 'The personal artistic process of the art therapist as a basis for supervision', *International Journal of Art Therapy*, 4: 32–36.

Searles, H. F. (1955) 'The informational value of the supervisor's emotional experiences', in *Collected Papers on Schizophrenia and Related Subjects*, New York: International Universities Press (1995 edition), pp. 157–177.

Sue, D. W. (1981) *Counselling the Culturally Different*, New York: John Wiley & Sons.

Williams, A. (1995) *Visual and Active Supervision*, New York: Norton.

Wilmot, J. and Shohet, R. (1985) 'Parallelling in the supervision process', *Self and Society: European Journal of Humanistic Psychology*, 13 (2): 86–92.

Wilson, L., Riley, S. and Wadeson, H. (1984) 'Art therapy supervision', *Art Therapy*, 1 (3): 100–105.

Woodmansey, A. C. (1987) 'What's wrong with psychotherapy?', *British Journal of Clinical and Social Psychiatry*, 5 (3): 73–75.

# Theoretical innovations in individual supervision

# Chapter 2

# The supervisor's eyes[1]

*Barrie Damarell*

## Introduction

The aim of this chapter is to explore the significance of topographical material in relation to art psychotherapy supervision. There is an emphasis on supervisory activity with art therapists who work with people with learning disabilities. However, I believe the universality of material will make it useful for art psychotherapists practising in other fields.

Much of what you are about to read flows from my sculptural background and practice. My belief is that, despite the relative lack of attention given to sculpture in art psychotherapy literature, there are many benefits that could transcend the three-dimensional divide and inform practice and supervision in the two-dimensional realm of the image.

A glimpse of what might be possible emerges from an exhibition commentary on the work of arguably Britain's most revered living sculptor, Anthony Caro. Moorhouse (2005) writes, describing the Child's Tower Room (1983–4):

> With this work, Caro advanced the idea of sculpture that is no longer a purely visual experience. Continuing his earlier dialogue between exterior and interior, the sculpture can be read as a kind of tower, with steps that lead from the outside into a contained, interior space. To experience the sculpture fully, the viewer enters the sculpture and responds physically to the interaction of its different shapes. Recalling the child's exploration of the tree-house or the space beneath the table, the sculpture evokes a world that is both real and make-believe.
>
> (Moorhouse 2005: 34)

The same commentator later describes two pieces (Halifax steps: Spirals 1994 and Babylon 1997) as

> . . . both [*using*] steps as a basic, instantly recognisable element. However, it is equally clear that the context of sculpture places this feature beyond use. Caro's engagement is with the idea of steps. He

deploys these elements freely and poetically; creating new structures that occupy the real space of the world but at the same time, stand apart from it.

(Moorhouse 2005: 45)

From these two brief extracts it is possible to see the richness of sculptural language and ideas. Notions of inside and outside take on a different quality associated, I suggest, with haptic (touch) sense that informs and gives depth to our perception of space. Negative and positive space, tension, dynamic, object(s), texture, surface and form are all terms that are not exclusive to sculpture but nevertheless find a uniquely powerful expression through that medium.

The commentary on 'Child's Tower Room' is also useful in the context of art psychotherapy in its link with early experience: '. . . Recalling the child's exploration of the tree-house or the space beneath the table . . .' (ibid.). Interestingly, further significance can perhaps be found in Caro's title in that it reminds us that not all childhood spaces are benign and nurturing[2]. I also detect fascinating associations with the *mirror* (both psychoanalytic and Foucauldian[3]) in the phenomena of '. . . structures that occupy the real space of the world but at the same time, stand apart from it' (ibid.), to which I will return later in this chapter.

The significance of sculptural thinking rests on the fact that we are born into a three-dimensional world of shape, mass, texture and distance, and our earliest activities are devoted to its exploration. For instance, the oral phase is as much dominated by the infant's assay of three-dimensional body-parts – the breast, fingers, thumb, and so on – as it is in gaining satisfaction. And later, when the child develops mobility, both physical space and the objects that populate it come within reach of the infant's curious mind. Importantly, there is a familiarity with three dimensions that significantly predates our later emerging interest with two-dimensional representation. This familiarity becomes a kind of haptic knowledge that later unconsciously informs our complex perceptions of space.

## Art psychotherapy supervision, its rituals and learning disability

As with the situation with sculpture, there is very little written about art therapy supervision in the context of learning disability. One exception is Rees (1998) who provides a chapter on the subject in which she describes models of supervision and highlights the character of countertransference material commonly experienced in work with the learning disabled. Examples of such are feelings of incompetence, disempowerment and boredom, all of which appear linked to the learning disabled person's experience of being, perhaps apologetically, in the world. Rees (1998) also speaks of the existence of 'unconscious processes at a societal level' that can lure the art therapist into acting out disabling attitudes held at a wider cultural level, to which I intend to add throughout this chapter.

My main challenge is to a ritual, played out each day by art psychotherapists across the land, whereby the client's artworks are predominantly laid horizontally upon a tabletop or quite often the floor for the purpose of looking. This ritual is almost certainly learned and passed on, ritualistically, through our training, supervision and general practice. It is an inherited way of *doing* that is, in my experience, rarely questioned or even much thought about and therefore repeated endlessly as an integral aspect of supervisory practice.

This culturally altered attitude to the image whereby the horizontal takes precedence over the vertical convention adopted in respect of pictures in both home and gallery alike seems to me to reveal something of the supervisor and therapist's longings for the image and the true activity of the converging gaze of their eyes.

I will argue that this culturally contradictory practice not only represents a kind of disrespect or undervaluing of the art object – the client, I suggest, visualises the vertical whilst engaged with the art materials – but also illuminates the scopic-regime, adopted or perhaps inherited and certainly active in both session and supervision.

It bothers me, on several levels, that the image is viewed horizontally. What does it say about this art that it is deprived of the vertical? We know only too well that art that did not make it onto the wall – the hallowed vertical – at school frequently marked the impending end to artistic interest. Instead artworks, implied unworthy, languished in the eternally dark horizontal of the art folder. I suggest that either consciously or not, and I suspect not, our horizontal attitude belies some inherent belief about imagery made in the context of art psychotherapy that marks it out as inherently different and indeed, by inference, this attitude extends to capture its maker.

## The topological dynamics of art therapy supervision

When thinking about the image in supervision the familiar visualisation of the triangle arises with, at each of its corners respectively, the client, the therapist and the supervisor. In this configuration only two subjects are actually present and taking part in the supervision process, with the absent client represented by their artwork. Due to the non-presence of the subject/client it is vitally important to consider the status of the art object/client in the supervision environment and in this respect the positioning of the art object/client is crucial. When visiting a gallery it is clear that attention has been given to the height and positioning of a given image. In this context eye-level is all-important and clearly not just for visual convenience.

If one imagines the painter at her easel the likelihood is that the position of her eyes will correspond with that of the gallery viewer: meeting eye-to-eye so to speak. Yet this eye-to-eye encounter in art therapy supervision often has a different and perhaps unequal dynamic.

It occurs to me that *looking down* – an ocular position common in art therapy supervision – has embedded in it an orientational attitude suggestive of power. Even the word *super*vision itself suggests a position of visual authority. The *eye* seems to command the image through its elevation and if the art object stands in the stead of its maker it evokes a cohabitant aspect of supervision, namely observation, that has echoes, due to the client's absence, of Bentham's Panoptican, the design of which enabled the observation of prisoners without their awareness and knowledge of the observer's identity. Although I have exaggerated in order to make my point, the client, although made aware of the supervisor's existence at the point of consent[4], *is* nonetheless unaware of their identity and location.

## Observation and the learning disabled person

There are few other groups of people in our society more closely observed than people with learning disabilities. It is common for the most meticulous observations to take place often around the areas of behaviour, sexuality and risk. These enquiries are endlessly recorded and discussed and infiltrate every intimate area of life and living imaginable.

Even when out of the home, people with learning disabilities are subjected to another form of observation in the form of the public gaze and, as pointed out by Foucault in the following passage, this is powerfully internalised to the detriment of the observed subject:

> There is no need for arms, physical violence, material constraints. Just a gaze, an inspecting gaze, a gaze which each individual under its weight will end by interiorising to the point that he is his own overseer, each individual thus exercising surveillance over and against himself.
>
> (Foucault 1977: 155; cited in Butler and Parr 1999: 208)

One unifying quality of such gazes is often in the form of tragedy (Swain, French and Cameron 2003): the learning disabled person is construed as a tragedy at birth and carries this construction throughout their life.

The problematic of the *looking down* dynamic in art therapy supervision is that it closely mirrors the learning disabled person's experience of life as a marginalised, isolated and tragic figure inhabiting a kind of *under*class. The ocularity of the supervision topology and the representation of the absent subject need an alternative approach away from the horizontal and towards the eye-meeting capacity of the vertical.

Grimshaw (2005) describes one such ocular change in the visual arts at the introduction of Cubism by Picasso and Braque at the beginning of the twentieth century. The previously dominant Renaissance-orientated visual ideology had placed the spectator at the centre of the world. Cubism brought an end to this scopic regime and in place of it offered a plethora of viewpoints to the observer's gaze. Even though the observer remained in the same special relationship to the image on the wall, the eyes were afforded free range by the multi-dimensionality of the cubist representation. Of course this had been an innate faculty of sculpture since the very beginning, although the eyes *and* the body had to work for their sweet reward in terms of geographical approach, to which I will return to later.

However, this said, Romanticism was an earlier movement, with a focus upon the expressive flow of the imagination from within the individual, whose influence and legacy can be detected in later movements such as Expressionism and Surrealism (Hughes 1996; Edwards 2004) and of course art therapy and its theory, training, practice and supervision processes. The position, I visualise, places both therapist and supervisor atop a high board preparing to dive into the client's material. This snapshot of the moment of intentionality is, in my mind, associated with the nature of allegory in relationship to visual art and its embeddedness in art therapy practice.

'The word "allegory" means "saying something else", that is, saying one thing and meaning something else' (Sheppard 1987: 130). Simply put, works of art are either deliberately allegorical or not. Sheppard (ibid.) points out that:

> Deliberate allegory is often defined as extended metaphor and allegorical interpretation is interpretation which treats literature (and for the purposes of this chapter I substitute visual art for literature) as metaphor capable of paraphrase, as a system of meaning which can be systematically decoded, as a language which can be translated.
>
> (Sheppard 1987: 129)

Sheppard suggests '. . . for deliberately allegorical works, the allegorical interpretation captures all the meaning; the rest is ornament' (ibid.: 130–131). The second position considers the case of the allegorical interpretation of works not deliberately made to function allegorically, as, I suggest, is occasionally the case with art objects made in the art therapy studio. For instance, Summers (1989) considers the spectrum of allegory and draws attention to the exclusive potential of the phenomenon and again the higher emphasis on meaning as opposed to appearance. For Summers:

> Allegory, like naturalism itself, may be said to depend on a kind of transparency of means in the simple sense that, as a metaphorical language of usual interpretation implies, it is possible to 'see through'

the surfaces of the work to its meaning . . . the pattern is always the
same: the opposition between lower appearance and higher meaning.

(Summers 1989: 133)

Owens (1980) refers to the 'allegorical impulse', which, in my view, aptly
describes the pull of the eye, and its attention, deep into the confines of the
frame.

My intention in this chapter is to persuade the gaze to take note of the
space within which the frame is set and to ponder what is unseen when
abiding to the traditional rituals of art therapy supervision.

### Vignette 1

In this scenario I am supervising an art psychotherapist working in an
adolescent service. In one particular session the art psychotherapist shares a
case that had been causing her some concern. The main difficulty, as she
put it, was that she was finding it difficult to concentrate on and connect
with the imagery of a teenage male client she had been working with for a
while. My supervisee fetched and placed upon the table a drawing made
on A3 (353 × 500 mm) white paper. The monochromatic and apparently
quickly made drawing depicted a warplane, bullets issuing from its wings as
it flew through the sky. In its horizontal orientation upon the table it was
indeed difficult to feel anything in response to it, no matter how hard I
tried.

After a period feeling absolutely stuck and struggling to think of something to say, it occurred to me that this way of looking at an aeroplane was
somewhat unnatural to say the least. I decided to pick up the picture and
hold it as high as I could above our heads. The outcome of this simple act
was astonishing. The picture that had previously been hard to feel an
emotional response towards now created a powerful feeling of aggressive
threat and foreboding. As we gazed up at it we both shared feelings of
vulnerability and exposure under this now malignant sky.

At this point my supervisee was able to make connections between her
teenage client's past experiences and the countertransference responses she
was now experiencing. I suggest that it is possible to see from this supervision vignette that positioning was vital to the countertransference experience in this supervision session, and that the initial and familiar scopic
regime – that of looking down at the horizontal image – was incapable of
the sensitivity that gazing up could achieve.

The ocular approach, described above, opens out the whole three-
dimensionality of the supervision space and challenges the dominant mode
of image perception. Picture, for a moment, a man in an art gallery looking
at a painting hanging upon the wall. You may observe him moving back
and forth before the image whilst his eyes dance upon the canvas. You

might further notice that his gaze seldom strays beyond the constraints of the frame, until after satiation he moves on to the next image within the same space. The framing of images, ornate or merely defined by their edge, insists on a kind of exclusivity of view, distracting our gaze from other concerns. Sculpture is not like this. Sculpture demands we take in the larger picture. For the sculptural object, external space is a necessity that provides its relatedness and forms its identity as a place within a wider space environment, be it gallery or hillside.

Now imagine the same man encountering a piece of sculpture. The dancing eye in painting evolves into the roving and unified body-eye of sculpture. In this scenario you might notice the man traversing the entire three-dimensional space in his appreciation of the object. The sculptural form discloses new visual information as the spectator's eyes, transported by his moving body, roam the contours of the form. Wittgenstein (1958) makes a similar point with respect to philosophical thought in which he states '. . . the same points were always being approached from different directions, and new sketches made' (p. vii). Wittgenstein suggests that through this process the whole landscape arises.

## Humanistic geography and art therapy supervision

A rather strange and unexpected source for the exploration of art therapy supervision emerges in the form of humanistic geography, which emerged during the 1970s as a reaction to the positivist discourses that dominated geography at that time.

Some humanistic geographers were attracted to philosophy, in particular phenomenology, in their inquiries into everyday experiences of place and the meanings attributed thereof. Adams, Hoelscher and Till (2001) quote Daniels (1992), in his explanation of the specialism:

> . . . the move from 'knowing about places' in an objective way, their facts and features, to 'understanding' places, in a more empathetic way, their character and meanings, that remains the hallmark of humanistic geography.
>
> (Daniels 1992: xix)

Tuan (1977, 2004), a central figure in the development of humanistic geography, explores how human identity is formed by place and has gone further by proposing that the image functions as a virtual space that one can enter. This is an interesting proposition that links the picture 'place' to the art therapy studio, and by extension the flux of identities within and between both. In this respect there seems to exist a clear relationship between what lies within the frame and what lies without.

*Vignette 2*

In this scenario I am supervising an art psychotherapist who works with adults with learning disabilities. She shows me an A1 (594 × 841 mm) sized image made predominantly using an earthy mauve pigment. I am sitting at a table set in the centre of the art therapy studio in which the picture was made. As I sit and look, I realise that I am vaguely aware of the similar colour at the periphery of my retina. Focusing more intentionally I saw that it was in fact the art therapist's coat hanging upon the peg in the studio. This appeared to link the studio with the virtual place described within the frame of the image and symbolically the therapist with the client.

In a later supervision session concerning the same client and with the consciousness of our previous experience we were less resistant to seeing the connectivity inherent in the image. In this case the colour of the table upon which the image was painted was represented upon the paper, as were areas of red in the same special relationship to red chairs in the room opposite to the client as she worked. I believe that this supervision vignette illustrates something qualitatively different from the earlier vignette. In the first, positionality was the key that unlocked the countertransference, whereas the second connects the studio and picture worlds and appears to map the topology of both real and virtual places.

## The art therapy studio

At this point it is important to consider what the studio space might mean to the learning disabled client. Learning disabled people get to make an extraordinary amount of art, much of which seems to function as a kind of *work* that passes the time in otherwise unfulfilling environments and importantly, and almost exclusively, is done in isolation with no real audience. Involvement in art therapy changes this but, in doing so, sometimes introduces problems associated with the notion of the artist and artistry. In my experience, the art therapist is often called the 'artist' by the learning disabled client and I have written elsewhere (Damarell 1999) on how 'high art' images are appropriated and adapted by the client in art therapy. There are others who seem not to see the artist's studio but who instead experience the art therapy studio as a classroom, often with negative reverberation. Underpinning both is an alignment of power that hinges upon the axis of competency, empowerment and social construction, awareness of which is vital to the supervision process.

## Heterotopias and the art therapy studio

In 1967 Foucault gave a lecture entitled 'Of Other Spaces'. Foucault's main concern was external space as opposed to internal mental space. He charted the configuration of space from the hierarchical nature of medieval society to the present, where the certainties of the pre-Galileo epoch dissolved and reconfigured in the face of the limitless expanses of outer space. Foucault proposed that oppositions such as private and public space were '. . . still nurtured by the hidden presence of the sacred' (p. 23) which is seen as an area of contemporary society where the sacred had not been challenged.

Essentially, he defined two types of site. The first of these he conceived as utopia and was defined as a kind of ideal imagining without concrete form. The other was conceived as a different sort of space altogether. Foucault described this as . . .

> something like counter-sites, a kind of effectively enacted utopia in which real sites that can be found within the culture, are simultaneously represented, contested and inverted. Places of this kind are outside of all places, even though it may be possible to indicate their location in reality.
>
> (Foucault 1967: 231)

To illuminate this somewhat complex concept, Foucault offered the example of the mirror . . .

> The mirror functions as a Heterotopia in this respect: it makes this place that I occupy at the moment when I look at myself in the glass at once absolutely real, connected with all the space that surrounds it, and absolutely unreal, since in order to be perceived it has to pass through this virtual point which is over there.
>
> (Foucault 1967: 232)

Foucault appeared to see heterotopia as originating out of the distant past and associated with rituals such as adolescent transition. These he named 'crisis heterotopia', the remnants of which can be found in the honeymoon tradition of today.

Foucault claimed that the crisis heterotopia was on the wane and was being replaced with what he described as 'heterotopias of deviation'. These are places where those who do not *fit* inhabit. There are five principles of heterotopia suggested in all, but only four are of particular interest to this chapter. The first principle, in the context of the present discussion, is Foucault's proposition that spaces such as rest homes, psychiatric hospitals and prisons are all examples of heterotopias of deviancy.

The second principle concerns the capacity of one space to hold and represent several others. Foucault suggests that both the theatre and the cinema are examples, as each is transformed by every individual and essentially unrelated performance and yet the fabric of these spaces remains essentially unchanged. The capacity for heterotopias to be linked with 'slices of time' (p. 234) represents the third principle. Foucault named this type of heterotopia, 'heterochrony'. These manifest in different forms, for example the festival is seen as transitory and essentially ephemeral, whereas a heterochrony in the form of the library or museum is the antithesis of the festival. Here time is accumulated, added to and stored.

The fourth and last principle concerns the quality of heterotopias that '. . . presuppose a system of opening and closing that both isolates them and makes them penetrable' (p. 235). Access to heterotopias is characteristically regulated and certain conditions govern passage. For instance, Foucault points to the prison as a site where access is compulsory for some whereas others are barred. Others are governed by ritual, only admitting those for whom these rites are appropriate.

This fascinating work by Foucault evokes many factors apposite to the art therapy studio and this present concern with art therapy supervision. For example, the art room, on any working day, is host to a myriad of different visual phenomena, art forms and enactments between the therapist and the client. At the end of each session, and exactly like the theatre, the room clears and returns to its natural state before the next space-altering occurrence. The linkage with time is shared and expressed in the curator activities embedded into art therapy practice. Each client's work is collected, dated, written about in clinical notes, catalogued and safely stored. This kind of 'time-freezing' is closely connected, as Foucault suggests, to the museum and its rituals.

The final similarity concerns the question of admittance. Many art therapists work in units where only some people are referred for art therapy. This creates a body of individuals who gain admittance to the art therapy studio and a group who are excluded, and exemplifies the conditional and selective nature of the art therapy space. The importance of Foucault's work for art therapists and their supervisors is in reminding us what our spaces represent, how they function within the culture and how they function as spaces apart, even while connected with a matrix of other spaces. But is the art therapy studio truly a heterotopia of deviance? I think not. Our practice spaces seem more congruent with the environments and rituals that Foucault appears to mourn, namely the heterotopia of crisis.

I believe this can be distilled from a passage by Shipton (1999) who charts the history of the mirror and its significance in the contemporary psychotherapy consulting room. In this example heterotopia is linked to the concept of self . . .

> The self serves to reflect both an internal and external reality, yet its source and its boundaries cannot be found to exist in any concrete way – the body is clearly not the same as the self. In times of crisis, we retreat into the self as a refuge.

> (Shipton 1999: 191–192)

In other words, in times of crisis the physical space of the studio and virtual art space of the art object combine to become potential refuges for the client. But this is not the end of the analogy for both also represent the transforming qualities that are so essential to the conception of the hetero-topia of crisis as set out and described by Foucault.

## The internal supervisor

Few discussions about supervision are complete without reference to the work of Casement (1985, 1990, 2002). The vital element of Casement's material is the concept of the internal supervisor. This faculty is visualised by Casement (1985) as developing through involvement in supervision. A key area in this process is described as 'trial identification' (pp. 34–35). Here the therapist learns to achieve a 'benign split' so 'his experiencing ego' can rove between himself in his shoes and the shoes within which the patient stands. The ability to simultaneously experience both states, as Casement (ibid.) puts it, enables the therapist, through her capacity for internal supervision, 'to be in two places at once'. The whole process, although often slow, enables a transition from a reliance on the external figure of the supervisor towards an interaction with a healthy split off and internalised representation of the supervision experience itself. This whole process suggests similar correspondences to what has gone before regarding spaces, both internal and external, and transitions, interactions and connections between the two. I would also like to suggest that Casement's model could be expanded to include the physical and metaphorical space within which both the therapist's and the client's shoes are located. It is entirely possible for the Casement 'observing and the experiencing ego' of both the art therapist and their supervisor to trial identify with the actual studio and virtual picture spaces of the client. In this configuration the limiting frame evaporates to reveal an open vista upon which the super-visor, be it internal or external, can rove with creative freedom.

## Conclusion

This has been a journey through a varied and sometimes surprising land-scape. I began by suggesting that sculpture, an art form rather neglected in the art therapy literature, had the potential to inform the discourse around two-dimensional imagery in art therapy supervision. This was intended to shake up the unconsciously ritualistic attitude apparent in supervision where the artwork is responded to by looking down on the object on the horizontal axis. I proposed that the position of the image equated with the social position of its maker and that in the context of learning disability this amounted to a repeating of the client's material.

Raising the image onto the vertical, a simple act requiring little energy, has the symbolic power of restoring respect and equality through which the absent client is able to take a valued and empowered position as part of the supervision triad. I also spoke of the dynamics between the therapist and the client in art therapy and the power-underpinned fantasies that might emerge in connection with the identity of the therapist as artist – an interestingly revealing insight into the profession itself.

Of course, the approach I suggest, as with all approaches, is not suitable for all supervision situations. However, this said, I believe it has the potential to form an aspect of the free-floating attention of both the therapist in her session and later in supervision. A crucially important aspect of this chapter relates to the gravitational pull into the centre of the frame. I have cautioned against this initial impulse for allegorical satisfaction as it encourages a peripherally blind trajectory into the supposed meaning-rich depths held within. As with allegory, there exists a tendency to value meaning above appearance which distracts the gaze from the outer world of the art object.

My approach has been to emphasise the supervisory importance of the space within which the art object is made, supported by the two supervision vignettes in which positionality was important – I refer to the warplane image – where the logical elevation of the image enabled the flow of countertransference response, and to the example where the image appeared to incorporate aspects of the studio within the virtual place represented by the imagery. In both examples, thinking out of the frame – an interesting variation on the contemporary business mantra implying the source of creative thought – was an important change in the traditional scopic regime in art psychotherapy.

This new point of view freed the observer from the near and far transitional activity driven by the needs of the inquiring eye and introduced the unity of both eye *and* body as it travels through three-dimensional space available to both the supervisor and supervisee. This active bodily and ocular paradigm has the power to confront the countertransference material pointed out by Rees (1998). This, I believe, can be achieved by the movement of both people within the supervision environment and in relation to the art object representation of the client, through which countertransference feelings of boredom and dullness can be acknowledged, not acted-out and converted into useful energy. The realisation that space can inform individual identity has often been sensed at a feeling level but the humanist geographers add much to our conscious awareness, the implication being that we ignore the influence of the creative context at our peril. In this regard it seems desirable, if not imperative, that supervision takes place in the same environment as the client used in her act of creation. For instance, the possibilities that flowed in vignette 2 would not have reached awareness if the supervision session had not taken place in the same art studio. The therapist's coat would have been absent, as would the all-important table and red chairs. This would have narrowed the perceptual and contemplative horizons so necessary in the gestalt figure–ground dynamic of the possible art psychotherapy supervision dynamic.

Foucault's thoughtfulness regarding the social significance of spaces promotes awareness of both the possible 'deviancy' of our studios as well as their healthy function as places of transformation (a heterotopia of crisis). It is interesting that the art therapy studio shimmers between the two depending upon the direction of approach. The most important message in this chapter is that people with learning disabilities occupy a position at the edge of our society. Typically they have limited possessions and rarely own their place of residence or hold a tenancy. Almost everything is shared and little is private. Space and place are therefore crucially unmet desires for this group of people. It is therefore unsurprising to see a person with learning disabilities carrying possessions or having adorned their clothing with objects and badges, as the body has become a vital *place* of existence.

Art therapy and its environment have the means to provide the expression of the socially suppressed topological desires of the learning disabled person. The studio becomes a landscape within which the place-related identity of the individual can emerge. Accordingly, the supervision process requires the sensitivity to distill this energy into useful awareness. Casement (1985) points the way in his concept of the 'internal supervisor'. This intriguingly spatial idea appears to offer the potential to consider the client's environment, be it virtual or physical and most probably a combination of the two, through the process of trial identification.

In conclusion, supervision in the context of learning disability has the responsibility of asking social as well as psychological questions, for disability is the product of our conditioning as much as it is a limiting construction of a fellow human being.

## Notes

1  I would like to acknowledge Anna Grimshaw whose book *The Ethnographer's Eye: Ways of Seeing in Modern Anthropology* inspired the title of this chapter.
2  Some people, with learning disabilities or not, begin their lives in the unusual environment of the incubator whilst others later might experience adversity and abuse behind closed doors.
3  From a psychoanalytic perspective, the significance of the mirror and the mirror-role have been described and explored by Lacan and Winnicott.
4  As part of my practice, I inform the client that supervision takes place and that our work together may occasionally be anonymously discussed. These processes are regularly enacted in work with the learning disabled because consent, due to possible memory and comprehension difficulties, cannot be assumed to span the whole period of therapy.

## References

Adams, P., Hoelscher, S. and Till, K. (2001) *Textures of Place: Exploring Humanist Geographies*, Minneapolis: University of Minnesota Press.

Butler, R. and Parr, H. (1999) *Mind and Body Spaces: Geographies of Illness, Impairment and Disability*, London: Routledge.

Casement, P. (1985) *On Learning from the Patient*, Hove: Brunner-Routledge.

Casement, P. (1990) *Further Learning from the Patient: The Analytic Space and Process*, London: Tavistock/Routledge.

Casement, P. (2002) *Learning from Our Mistakes: Beyond Dogma in Psychoanalysis and Psychotherapy*, London: Tavistock/Routledge.

Damarell, B. (1999) 'Just forging or seeking love and approval? An investigation into the phenomenon of the forged art object and the copied picture in art therapy involving people with learning disabilities', *Inscape*, 2: 44–50.

Dantels, S. (1992) 'Place and the geographical imagination', *Geography*, 77: 311.

Edwards, D. (2004) *Art Therapy: Creative Therapies in Practice*, London: Sage Publications.

Foucault, M. (1967 Lecture/1984 Published) 'Of other spaces', in N. Morozoff (ed.), *The Visual Culture Reader: Second Edition*, London: Routledge, pp. 229–236.

Foucault, M. (1977) 'Disabled bodies in the gay community', in R. Butler and P. Hester (eds), *Mind and Body Spaces: Geographies of Illness, Impairment and Disability*, London: Routledge, p. 208.

Grimshaw, A. (2005) *The Ethnographer's Eye: Ways of Seeing in Modern Anthropology*, Cambridge: Cambridge University Press.

Hughes, R. (1996) *The Shock of the New: Art and the Century of Change*, London: Thames and Hudson.

Moorhouse, P. (2005) *Interpreting Caro*, London: Tate Publishing.

Owens, C. (1980) 'The allegorical impulse: towards a theory of postmodernism', in D. Preziosi (ed.), *The Art of Art History: A Critical Anthology*, Oxford: Oxford University Press, pp. 315–328.

Rees, M. (1998) *Drawing on difference: Art Therapy with People who have Learning Disabilities*, London: Routledge.

Sheppard, A. (1987) *Aesthetics: An Introduction to the Philosophy of Art*, Oxford: Oxford University Press.

Shipton, G. (1999) 'Self-reflection and the mirror', in C. Mace (ed.), *Heart and Soul: The Therapeutic Face of Philosophy*, London: Routledge, pp. 180–193.

Summers, D. (1989) 'Form, nineteenth century metaphysics, and the problem of historical description', in D. Preziosi (ed.), *The Art of Art History: A Critical Anthology* (1998), Oxford: Oxford University Press, pp. 127–142.

Swain, J., French, S. and Cameron, C. (2003) *Controversial Issues in a Disabling Society*, Buckingham, Philadelphia: Open University Press.

Tuan, Y. (1977) *Space and Place: The Perspective of Experience*, Minneapolis: University of Minnesota Press.

Tuan, Y. (2004) *Place, Art, and Self*, Santa Fe, New Mexico: Center for American Places.

Wittgenstein, L. (1958) *Philosophical Investigations*, Oxford: Blackwell.

# Chapter 3

# Framing enchantment

## Countertransference in analytical art psychotherapy supervision

*Joy Schaverien*

---

*Enthral*: To hold spellbound, enchant, captivate (Collins Concise English Dictionary)
*Enchant*: Charm, to put someone under a spell (Oxford Dictionary of English)

### Introduction

In this chapter I consider enchantment[1] as a factor in the supervision of analytical art psychotherapy. I propose that there are times when the therapist, working with diverse and sometimes disturbed states of mind, is in a condition akin to enchantment. I mean this in a rather wide sense; it is not a romantic state but rather a very real and substantial embodiment, in the therapist, of a psychological shadow element – an unconscious counter-transference. It is as if the art psychotherapist is spellbound and is, literally, in need of the vision of another in order to break that spell. It takes *super*vision to extract both therapist and patient from the spell that has woven them together. My interest is in states that might be communicated unconsciously through the transference, as well as the pictorial image mediated within the therapeutic relationship.

This is about supervising art psychotherapists, whose clients make art in their sessions, but I am also drawing on my experience of supervising psychotherapists and Jungian analysts, whose clients sometimes bring pictures or art objects to their appointments. The Jungian theory of active imagination lends itself to the exploration of art within the therapeutic relationship (Schaverien 2005) and, extending this idea, supervision might be considered a form of shared active imagination. It emerges, between therapist and supervisor, as they conjure an essence of the therapist's experience of the client and the pictures. This is akin to what Ogden (2005) has called 'dreaming the patient' but, whilst for Ogden this 'imagined third' remains completely imaginal and intangible, in art psychotherapy an actual object from the session may be present in the supervisor's room.

The art object embellishes supervision, revealing both intra-psychic elements of the patient's unconscious and inter-psychic aspects, generated in-between patient and therapist. In supervision, the picture echoes, and to a degree represents, the dynamic field of the art psychotherapy encounter (Schaverien 1995: 196). The supervisor then has privileged access to a tangible object from the session and this adds another dimension to models of psychotherapy supervision (see Driver and Martin 2002; Wiener *et al.* 2003). In art psychotherapy supervision the art object reveals otherwise inarticulate elements of the session.

## Framed experience

In order to process complex supervisory experiences a clearly boundaried setting is necessary. Psychotherapy is often described as framed experience and this could be extended to supervision (Langs 1994). This might be envisaged as a series of ever-decreasing frames within frames that are both real and metaphorical. The outer frame is constructed by the physical reality of the bounded space of the art therapy studio, sealed by the walls and closed door. Within this there is the metaphorical, intangible frame, which is made up of the agreed limits of the therapeutic relationship, including the arrangements and formal structures needed for the safe conduct of psychotherapy. Times of sessions (or, in private work, the fee) and other practical arrangements are all part of this. Within these secure outer frames, a dynamic space is created in which the therapeutic relationship develops. In addition to this traditional psychotherapy frame, and contained within it, the artwork offers a central framed area that is often a focal point. Finally, if we draw back beyond the outer bounds of psychotherapy, supervision might be imagined as an encircling, outer frame that offers containment for the whole enterprise.

This idea of framed experience has parallels with other cultural settings and so, as I have done before (Schaverien 1989, 1991, 2003), I turn to the theatre, that home of enchantment. The theatre is a well-known metaphor for the psyche and for psychotherapy (McDougall 1986; Jenkyns 1996; Gordon 1989). However, as far as I am aware, it has not previously been applied as a metaphor for supervision. I turn to it now to illustrate the respective roles of therapist and supervisor within the symbolic space created in supervision.

In the traditional theatre the proscenium arch frames the stage where the drama takes place. Everyone concerned knows the implicit rule that the audience is admitted to the auditorium but not the stage. Accordingly, actor and audience play their part in this imaginal enterprise. On entering the theatre the spectator suspends disbelief. It is a cultural given that the play is a symbolic enactment and the action is imaginary. However, if the performance is good, both player and spectator experience real emotions.

Tragedy may move the spectator to tears, whilst aggression may induce fear; the effect may be cathartic, evoked by empathy, or identification with the protagonist. There may be vicarious enjoyment in witnessing an intimate drama but being removed from it (Aristotle 1965). The point is that all concerned enter voluntarily into a shared form of imaginative activity, lending themselves to the enchantment of the performance: and so the drama casts its spell.

The play is make-believe and to interpret it literally would be to confuse the frames of reference. A hypothetical, dramatic interaction illustrates this difference between a symbolic attitude and a literal or concrete response. Imagine a theatrical production where two actors are taking part in a fight on the stage. Suddenly one of them pulls a knife and threatens to attack the other with it; the tension mounts in the audience when he moves forward as if to stab the hero. At this point one member of the audience can bear it no longer and leaps onto the stage, grabs the wrist of the actor holding the knife and wrestles him to the ground. This is a misunderstanding of the implicit frames of the setting. In the process of entering the drama a category error is made; there is confusion between the symbolic and the real. In the usual course of a drama members of the audience make a psychological split that enables them to suspend disbelief and so, even though real emotions are experienced, the symbolic attitude is maintained. On this occasion, for this member of the audience, there is a loss of the make-believe element, the 'as if', and so the imaginal space collapses.

In considering this as a metaphor for supervision we might conceive of art psychotherapy as a drama, made up of different active elements. The first is the client's narrative, the story that is told or conveyed in their early pictures. Then, as the therapeutic relationship becomes established, the transference/countertransference dynamic engages the therapist, together with the client, in a live drama. In this the pictures sometimes become an embodiment, carrying aspects of both of the former and also introducing a new element. Through the transference the client attributes attitudes and responses to the therapist, some of which are ego alien to the therapist, but they may be so powerful that they lead to a temporary loss of the symbolic attitude. For a time the therapist may believe or sometimes embody the projection, temporarily becoming convinced that she is a bad therapist, an abusive or perfect parent/therapist or an idealised saviour, lover/therapist. The point is that the transference is a bit like a drama in which the protagonists experience real emotions but it is vital to remember that it is also a symbolic relationship.

When the symbolic attitude collapses – the projection is taken for real – then there is a temporary loss of the 'as if' meaning of the transference. Like our hypothetical member of the audience, the client, and sometimes the therapist, becomes identified with the transference and cannot separate from the unconscious projection. It is such identification with the projection that may lead to acting out; in such a situation the therapist mistakes that which should remain symbolic for real. Supervision plays a part in reinstating the symbolic attitude by helping the therapist regain a conscious stance. Supervision is then an essential form of emotional cleansing, offering separation from the projections and restoring reality.

When the therapist presents in supervision she might be seen like an actor, who moves from the position of protagonist to join the supervisor in observing the action from a critical distance. She or he may bring unprocessed and largely undifferentiated material to supervision. The very act of supervision requires the therapist to make a psychological split, simultaneously standing beside the supervisor, as a spectator of the drama, as well as observing her part in it. In this way the symbolic attitude is restored.

## Art psychotherapy supervision

For the therapist it may be a relief to discuss confidential material but first trust needs to be established. If the therapist is, for example, self-critical the supervisor may be placed in the role of a persecutory other. Alternatively there may be idealisation, conveyed in a pervading deference and a sense that the supervisor knows best (see Case, Chapter 6). The supervisor will resist the temptation to collude with such projections and attempt to help the therapist to find his or her own autonomy. The therapist needs to prepare for supervision by giving an account of the patient's history, sometimes a written, verbatim report of a session, and bringing the art objects or photographs of them. Once trust is established in supervision, countertransference responses can be explored in depth, including emotional and bodily sensations, images and fantasies generated within the therapeutic relationship (see Schaverien 2006, for detailed discussion of gender issues within supervision and Orbach 2006, for discussion of bodily countertransferences).

The supervisor, as if from the privileged position of the audience, witnesses the drama that unfolds in supervision. Whilst the therapist recounts the experience of the session, the supervisor closely attends, forming a picture of the therapeutic relationship as a whole, including the pictures. As the atmosphere of therapy is recreated the supervisor, like the spectator in the theatre, may be moved by tragedy, horrified by stories of abuse, saddened or angered on behalf of the client or fear for the welfare of the therapist. In this way she is drawn into the drama but at the same time maintains a dispassionate and watchful eye on her own reactions. The supervisor's task is to think with the therapist about the meaning of the therapeutic relationship; she is attuned to listen for the unconscious implications of the interactions presented. The therapist may be totally engaged with the drama of the session but the supervisor is not immediately involved and so her view is outside the dynamic. The point is that, at its best, the framed space of supervision creates a symbolic space in the mind of the therapist, a space to think.

## Unconscious enchantment – Therapist A

Therapist A, an experienced art psychotherapist, required supervision for an art psychotherapy group that she conducted in a psychiatric hospital one day a week. Her working week was divided between working as an art psychotherapist in the NHS and in part-time, private practice. She had been attending supervision for a year but recently her attendance had become erratic for a number of apparently practical reasons. On this occasion she arrived with an armful of paintings from the group that she wanted to discuss.

Top of the agenda for both supervisor and therapist was the lack of recent attendance and the related fact that the supervision seemed to be breaking down. Discussion evolved around the difficulty the therapist had in making the appointed time. Any other time that was available was impossible because of other commitments. Thus an impasse was reached and they were on the point of agreeing to terminate the supervision. Then the therapist said how much she valued the supervision and wished she could continue. It was difficult to make this time now, but in six months it would be possible, because she had a private patient who would be leaving. The rest of this morning in her week would then be free. The supervisor reflecting on this suggested that, from what the therapist was saying, it seemed that the supervision could continue if this patient was asked to come at another time. A look of total surprise and almost shock came across the face of the therapist and she said: 'Oh I can't do that'. The supervisor inquired, 'Why not?' A stunned silence followed and then relieved amusement.

Therapist A explained that she was considering other changes, including possibly moving to a different consulting room, but she could not do this either until the patient had terminated. Her other patients would be able to move but not this one. It became evident that the therapist was in the thrall of this patient. We could consider this to be a form of enchantment; it was as if she was spellbound, unable to think, to act autonomously or to conceive of the obvious solution to her problem. She was in a state of unconscious identification with the patient. She needed desperately to separate but, because it was unconscious, this was not possible.

This patient was not the subject of today's supervision and so this could have been missed. However it was evident that, before the group could be given attention, this particular patient had to be discussed; she demanded attention. It emerged that the patient was the child of a depressed and anxious mother who feared holding her baby. There was clearly a fragile attachment, which was compounded when the father took care of the baby, further undermining the mother's confidence. Later, as the patient was growing up, mother came between her and the father, breaking up any pleasant engagement between them, demanding his immediate attention and so making the patient feel abandoned. It is likely that this insecure attachment had produced a baby that had to hold on very tightly in order not to be dropped. Although she was an adult this was unconsciously replayed in the transference; she was now, psychologically, holding very tightly to the therapist. It was this transference dynamic that had the therapist in thrall.

A powerful countertransference made it unthinkable to move this patient, as if such a move would be disastrous in some unspecified way. For the therapist it was not 'as if' the patient were the baby that could not be put down: she just could not move her. The therapist had become unconsciously identified with the anxious attachment associated with the patient's fear of being dropped, and so she was unable to act autonomously. Now, as the patient's story was recounted, it was as if the shadow lifted: there was a lighter feel in supervision and consciousness returned. A separation from the transference, in the therapist's mind, now made it possible to imagine talking to the patient's adult part and asking her to change her appointment to a different time. Now the request would be accompanied by the therapist's empathic understanding that the client was quite able to make such a change, even though the child part of her might be unsettled by the request. The point is that once the unconscious, transfixing element is conscious it is possible to separate reality from the transference enchantment.

In supervision both therapist and supervisor together create a space to think about the patient and so to restore the symbolic attitude. In this case supervision enabled the therapist to separate from the projection and so to differentiate from the intense transference. The therapist's confidence to make this intervention benefits the patient by modelling that separation is not necessarily disastrous. I emphasise that this was an experienced art psychotherapist because it shows how we all continue to need supervision, literally the vision of another person, to help us untangle the powerful material that sometimes overwhelms us psychologically. In the supervision session described above, the original task, of supervising the art psycho-therapy group, temporarily had to take second place. The private patient was in the way of the 'sibling' group. This countertransference enchantment, evoked by the transference, influenced the therapist beyond the therapeutic frame. It was only when this patient's infantile anxiety was understood that the reality of the psychotherapeutic frame could be reinstated in the therapist's mind.

## Transference in supervision

Transference is a symbolic relationship, generated in psychotherapy and sometimes mediated in supervision. Transference reactivates past patterns of relating and brings them live into the present of the therapeutic relationship so that the psyche is mobilised and change becomes possible (Freud 1912, 1915, 1917). To discuss transference as a form of enchantment, or a spell, is unusual. On the one hand psychotherapy is a very practical and grounded endeavour and yet the therapist lends her/himself to the influence of the patient's psyche. Thus he or she may become subject to all kinds of projected affect and magical thinking. This may bear little resemblance to the grounded reality of the therapist. Jung (1946) writes:

> The transference . . . alters the psychological stature of the doctor, though this is at first imperceptible to him. He too becomes affected, and has as much difficulty in distinguishing between the patient and what has taken possession of him as has the patient himself.
>
> (p. 18)

This passage vividly conveys how the therapist [doctor] may lose the symbolic attitude and become imperceptibly altered by the transference: in other words, as we saw with Therapist A, in thrall to the patient.

Jung likened the analytic vessel to the sealed container of the alchemist's alembic. This is an image of a very securely framed space. Within the alembic, opposing elements are attracted, come together and mix, producing an intense chemical reaction from which something new emerges (Jung 1928a). This is a metaphor for the transference/countertransference dynamic, in which an initial attraction or repulsion occurs, followed by a mixing and finally a separating out of the elements. As a result a new, conscious state is born (Jung 1928a; Samuels 1989). The picture plays a part in this because here, like the alchemist's alembic, real substances are used. Within the analytic frame these substances (paint, pastels or charcoal) are applied, mixed and something new is created and the whole is understood to have a psychological parallel (Schaverien 1991: 155–157). Clearly the frame of the analytic vessel needs to be strong to withstand the pressure from such powerful unconscious forces, and supervision contributes to this. Supervision might be viewed as a sealed outer container, an extension of the bounds of the analytic vessel, adding to its power to withstand pressure from within (Schaverien 2003, 2006; Cwik 2006).

Transference does occur within supervision, as in all forms of human interaction, but it is not appropriate to analyse it. To distinguish between analysis and supervision I turn, as I have before (Schaverien 1991, 1999, 2003), to Greenson (1967). Greenson divides the therapeutic relationship into three elements: the real relationship, the therapeutic alliance and the transference. If this is extended to supervision the priority is altered. In supervision, the three parts might be the real relationship, the transference and *The Supervisory Alliance*. In supervision, as in analysis, *The Real Relationship* is a real relationship, which comprises attention to frame issues and the practical aspects of supervision.

The *transference* is central in analysis but not in the supervisory relationship. Transference may develop in supervision but it is rarely interpreted unless it inhibits the process of supervision, in which case it might indicate the therapist's need for further analysis. The supervisor might sensitively suggest this but would not engage in that process, as interpretation of transference fosters regression and so it would breach the frame of supervision. The imaginal drama that is transference is enacted on the analytical stage and not the supervisory one. The supervisor holds in mind a boundary between supervision and personal therapy.

The *supervisory alliance* is central in supervision. This is a real relationship in which there is an element of teaching, as well as modelling of good practice. It is influenced by the context, so that when the therapist is in training, the teaching role of the supervisor is more significant than when the therapist is qualified. With the experienced therapist, supervision may become a meeting between colleagues and the supervisory alliance may develop into one of mutual respect. In peer supervision, the alliance is between equals engaged in consideration of the material of one of them. When trust is established the drama that develops between psychotherapist and supervisor may be understood as parallel process: a reflection of the therapeutic relationship, which may indicate the unconscious dynamics at play (Searles 1955, 1962; Langs 1979, 1994). In good supervision there is an exploratory feel and a clear boundary between analysis and supervision.

## Countertransference

Countertransference in supervision is complex. Originally countertransference was considered to be the analyst's unresolved transference to the analysand that needed to be eliminated by further analysis of the analyst. Although this is still considered to be one aspect, today countertransference is more generally considered to be the analyst's response to the whole of the analytic situation (Heimann 1949; Little 1950). Countertransference is a means by which the therapist becomes attuned to the patient; it is therefore a sensitive instrument in analysis, which is honed in supervision.

In human relationships it is usual for love to evoke love and hate to evoke hate: the 'talion law' (Racker 1968: 137). It is similar in analysis and therefore a positive transference will evoke a positive countertransference, whilst a negative transference will evoke a negative response (Racker 1968: 137). Frequently the unconscious element is split off and attributed to the analyst. So, if the conscious affect is love, hate is probably split off whilst, if the conscious attitude is hate, it is likely that love is its unconscious counterpart. The therapist's task is to observe rather than to act on the impulse to retaliate, whether that is to return love with love, or hate with hate. At times supervision can be essential in managing such a dynamic and especially when it manifests itself in projective identification. This is when the feelings of the patient are so effectively split off and projected that the analyst experiences them as her own (Klein 1946).

Jung introduced the term participation mystique, which he borrowed 'from the anthropologist Levy-Bruhl' (Jung 1921: para 12; Samuels 1986: 106). It is applied to describe a form of magical thinking in which there is no separation between subject and object; all things are connected. There is a similarity between this and the Kleinian projective identification but participation mystique opens up a wider domain. Gee (1996: 547) compares these two terms favouring participation mystique, which he reminds us Jung also called unconscious identity (Jung 1928b). In applying the work of Cassirer (1955) I have discussed such magical thought processes in relation to art objects created within analytical art psychotherapy. Magical thinking may be embodied in an artefact which is then experienced as having power, and so unconsciously carries something of this belief system (Schaverien 1991: 41–46). The artwork may engage the patient in this way but the therapist too may be affected. Communication is picked up through unconscious and non-verbal experiences that might be called 'participation mystique' or 'projective identification'. I am using enchantment in this context because it incorporates both of the former and perhaps adds something new for consideration of supervision.

## Countertransference in supervision

Countertransference in supervision is made up of:

- The therapist's countertransference to the patient.
- The supervisor's countertransference to the patient.
- The supervisor's countertransference to the therapist.
- The countertransference of therapist and supervisor to the pictures.

The *therapist's countertransference* is revealed in supervision through reporting the therapeutic dialogue, presenting the pictures, as well as considering bodily responses and mental images. These may not be very obvious at first, however on occasions they are very marked. For example it may emerge that the therapist dreads the sessions with a particular patient, or excitedly anticipates them. The therapist might find the pictures of one patient to be very appealing or others repulsive. Understanding such extreme responses may reveal some, as yet, unintegrated potential that is trying to break through to consciousness. Thus such responses, and those that are less obvious, might be regarded as possible unconscious communications from the patient and so material for supervision. The supervisee learns to use supervision in this way.

At times the *supervisor has a countertransference response to the patient* as presented in supervision but this cannot be separated from the therapist's presentation. For example a supervisor, listening to the report of a patient to whom the therapist is apparently attuned, may rather unexpectedly become irritated or impatient. If this is explored it may reveal a state of identification or some negative aspect of the transference that was previously unconscious. Conversely the therapist may be angry or frustrated with the patient; then the supervisor's empathy for the patient may soften the therapist's attitude. Thus the supervisor takes account of the whole supervisory relationship, its feeling tone and the way the patient is presented. Given the confidential and sealed nature of the analytical vessel, the witnessing function of the supervisor is significant. The supervisor, as witness, may bring to light the opposite element in a stuck transference situation. This use of the supervisor's countertransference may eventually facilitate the therapist's ability to think about the patient in new ways.

The *supervisor's countertransference to the therapist* is complicated. Wiener (2007) discusses some of the challenges that may emerge in this relationship. The supervisory one is a real relationship but even so it may contain transference elements and at times these may emerge from supervisor to supervisee. The supervisor's sibling relationships may be activated: for example the supervisor may find she envies the therapist, perhaps for having such an interesting patient or for doing good work. Alternatively the supervisor may be irritated by the therapist's inexperience and feel that she could do better with the patient. Idealisation may lead the supervisor to expect more of an inexperienced therapist than is reasonable. The point is that such transferences from the supervisor to the supervisee need to become conscious and, if necessary, be worked through in supervision or the therapist's own analysis. The countertransference issues that reveal parallel process can only emerge once such personal material is conscious. In order to be available to facilitate the separation and differentiation of the individuation process for the patient, both supervisor and supervisee need to separate from mutual projections.

In art psychotherapy there is also the *countertransference to the pictures* to consider. As the therapist and supervisor view them together, countertransference enchantment may be revealed. Art, whether good, bad or indifferent, evokes some form of aesthetic response, a form of 'aesthetic countertransference' (Schaverien 1995). This is different in each case but the point is that the aesthetic impact of art created in or brought to a session influences the therapeutic relationship and so plays a part in supervision. The art object may bring some of the actual physical chaos and mess of the art psychotherapy session into supervision. With adults this usually remains in the pictures and so leaves with the therapist. However in supervision of art psychotherapists working with children (the type of work so vividly described by Aldridge 1998, O'Brien 2003, Case 2005), real traces may remain behind in the supervisor's room, such as bits of glitter that spill onto the carpet, embedding in it. It is sometimes as if a tiny fragment, a reminder of the child client, has been left in the supervisor's room until the therapist returns. This may well go unnoticed but it could evoke a range of feelings. The therapist may be concerned about leaving a mess in the room. However she may feel held in mind by the supervisor and so supported in her work with a difficult child and this may be symbolised by these little shards from the session.

### The spellbound supervisor

Not all enchantment is vibrant or seductive: it may include boredom, anger and hate as well as seduction and even love. The supervisor's task is to break the spell, in the sense of helping to bring consciousness. In the following example it was the supervisor who became enchanted and so transfixed. Boredom in supervision, as in analysis, may indicate something of the unconscious dynamic between the participants. Therapist B talked throughout his supervision session, apparently presenting a patient. The supervisor, to her own distress, was at first bored and then, as the session continued, found it almost impossible to stay awake; the feeling was overwhelming. She was drifting and then pulling herself back from the edge of sleep. Unable to get a sense of the patient being presented or the question being asked by the therapist, she became very concerned. She blamed herself, inwardly, for being an inept supervisor. The session passed and the supervisor reflected on the experience in her own supervision, coming to realise that something must have been communicated by this experience.

In the following session the supervisor decided to comment on the compelling atmosphere in the last session, wondering if the therapist had been aware of it. In raising the topic she was not specific about the nature of her experience of that session. This was enough to open the topic for discussion and it enabled the therapist to explain that, the day before the last session, he had had some bad news in his personal life; a relative had died. He had decided that it would be best not to mention it and throughout had been trying to steer the supervision away from reference to anything that might upset him. Thus the atmosphere of the supervision session had been inauthentic. Unconsciously the therapist had been communicating this and so the supervisor was overwhelmed with sleep.

This countertransference enchantment was played out in the supervision session but it was not apparently related to the client's material. It would be interesting to know what the client had brought to the session because exploration might reveal this to have been a parallel of the therapeutic situation but we do not have that information. My point is that this spell was cast, unconsciously distracting the supervisor, and so protecting the therapist's vulnerable state. The supervisor lacked the confidence to challenge the atmosphere in the room and, thinking it was merely her own sleepiness, blamed herself and so said nothing about it. If she had been able to challenge the boredom she was feeling at the time, the spell might have been broken. Therapist B would probably have broken down and his very real distress would have emerged. Although consciously he did not want to be touched emotionally, it is likely that he would have been relieved to have his emotional state recognised.

This spell, created in the supervision session, demonstrates how impossible it is to work in supervision if all is not well with the frame. If Therapist B had been able to tell of his personal state first, then supervision could have proceeded. It is important for the therapist to feel able to relate current aspects of their personal life that are likely to affect the supervision. This is a delicate balance between supervision and personal therapy; sometimes it is difficult to separate the two and so sensitive attunement is required to draw this line.

### Parallel process

My next two examples bring the picture centrally into the frame. Therapist C brought a series of pictures made by a client from her private art psychotherapy practice. She was unable to understand why she could not get a sense of their meaning. The patient was an artist and so very able with the medium of art psychotherapy. The presenting problem was his dissatisfaction with his current post and he wanted a change of career and was considering training as an art psychotherapist.

The pictures were vibrant and well executed, as might be expected of someone who had trained as an artist. They were full of coloured abstract patterns made with some expertise. There were swirls and circles and wild marks. They were accomplished pictures, however the supervisor was unmoved by them. Each week the therapist brought a picture and reported that week's session in detail. Each week the supervisor listened and thought that she was missing something because she could not feel engaged with these images. Then, gradually, she realised that there was no real story to re-animate them in supervision. There was no connection with the person who made them – he was not coming through in the therapist's presentation. After bearing with this for a while, and struggling with the feeling that she was watching something in which she could not participate, the supervisor challenged the therapist by admitting to her that the pictures left her unmoved.

This opened up discussion, which quickly came to centre on the pervading sense of discomfort that the therapist experienced in the sessions, most of which were taken up with painting so that there was little room left for processing the material. The patient recounted the situation at work but avoided discussing his personal life in depth. In this way he controlled the sessions and left little or no time for the therapist to speak. The therapist was placed in the position of voyeur. She was troubled because she felt very little for the pictures but she was in awe of their aesthetic qualities and admitted to being impressed because he was a professional artist. She thought this was merely her own feeling, that she was not a good enough artist/therapist for the patient.

Gradually, these feelings began to make sense in terms of the patient's history. It was likely that it was the patient who felt inadequate. Watching him paint was rather like watching masturbation: there was no real intercourse between them and so the patient was not in a relationship with her. He could perform through art, which had been his way of dealing with difficult times in his early years and the death of his father when he was a young teenager. Now he was showing off his expertise and the therapist felt inadequate. However she began to realise that this was, to a degree, a false-self projection. The therapist felt useless in the face of his apparent expertise but it seemed that this was projective identification. The patient's shadow split off and inadequate feelings were lodged in the therapist. She embodied his vulnerable child self. Thus the pictures were repetitive and unconsciously defensive.

It took much discussion in supervision to begin to understand the very real fear of intimacy that lay behind these attractive but repetitive pictures. Once the therapist was able to understand her own inadequate feelings as linked to the state of the patient, she was able to speak with him about his own inadequate feelings. At first this too was denied and resisted but over time a dependent, erotic transference emerged. He permitted himself to need the therapy. As a result his pictures filled less of the space but those he did make became more meaningful. He began to relate to the therapist.

There was a lack of life in this therapy, which was replayed in supervision and reflected in the pictures. The spell, which cast a deadening effect, was broken by the supervisor's intervention, but it took time for the therapist to become conscious and process this with the patient. Sometimes the supervisor has to bear the not-knowing, alongside the therapist, before the enchantment can be mediated and transformed through interpretation.

In supervision, as in art psychotherapy, a distinction needs to be made between form and content: between the effects of the presentation of a material art object and the imagery that it reveals. The pictures made in analytical art psychotherapy may embody the transference, acting as a talisman or a scapegoat, depending on the psychological investment in them (Schaverien 1991). This is an effect of both their object nature and the imagery they reveal. Pictures made in therapy may be aesthetically rather weak and so they do not immediately connect with the viewer. It is only as the context in which they were made is animated by the therapist's account that the picture becomes meaningful (Schaverien 1991: 152).

Therapist C's patient did not at first invest in his pictures and as a result he did not treat them as meaningful: talismans to be valued. Rather they were scapegoats, in the sense of externalising and showing off; they embodied his flamboyant disguise/persona. In supervision it was the combination of observing the interpersonal relationship, combined with the scapegoat transference embodied in the pictures, that gave access to the real person of the patient. It is a combination of the therapeutic relationship and the picture that weaves the therapist into its spell and enchants. This does not always immediately communicate in supervision. It is when the therapist conveys the context from which the picture emerged that it becomes animated. Then the supervisor is admitted to the inner frame of the drama of the therapeutic relationship and its atmosphere begins to permeate the supervision.

### Enchantment in the picture

My final example raises questions regarding the manner of presentation of art objects in supervision. Therapist D explained that she had not brought her client's picture to supervision with her. From her discussion of the session in which the picture featured it was clear that something about it had profoundly disturbed her. She described the picture, which contained some very unsettling imagery, but it was unclear why it was so disturbing. The supervisor was finding it difficult to visualise this troubling picture. Despite Therapist D's description, the supervisor was frustrated that, literally, she could not see what the therapist meant. The picture seemed to be central in the supervision session despite its absence.

The supervisor commented on this, explaining that it was very difficult for her to visualise the picture. It was clear that something about it troubled the therapist and it was evidently important, so she was curious about why the therapist had not brought it with her. (The therapist kept the picture, along with others, in a folder, in a cupboard in the art room.) Without hesitation Therapist D said that the picture felt too confidential to bring on the journey to the supervisor's consulting room. At first this seemed understandable and respectful; it was evident that the imagery was very disturbing for the patient. This raised the question of the patient's consent and as this was discussed the therapist explained that she felt it would disrupt the therapy to ask permission to bring these highly charged pictures to supervision. Moreover the imagery was very vivid and rather violent and she would not want to carry it with her. She felt that to bring a real and physical object created by the patient out of the sealed container of the art room would violate the sacrosanct nature of therapy. Moreover, as they further discussed it she considered that some unspecified person might see the picture on the journey. It seemed that there was transference material mixed up with the reality of this situation.

Therapist D had brought pictures of other patients before, without having the same anxieties, so it seemed that something was being activated in her. Clearly the picture was disturbing for the therapist, as well as her client, but it seemed that there was some magical thinking operating; there was a general concern about something magical getting out of control. At this stage it was unclear whose concern this was – was it that of the therapist or the patient or both? I propose that this therapist was in the thrall of the transference and that was embodied in the picture: she was captivated by it.

Therapist D's concern about violating the therapeutic vessel by taking the picture out of the art room was a real and respectful concern. She was guarding the patient's right to privacy. At this point the supervisor could have closed the topic, agreeing with the therapist and thinking no further about it. However the supervisor might be curious and suspect that it could be fruitful to explore this in more detail. How would it be if this were treated as an unconscious communication from the patient? In magical terms we might say Therapist D was spellbound – unable to move freely and captivated by an unconscious atmosphere. She was in a state of unconscious enchantment. The patient had unconsciously communicated her state of anxious fear to the therapist who was now embodying it. The therapist had worked with this supervisor for a long time but it seemed as if the trust they had established was now in danger of breaking down.

This needed to be tackled and the supervisor pointed out that this problem was unusual and so needed further discussion. Therapist D had real concerns about bringing the picture out of the framed space of the consulting room to the supervisor's room. It was the journey in-between that troubled her most. Attention now focused on the patient: how she had made the picture and what had been discussed in the session. The client had suffered intrusive bullying in her early years, both at home and on her way to school. There was also a question of whether the abuse she had suffered had been sexual. Although there was no specific memory of this there were bodily symptoms that led her to suspect this herself.

Therefore, it was evidently very important that Therapist D felt compelled to scrupulously respect the bounds of this therapy. This may have been a magical form of countertransference but it needed to be respected. As it was discussed further, it seemed that a possible solution might be a photograph. Many art psychotherapists keep a digital camera in the art room for the purposes of recording the artwork and so Therapist D considered this and realised that this would feel less exposing. She decided to ask permission to do this, explaining the practice of consulting a senior colleague in order to help her to think about the patient. Sometimes a patient appreciates this attention: it is as if she is being borne in mind by two parents. The patient agreed and so the therapist brought a photograph of the picture two weeks later. The frame issue, of the form of presenting the object, had thus been dealt with and it was then possible to begin to process the imagery.

On viewing the picture there was an initial shock; it was indeed a very disturbing image. The paper was black and on it, painted vividly in red and yellow, a face that appeared to be in great torment. A hand with a knife was pointing at the figure. It suggested the feel of an abusive intrusion – a threat of some archetypal immensity. This image was both a picture of the sense the patient had of being bullied and, at the same time, it was what she would like to do to the bullies. It was this exposure of her own murderous aggression, and a fear that it could get out of control, that had terrified her and communicated itself to the therapist. Moreover as it was explored it seemed likely that the therapist's anxiety about an unspecified person seeing the picture, on the journey to supervision, replayed the patient's experience of being exposed to bullies on the way to school. The imagery was indeed the stuff of repressed fears and its impact was considerable.

I will not discuss the implications of this imagery in more detail but there was a complex and lengthy process of becoming familiar with the imagery and integrating understanding of its meaning, in both supervision and therapy. The photograph clearly had less impact than the actual image would have done. A photograph is no substitute for a picture presented in its actual, raw, state but for the therapist the threat, expressed in the image, was safely contained in the photograph.

This example demonstrates how the pictures in analytical art psycho-therapy may influence the therapist. Initially Therapist D was uncon-sciously identified with the picture (Jung 1927; Gee 1996). This was a concretisation of the transference state. The object was not separate from the person; there was no psychological separation, no differentiation. Dis-cussion of the means of bringing the picture, as well as the ethical issues around presenting it, created a distance, a space so that the symbolic attitude could be reintroduced. If we recall our example from the theatre, where the member of the audience leapt onto the stage to save the actor, we might see a similar process in operation here. For this patient this was a living image. She, and for a while the therapist, experienced the picture in a very concrete way, it was not 'as if' it was the thing depicted, it was the same as the act. In supervision the 'as if' was reinstated so that it was no longer the act: it was a picture of the act. The therapist had to experience the 'as if' in order to be able to work symbolically with the transference and the image.

## Conclusion

I have proposed that countertransference is a form of enchantment to which we readily lend ourselves in the consulting room and from which at times it is not easy to extract ourselves. There is an unconscious mixing, which could be seen as a form of contamination, to which the therapist lends herself. The therapist travels with the patient into the recesses of the conscious mind and permits the dark material from the psyche to permeate a layer of her being. Psychotherapy is rather dangerous work in this sense. Like the miner who goes deep underground to find the coal or precious metals hidden there, the therapist takes risks with her own health and welfare.

Thus the role of the supervisor is an important one in confronting the shared imaginal world of the patient and therapist and breaking the spell of the countertransference enchantment. Supervision is then essential: a kind of moral and emotional cleansing to which we subject ourselves. It is like a shower where fresh water is poured over the therapist permitting her to separate herself from the shadow of the patient's material and to see it in a new light.

## Note

1 Although this use of the term enchantment is not the same as that of Bettelheim (1976) in his book on fairy tales, *The Uses of Enchantment*, I would like to acknowledge his use of this term.

## References

Aldridge, F. (1998) 'Chocolate or shit: aesthetics and cultural poverty in art therapy with children', *Inscape*, *3* (1): 2–9.

Aristotle (1965) *On the Art of poetry* (translated by T. S. Dorsch), London: Penguin Classics.

Bettelheim, B. (1976) *The Uses of Enchantment: The Meaning and Importance of Fairy Tales*, Harmondsworth: Penguin.

Case, C. (2005) *Imagining Animals: Art, Psychotherapy and Primitive States of Mind*, London: Routledge.

Cassirer, E. (1955) *The Philosophy of Symbolic Forms. Mythical Thought, Vol. 2*, New Haven: Yale University Press.

Cwik, A. J. (2006) 'The art of the tincture: analytical supervision', *Journal of Analytical Psychology*, *51* (2): 209–226.

Driver, A. and Martin, E. (2002) *Supervising Psychotherapy: Psychoanalytic and Psychodynamic Approaches*, London: Sage Publications.

Freud, S. (1905) *Three Essays on the Theory of Sexuality* (Standard Edition; vol. VII), London: Hogarth.

Freud, S. (1912) *The Dynamics of Transference* (Standard Edition; vol. XII), London: Hogarth (1963 edition).

Freud, S. (1915) *Observations on Transference Love* (Standard Edition; vol. XII), London: Hogarth.

Freud, S. (1917) *Transference* (Standard Edition; vol. XVI), London: Hogarth.

Gee, H. (1996) 'Developing insight through supervision: relating then defining', *Journal of Analytical Psychology*, *41* (4): 529–553.

Gordon, R. (1989) 'The psychic roots of drama', in A. Gilroy and T. Dalley (eds), *Pictures at an Exhibition: Selected Essays on Art and Art Therapy*, London: Tavistock, pp. 189–197.

Greenson, R. (1967) *The Technique and Practice of Psychoanalysis*, London: Hogarth.

Heimann, P. (1949) 'On countertransference', *International Journal of Psycho-analysis*, *31*: 81–84.

Jenkyns, M. (1996) *The Play's the Thing*, London: Routledge.

Jung, C. G. (1921) 'The type problem in classical and medieval thought', *Psychological Types* (CW 6), London: Routledge (1989 edition).

Jung, C. G. (1927) 'Mind and earth', *Civilisation in Transition* (CW10), London: Routledge (1974 edition).

Jung, C. G. (1928a) 'On psychic energy', *The Structure and Dynamics of the Psyche* (CW 8), London: Routledge & Kegan Paul (1972 edition).

Jung, C. G. (1928b) 'Child development and education', *The Development of the Personality* (CW17), Bollingen: Princeton University Press.

Jung, C. G. (1946) 'The psychology of the transference', *The Practice of Psychotherapy* (CW 16), Bollingen: Princeton University Press (1954 edition).

Klein, M. (1946) 'Notes on some schizoid mechanisms', in *Envy & Gratitude*, London: Hogarth, pp. 1–24.

Langs, R. (1979) *The Supervisory Experience*, New York: Jason Aronson.

Langs, R. (1994) *Doing Supervision and Being Supervised*, London: Karnac Books.

Little, M. (1950) '"R" the analyst's total response to his patient's needs', in M. Little (ed.), *Transference Neurosis and Transference Psychosis: Towards Basic Unity*, London: Free Associations Press (1986 edition), pp. 51–80.

McDougall, J. (1986) *The Theatres of the Mind: Illusion and Truth on the Psycho-analytic Stage*, London: Free Associations Books.

O'Brien, F. (2003) 'Bella and the white water rapids', *Inscape*, *8* (1): 29–41.

Ogden, T. H. (2005) 'On psychoanalytic supervision', *International Journal of Psychoanalysis*, *86* (5): 1265–1280.

Orbach, S. (2006) 'What can we learn from the body?', in J. Schaverien (ed.), *Gender, Countertransference and the Erotic Transference: Perspectives from Analytical Psychology and Psychoanalysis*, Hove: Routledge, pp. 198–209.

Racker, H. (1968) *Transference and Countertransference*, London: Hogarth.

Samuels, A. (1986) *A Critical Dictionary of Jungian Analysis*, London: Routledge & Kegan Paul.

Samuels, A. (1989) *The Plural Psyche: Personality, Morality and the Father*, London: Routledge.

Schaverien, J. (1989) 'The picture within the frame', in A. Gilroy and T. Dalley (eds), *Pictures at an Exhibition: Selected Essays on Art and Art Therapy*, London: Tavistock, pp. 147–155.

Schaverien, J. (1991) *The Revealing Image: Analytical Art Psychotherapy in Theory and Practice*, London: Jessica Kingsley (1999 edition).

Schaverien, J. (1995) *Desire and the Female Therapist: Engendered Gazes in Psychotherapy and Art Therapy*, London: Routledge.

Schaverien, J. (2003) 'Supervising the erotic transference and countertransference', in J. Wiener, R. Mizen and J. Duckham (eds), *Supervising and Being Supervised: a Theory in Search of a Practice*, Basingstoke: Palgrave/Macmillan, pp. 167–184.

Schaverien, J. (2005) 'Art and active imagination: reflections on transference and the image', *Inscape*, *10* (2): 39–53.

Schaverien, J. (2006) *Gender, Countertransference and the Erotic Transference: Perspectives from Analytical Psychology and Psychoanalysis*, Hove: Routledge.

Searles, H. (1955) 'The informational value of the supervisor's emotional experiences', in *Collected Papers on Schizophrenia and Related Subjects*, London: Maresfield (1986 edition), pp. 157–176.

Searles, H. (1962) 'Problems of psychoanalytic supervision', in *Collected Papers on Schizophrenia and Related Subjects*, London: Maresfield (1986 edition), pp. 584–604.

Wiener, J. (2007) 'The analyst's countertransference when supervising: friend or foe?', *Journal of Analytical Psychology*, *52* (1): 51–69.

Wiener, J., Mizen, R. and Duckham, J. (2003) *Supervising and Being Supervised: A Practice in Search of a Theory*, Basingstoke: Palgrave/Macmillan.

# Chapter 4

# Piecing together the jigsaw puzzle

## Thinking about the clinical supervision of art therapists working with children and young people

*Tessa Dalley*

## Introduction

As the title of this chapter suggests, the process of supervision is rather like piecing together a jigsaw puzzle. In the presentation of clinical material from a session with a child in art therapy, there are a myriad of projections, thoughts and feelings brought by the art therapist to supervision. In mulling over the material, there is an impression or an idea that begins to form in the supervisor's mind of what the puzzle might look like as it grows towards completion. Finding a piece of the jigsaw that fits involves making links and transforming what was unknown into something that is known and becomes 'seen'. Working on this together with the supervisee involves a slow and careful process of thinking and understanding how the various pieces may or may not fit together.

This way of thinking is helpful because of the complex nature of the therapeutic encounter as well as the complexity of the relationship that builds between supervisor and supervisee. There are many parts to this process. The frame of the supervision is established first, like the corners and outside edges. This involves frequency, duration, place and the manner in which cases are to be brought and is largely dependent on the theoretical orientation of the supervisor. Once these outside edges or the frame of the supervision are in place, there is a sense that the real work can begin.

The supervision work involves the task of joining up inner pieces of the jigsaw by attending to the detail of the therapeutic process. Different parts of the puzzle involve understanding the communication of the child, the transference and countertransference relationships with the art therapist and consideration of the artwork made in the session. These may resonate, in parallel, with the relationship with the supervisor. The puzzle is undertaken jointly and in the course of this activity the relationship between supervisor and supervisee has an evolving life of its own that includes attending to the unconscious aspects of this relationship and all its vicissitudes.

Supervision is a complex process and is a central vehicle in the teaching of therapeutic practice. Supervision makes it possible for the supervisee to learn from the therapeutic process, and have insight into the experience of the patient. The three parts of the training of art therapists in the UK include theoretical seminars and lectures, personal therapy and clinical practice under supervision, and these are integrally linked in the growth and development of a qualified practitioner. Post qualification however, the necessity to continue in both personal therapy and clinical supervision is paramount and, in my experience, this is often when the real learning begins.

Winnicott introduced the concept of the 'good enough mother' – the mother who is able to respond appropriately to her infant's needs and demands and understands these as her child expressing his temporary inability to cope with the external world, rather than experiencing these as a personal attack about which she then feels overwhelmed and guilty. If the good enough mother herself is held and supported, either by the child's father or another supportive adult, this provides the 'nursing triad' enabling the child to be contained emotionally even when he expresses his rage. Hawkins and Shohet (1989) suggest that this concept provides a useful analogy for supervision in order that the 'good enough' therapist can survive the negative attacks of the patient by being held within and by the supervisory relationship. Supervision thus provides a container that holds the relationship within the 'therapeutic triad'.

This is particularly important when working with children who bring chaotic, primitive feelings and thoughts to therapy. The therapist's task is to take in these projections, process them and enable the child to take them back in a meaningful way. This can take some time and may occur over many weeks and months. The therapist may remain confused about the child's communications and in a position of not knowing what is happening in the therapeutic relationship. The supervision provides the space where thinking takes place and these undigested, unprocessed thoughts and feelings are understood and meaning takes place. The therapist is then able to take her experience of being contained and understood back to the therapeutic setting, which helps the understanding of the communications of the child. In the course of this process, the supervisor, who may receive similar projections from the supervisee, remains in a position to think and reflect. The capacity to process these thoughts offers an intermediate space for creative thinking and play. Learning is most creative when it emerges in play (Winnicott 1971). Without the capacity to play none of the creative work that Winnicott regarded as central to the analytical endeavour takes place. This 'playfulness' requires trust and a sense of feeling contained. Putting the jigsaw together involves moments of pleasure, excitement, frustration, feelings of inadequacy and despair and also success in making links and a feeling that the picture is building into a configuration that makes sense.

## Putting together the outer frame: establishing a working contract

Much has been written about the appropriate setting for supervision (Hess 1980; Hawkins and Shohet 1989; Case and Dalley 1992, 2006 2nd edn; Langs 1994; Grinberg 1997; Martindale *et al.* 1997). A secure supervision frame is necessary to establish a system of ground rules, conditions and boundaries for effective supervision to take place. A supervision contract includes a firm frame of a set time, set fee, set hours and place to ensure privacy with strict confidentiality. There is a need for the relative neutrality and anonymity of the supervisor (Langs 1994). When these conditions are not all fully in place Langs describes the situation as 'frame deviant'. It is certainly important to attend to both conscious and unconscious components to this process to create a 'working alliance' between the two members of the supervising experience to ensure the process may develop under the best possible circumstances. In this way, the supervisor offers herself as a model of identification.

Over the years, I have supervised art therapists who work with children and adolescents in a variety of different settings. These settings have included CAMHS teams (Child and Adolescent Mental Health Service), special schools for children who have emotional and behavioural difficulties or learning difficulties, specialist units for autistic children, mainstream schools both at primary and secondary level and specialist services for looked-after children, which include residential children's homes. In most of these settings the art therapist works as a member of the multi-disciplinary team. In some cases, such as those art therapists working in private practice, they may be a sole practitioner where it is necessary for the therapist to make the links with the care network of the child.

In supervision of therapeutic work with children, there may be a large chunk of the jigsaw that needs to be considered in a different way, such as thinking about the looked-after child who may be in transition between foster carers, the complexity of the care network that supports the child, child protection procedures and so on. When the frame for the child moves, the supervision follows. Different clinical settings may involve other approaches such as the supervision of group work. The art therapist will bring the material from an ongoing therapeutic group so that there are a number of children and group dynamics to consider. If both group facilitators attend supervision together, the interaction between them can also be explored. The use of video can be helpful for supervision purposes in tracking the detail of the many interactions and dynamics within the group. Occasionally art therapists themselves are supervised in a group situation rather than individually. The group can provide a supportive atmosphere in which anxieties, reflections and feedback from peers can be shared. Sometimes this is requested for reasons of economy of time or money.

An important part of the supervision frame is providing a platform for learning about child development and a basic understanding of normal and abnormal developmental processes. This may include introduction to the range of childhood disorders that the art therapist may encounter in the course of her work, such as general anxiety states, school phobia, autism, attention deficit hyperactivity disorder (ADHD) or conduct disorders, anorexia or bulimia. Theoretical knowledge of the work of child psycho-analysts such as Melanie Klein, Anna Freud and Donald Winnicott is a requirement for therapeutic work with children as well as having a working knowledge of attachment theory (Bowlby 1969), parent–infant psychology such as concepts of attunement and intersubjectivity (Stern 1973) and the latest theories on neurobiological development in children (Schore 2001). Understanding early infantile processes and stages of psychosexual development is helpful when thinking about the pressures that bear on children's social and emotional development. For example the adolescent may present with aggression, acting out self-destructive behaviour that can be anxiety provoking for the art therapist. This knowledge helps the less experienced therapist to understand more fully the vast range of projections, feelings and behaviour that a child may bring to the therapeutic relationship.

One central aspect of the supervision is to provide the supervisee with a good enough understanding of her patient. Because respect for the clinical material is perhaps one of the most essential attitudes that should be transmitted to the supervisee (Grinberg 1997), it is necessary to have process notes of clinical sessions and the artwork made in the session. In this way it is possible to listen, observe and reflect on the supervisee's interventions, observing the dynamic interaction established with the child and how the art therapist makes use of the communication, both conscious and unconscious. The artwork is important to include in this process as supervisor and supervisee can look together and reflect on the many layers of meaning contained in the image. There may be a variety of images to consider, such as paintings, clay models, sand play and so on. Sharing associations and responses to the work assists in the understanding of the material at a deeper level.

## Peter

For the purposes of this chapter I will give a condensed account of one case that I supervised over the course of six years. This was a complex and challenging puzzle. The art therapist had been in supervision with a psychoanalyst at her work place, a residential children's home for children aged 11–16. She wanted to change supervisors as she was looking to work more specifically with the artwork and images made by her patient and gain a deeper understanding of the art therapy process. The art therapist had been working there for a couple of years and was in her own personal analysis. The home was staffed by two managers, care staff, teachers and a drama therapist who worked offsite. The high turnover of staff affected the therapist's sense of membership of a team that was constantly changing. The art therapy room was small and situated away from the main body of the home. The care staff worked closely with the art therapist to support the children's attendance. (For a detailed clinical account of this case see Retford-Muir 2007.)

> Peter was ten years old and one of the youngest residents in the house. He was on a Full Care Order and had been looked after since he was four months old. His mother was unable to care for him and there was no contact with his father. His mother subsequently gave birth to another child. Peter's younger sister remained in her care, which was very painful for Peter and exacerbated his sense of rejection and abandonment. Peter had experienced a number of different foster placements that broke down due to his aggressive unpredictable behaviour. In one of his foster placements he was sexually abused by an older foster child. This was not disclosed until the art therapist had been working with Peter for some years. In the home there was a system of key workers with whom Peter formed close dependent attachments. During the course of his therapy, which lasted for six years, the change of these workers, often at short notice and without prior warning, was another de-stabilising problem for Peter. He had few friends, finding it very difficult to relate to his peer group.

Once the supervision frame is established, the work starts with gathering information regarding the outer frame or external world of the child and the network that supports him. A detailed developmental history of the patient from birth includes developmental milestones, past medical history, care situation, his family circumstances with regard to parents, siblings, particular traumas or significant life events and also the wider network of school, hobbies and friendship groups.

> Peter's presentation was extremely complex. He was emotionally immature for his age, presenting like a much younger child in his lack of capacity to think for himself, or master his anxieties. He had quite severe obsessive–compulsive rituals, which included compulsive eating and an inability to control his own food intake. He had poor speech, very low frustration tolerance and a lack of impulse control. The most challenging aspect of his behaviour was that he was incontinent of urine and faeces and would defaecate anywhere in the house,

such as on the stairs. Attempts by the home staff to make him use the toilets ended up with him smearing faeces on the walls.

## Working from the outside in

The role of the supervisor supports the supervisee in fostering her potential to become a competent therapist. At this point in the work, the art therapist had doubts about her capacity to work with Peter as his presentation was so complex and his behaviour difficult to manage. She was overwhelmed and bewildered by her young patient. She had been working with him for six months in twice-weekly therapy. In order to help build up a psycho-dynamic picture of the child and his internal world, the supervisor aims to listen to these worries of the supervisee but give full attention to the inter-action between the art therapist and child in the session being presented. The intention is that the supervisee may find her own way of thinking in subsequent sessions.

Casement (2002) advocates the use of an 'internal supervisor', which involves the supervisee developing a capacity to process for herself what is taking place with the child in the moment to moment interaction of each session. This includes a sense of timing for interventions: when to interpret, when to stay silent, how to think about the use of the art materials in the session. Casement describes this as the establishment of a 'mental island' with which to reflect on the session at the time rather than later. This capacity helps the therapist make sense of her response to the child, par-ticularly when under pressure and flooded by feelings without being incapacitated by them. 'This allows greater freedom for the therapist to be drawn into the dynamics of the session whilst still preserving, in the observing ego, sufficient detachment for monitoring the vicissitudes of a session' (Casement 2002: 27).

The 'internal supervisor' is distinct from that of the 'internalised' supervisor. Over time the supervisee will 'internalise' the experience of her supervisor and may anticipate what she might say or think. This does not take over the therapist's capacity to think for herself but creates an inner dialogue between the internal and internalised supervisor whilst with her patient. By presenting this clinical situation to her supervisor, the super-vision frame brings together this inner dialogue with the external supervision process.

## Relationship between supervisor and supervisee

The supervisee has the most difficult task as the pivotal person in the process of supervision. She takes responsibility for taking in and processing therapeutic work, which she conveys to her supervisor. The experience of supervision and her supervisor's responses are received and taken back to the therapy setting and to the supervised patient. The dynamics between the supervisory triad of supervisor, supervisee and the patient are therefore complex and both conscious and underlying unconscious processes need to be addressed. Langs (1994) highlights two distinct dialogues that are set up in the supervision process: firstly, the supervisor's conscious response to the presentation of case material and images, which may include theory and technique; the second level of communication and experience is unconscious and expressed indirectly through exchanges that centre around the frame-work of supervision. Langs suggests that these conscious and unconscious components may be in conflict. He describes how the conscious system is 'frame insensitive and inclined towards frame alteration', that is, any pro-posed change in the frame seems, on the surface, acceptable to both super-visor and supervisee but the unconscious system is highly 'frame sensitive and inclined towards frame securing efforts' (Langs 1994: 254). These ideas are helpful when there are pressures on the organisation of the outer frame, which may or may not be conscious. Both supervisor and supervisee need to be receptive to these processes and how this then affects their relationship. If the outer frame of the jigsaw gets dislodged or removed, there are holes and gaps in the emerging picture. This may also resonate in the containment between therapist and patient.

Once the supervision has become established, problems may surface for either supervisor or supervisee. Difficulties can arise in the understanding of the way the pieces of the jigsaw fit together. There may be many reasons for this. For example, transference difficulties such as projection of critical or uncontaining parental images may affect working in the supervision rela-tionship. At the beginning of clinical supervision the supervisee may project her ideal ego into the supervisor and invest too much in the authority and assumed wisdom. When this happens the supervisee may feel obliged to work in a way that she anticipates the supervisor would prefer and the dependence on the supervisor is exaggerated. Supervision can awaken per-secutory anxieties and it may be difficult for the supervisee to bring feelings of vulnerability, that 'they have not done it right'. Rather than feeling exposed there is sometimes a need on the part of the supervisee to protect herself from being judged and she becomes her own harsh critic. 'Develop-ment will stop when the supervisee is fixed in an idealised transference. The supervisee risks becoming an echo of the supervisor, losing his own devel-oping identity as an analyst and becoming a mere clone of the supervisor, negating his capacity to think and to create' (Casullo and Resnizsky 1993).

Supervision is not about prevention of mistakes but learning from them and understanding them. The supervisor may feel that the art therapist is resistant to close scrutiny of her work. This may be to do with a reluctance to enter into the necessary hard work that the work of supervision entails.

The art therapist may bring artwork to show to her supervisor as a way of not putting herself sufficiently into the therapeutic relationship. In order that the supervision can progress, it is helpful if these difficulties can be addressed and discussed in the supervisory relationship. In this way, it may be possible to turn the jigsaw pieces around, upside down and look at them from a different angle to re-establish the supervision process. It is also helpful if the issues can be explored in the supervisee's personal therapy.

> Peter was belligerent and defiant towards the therapist. He used many art materials in a very messy way with paint spilling everywhere. He was unable to settle to any particular activity and talking with him seemed impossible. He was uncontained and chose to run out of the room when he became most anxious. He would then hide and refuse to come back in, leaving the therapist with the feelings of abandonment and rejection that he also experienced.

In supervision we reflected on his predicament and the meaning of his behaviour: a ten-year-old boy who remained stuck at a pre-oedipal level of development with a precarious care situation. This was compounded by his confusion and underlying aggression, which is overwhelming for children at this stage of development. We understood this aggression as being channelled into his lack of bowel control or his deliberate incontinence, as the care staff understood it. There is a question about whether he had ever been toilet trained. He lacked stable, male role models. His insecure attachments were compounded by his sense of abandonment by his mother whose affection he craved. He had very little sense of self.

In supervision it was difficult to get a detailed account of the process of each session as they were so chaotic. Peter would flit from activity to activity, creating a lot of mess in his wake. We thought about the 'messy' unformed aspect of his internal world and lack of object constancy. An early transference developed with the art therapist as a maternal object who he craved and yet wanted to 'rubbish' and 'defaecate on'. The aggression towards his mother (therapist) remained unconscious. These feelings were poured into his 'rubbish' paintings, which needed to be 'chucked out'. It was necessary to begin with holding and containing by the therapist as a mother would do with her new infant.

The art therapist used the supervision space to reflect on this as Peter attacked her capacity to think in the sessions. The mother/baby relationship provided an important model for us to understand the infantile needs and projections that Peter brought to his therapy. The art therapist experienced her patient as needy – like an infant at the breast – but her experience was that he was not able to take her food in a way that was satisfactory. At this stage, although he was emotionally 'hungry', he did not let her 'feed' him.

The therapeutic alliance was still precarious. The art therapist felt she was battling with him and at the same time being the object of his projections, which she also felt unable to take in. We thought together about this feeling of 'unconnectedness' and how to make links so that meaning could develop and communications be understood. The idea of 'trial identification' came to mind in order to think about how Peter might experience what is being said by the therapist. It can be helpful to re-think from his point of view what has just been said as this might be different from what was intended by the therapist (Casement 2002).

In this way, we thought about his turbulent state of mind. The containment experienced by the therapist in supervision enabled her to contain Peter. Working on keeping him in the room, providing a concrete container, gave Peter the sense that he was wanted and that the therapist was not going to repeatedly abandon him, which was a pattern set up internally in Peter and why he continued to act this out. Slowly over time he stopped trying to leave and was able to stay in the room and allow the therapist to enter his world emotionally. His trust began to build, as it was in the supervision. As a maternal object, the therapist represented something Peter had never experienced, someone who could begin to contain him and understand his emotional world, process and think about his experience and give it back to him in a manner that he found tolerable. Many of these intolerable feelings were channelled into the image making, which was messy, fell apart and 'rubbish'. The rubbish part of Peter was acknowledged and he began to build a capacity to think and put words to his experience. His lack of bowel control compounded his sense of being the pooey dirty little boy. Symbolically this was expressed in the sessions, as the art therapist was the receiver of his 'mess'. In the same way, the supervisor received the account of this 'mess' by looking together with the therapist and reflecting on his images. By understanding this in supervision, the art therapist was able to tolerate this. Having felt out of her depth, she was beginning to build her relationship with Peter, gain confidence and develop her internal supervisor.

## Transference and countertransference

The complex nature of psychodynamically oriented art therapy work involves the transference relationships that develop between therapist, child and the image. The supervisor assists the process of enabling the supervisee to work this through and learn from the experience. The question about whether the supervisor's role is to help clarification of the supervisee's countertransference responses is complex as this begins to stray into the realms of personal therapy. de Folch (1981) maintains that it is important to teach the supervisee to observe her emotional reactions, to verbalise them and talk about them with the supervisor. In her opinion focusing on the supervisee's countertransference is a means of understanding the patient's transference but she acknowledges the risk of stepping over the boundaries between supervisor and therapist.

As the therapeutic work progressed, Peter's use of images changed. He did not need to evacuate so much of his 'mess' and rubbish as the containment in the sessions enabled more thinking to take place. He began to involve the therapist in some elaborate role play and requested they enact various scenarios. Peter was expressing his need to be more in control of his objects and play more like a toddler with his mother. We thought together about her participation and how Peter wanted to dominate and control. Firm limits and boundaries, such as not hurting each other or damaging anything in the room, were placed on these activities by the therapist to maintain the feeling of safety. The intensity of the work deepened with the interpretation of the transference. Peter found the therapeutic breaks extremely difficult to manage. His behaviour significantly regressed during the breaks. A relapse of soiling occurred while the therapist was away. As he began to experience a containing maternal presence in the relationship, he felt the abandonment by his mother/therapist more acutely. His mother often failed to attend arranged contact visits. During holiday breaks, many children went home to see their parents but Peter stayed in the house. The therapist expressed her own feelings of guilt about taking her breaks, experiencing her own sense of abandoning her patient.

The transference–countertransference relationship between supervisee and the child can become present in a displaced way during supervision. If a parallel process does emerge, this needs to be acknowledged in the 'here and now' of the supervision. The supervisor listens to her own emotional reactions in relation to the supervisee. At this stage in the work, the planned breaks in the supervision also resonated with the issue of guilt and abandonment.

Outside of the sessions, Peter's challenging behaviour began to improve. He stopped soiling in the house and for the first time they were able to take him on an outing, which he managed very well. Significantly his speech was improving and he was beginning to put his feelings and thoughts into words and make sense of his experience. Adolescence began early as he entered puberty at the age of 12. He grew very quickly and became awkward in his rapidly changing body. He began smoking, copying the older people in the house. His behaviour became risky and unpredictable as he started to abscond and become increasingly defiant. His behaviour became more overtly sexualised as he brought to his sessions fantasies about becoming a woman and a desire to cross-dress. His drawings became full of sexually explicit and graphic imagery.

In supervision we now had to consider the therapeutic work in the context of a young confused adolescent beginning to struggle with issues of separation and individuation. Peter had not consolidated earlier stages in his development and therefore was not socially or emotionally prepared for the upheavals of the adolescent process. As his adolescence developed, the confusion around his sexuality and the extent of his gender identity problems became manifest. Understandably this stirred up difficult feelings in the art therapist and she struggled with her responses to Peter and how to help him work this through. In the transference, she had become a sexual object for him but this was confused with the idea in his mind that if he was a girl his mother may not have rejected him. It was during this phase of the work that he disclosed his sexual abuse.

Disclosure of abuse necessitates another important function of the supervision work in managing confidentiality issues, child protection procedures and clinical material that might be needed for court proceedings should the therapist be required to give evidence. These disturbing events were difficult for the therapist to process, and highlights the importance of being in personal therapy when working with such disturbed patients. Consideration of the therapist's countertransference was paramount. This helped to understand and contain the therapist's anxieties in managing the process of the sessions and also the events that were rapidly unfolding in Peter's life.

Sedlak (1997) describes his experience of supervising therapists who were either untrained or had not engaged in their own personal therapy. He outlines how the therapist's work deteriorates when she is unable to deal with the countertransference in a professional manner. Problems potentially arise when the therapist fails to manage negative countertransference and may lead to acting out on the part of the therapist. A supervisor who recognises this problem encourages the supervisee to engage in her own personal therapy so that both the supervision work and therapeutic endeavour can continue. A similar point is emphasised by Martindale et al. (1997):

> If counter transference reactions are not able to be made conscious and reflected upon, there can be many forms of harmful enactments or verbal communications to patients or avoidance of emotional contact

with them and their problems. The more disturbed the patient, the more likely are disturbing counter transferences and the more vulnerable is the patient to these reactions by staff.

(Martindale *et al.* 1997: xv)

Peter re-experienced and re-enacted his abuse through his drawings and fantasy games and was able to find some words to his torment. He found containment as the art therapist was able to bear it and manage her own countertransference response. Although he was making progress in working this through, at the same time it was helpful to acknowledge just how damaged Peter was and what powerful anti-developmental forces governed his behaviour. There can be some resistance to the supervisee acknowledging this damage and the purpose of keeping this in mind was not to destroy the therapist's optimism but to enable her to take a realistic view of the patient and to be aware of the limited progress he might make. 'A tolerant awareness of these grave limitations can in itself be a powerful container of the therapist's difficult counter transference feelings' (Sedlak 2000: 36).

> During this difficult phase of the work, new management took over running of the home. The new manager had a completely different way of understanding the children and, without consultation, imposed change on the whole structure and activities of the house. This was deeply disturbing for Peter but also for the art therapist who was put into the position of renegotiating her own contract. Many weeks were spent in supervision thinking about the impact of this change on the art therapist and therefore on her patient. It was important to include this in the work in order to keep the container safe for Peter. It felt as if some of the outer edges of the jigsaw had been drastically removed and we had to work hard to restore the therapeutic frame and also the supervision frame. Peter's anxiety escalated, although this was largely contained in his therapy, as inappropriate sexualised behaviour in the house with staff and the other children diminished. His therapy was established as a safe place to bring these deep insecurities, which were stirred up by the changes in his external world.

Peter slowly began to feel safer and settled down after these changes and began to achieve well at school. He continued to bring his sexual confusion and fantasies about being a girl, wanting the art therapist to participate in the acting out of these fantasies. With this presentation of such a specific gender identity problem, we discussed the idea of an external consultation with an expert and agreed that the art therapist would seek a one-off consultation at a specialist unit for young people with gender identity problems in order to get a deeper understanding of the nature of Peter's disturbance.

## Completing the jigsaw: termination

As with any therapeutic relationship the termination phase of a supervision contract is planned. The supervision relationship may come to a natural end for different reasons for either supervisor or supervisee, such as change of employment circumstances, end of a particular piece of clinical work, moving away and so on. If the working relationship has been 'good enough', the ending will be planned in advance and a termination phase agreed.

> Peter was approaching 16. He expressed his anxiety about what would happen to his care following his 16th birthday. We understood that the heightened institutional anxiety directly contributed to Peter's renewed outbursts of aggression that were once again recurring in the house. There was also another change of management. Internal pressures were mounting in managing his own anxieties about separating and moving on. Together we speculated whether Peter was going to do something so severe that it would cause him to be asked to leave the home and therefore his therapy. (Historically in the home, planned moves were rare. Most children left because they had to as their behaviour had become unmanageable.) Peter's own abuse had impacted on him in a way that he found unbearable. When another child accused him of sexually abusing him, Peter was removed immediately from the house. The art therapist was understandably shocked at the sudden removal of her patient and abrupt termination of his therapy.

The external consultation on Peter's case at the specialist unit for gender identity problems had clarified some thinking about the complexity of Peter's predicament. There was now an emerging concern about how to link up thinking in the supervision frame and take this back to the care network. This was difficult for the art therapist. The staff team in the home were constantly coping with crises and were unable to make links with Peter's anxieties and how these were being acted out in the home. In supervision we discussed how to proceed, thinking through all the different meanings of this behaviour. Peter was placed temporarily in a medium secure unit while he waited to hear whether the case would go to court or, due to his age, he would be referred under a Treatment Order. The art therapist arranged to visit him pending this decision. She was left in the same situation as her patient – perplexed and not knowing what was going to happen to him. In supervision, it was acknowledged that being locked up in a secure setting was how Peter was going to manage his anxieties about independence and moving into adulthood. This was the ultimate container and he could feel safe.

There were many months of indecision about Peter's final placement. The art therapist re-established his sessions to maintain the therapeutic continuity. Once his placement was settled, they agreed a termination phase that could be planned and managed appropriately in order not to repeat the pattern of abrupt endings of relationships, loss and abandonment. Peter had matured emotionally through his ordeal and become a more thoughtful young man. He was able to appropriately work through the ending of his therapy and felt able to manage his future. He wanted to leave his artwork with the therapist on leaving.

The therapeutic work was terminated at a time when the art therapist felt Peter was ready to move on. He had become more able to think and reflect on his predicament and the meaning of his behaviour. The therapist was satisfied that he was being well cared for in a contained environment as a young adult. There are, however, often situations working therapeutically with children who are looked after when both therapist and young person are faced with unpredictable endings that cannot be managed. As in the case of Peter, the child is removed from the placement, sometimes without warning, and the attachment is broken. This pattern of broken attachments mirrors the child's early experience, repeated by moving between placements and thus replicated by the very system that is meant to care for them. This is a difficult dynamic to work with as the therapist is often unable to address the damaging effect on the child and at times feels powerless and hopeless in the face of decisions about her patient being taken out of her hands. She therefore can identify with the child's predicament within a system, which repeats patterns of loss and abandonment. Exploring these feelings within a supervision relationship provides the necessary containment and consistency. Paradoxically, the abrupt ending of a therapeutic contract can also resonate with the supervision contract, which may also have to be terminated.

This complex case highlights many aspects of the supervisory role. Hawkins and Shohet (1989) describe the supervisor as needing a 'helicopter ability' – the ability to switch perspectives – to be able to focus on the patient that the supervisee is bringing, to focus on the supervisee and her process, to be able to focus on the supervisor's own process and the 'here and now' relationship with the supervisee, to be able to see the client in the wider context and help the supervisee do likewise, to see the work in the wider context of the organisation and inter-organisational. In supervising the case of Peter, the complexity of the jigsaw needed careful consideration with powerful transference and countertransference issues that surfaced in both the therapeutic and supervisory relationship. Working through and understanding in supervision enabled thinking to be joined up and the pieces to be put in place. At the same time the supervisor learns from the experience. Putting in the final pieces and completing the puzzle makes a closure to the supervision work and the final picture can be reflected upon.

## The final picture

Supervision requires what Dispaux (1994) calls the 'learning position'. This is a personal attitude that predisposes the art therapist to think, to reflect upon feelings and to feel the thoughts experienced in the art psychotherapeutic relationship with the patient and with the supervisor. This emerges from the healthy dynamic interaction between supervisor, supervisee, patient and their images. It is a question of being 'touched', affected or altered by the supervision process. These 'feeling thoughts' invite deep reflection about the patient and develop an integration of knowledge with practice, as well as with the therapist's own internal world, assisted by her own personal therapy. With experience, 'feeling thoughts' therefore become less defensive and stereotyped, and increasingly personal and available for creative use. The 'learning position' implies that the art therapist has sufficient capacity and sensitivity to experience her own anxieties and defences instead of projecting them. She is thus better able to understand herself and her patients.

## References

Bowlby, J. (1969) *Attachment and Loss*, London: Hogarth Press.
Case, C. and Dalley, T. (1992, 2006 2nd edn) *Handbook of Art Therapy*, London: Routledge.
Casement, P. (2002) *Learning from our Mistakes*, London: Brunner Routledge.
Casullo, A. and Resnizsky, S. (1993) 'Supervision Psicoanalitica', paper presented at the Sixth Conference on Training Analysts, Amsterdam.
Dispaux, M.-F. (1994) 'How to become a psychotherapist with a psychoanalytic orientation: the place of supervision in the training process', EFPP Adult section, European Conference, Luxembourg (October).
Folch, T. E. de (1981) 'Some notes on transference and counter transference problems in supervision', *Bulletin of Psychoanalytic Federation, 16*: 45–54.
Grinberg, L. (1997) 'On transference and counter-transference and the technique of supervision', in B. Martindale *et al.* (eds), *Supervision and its Vicissitudes*, London: Karnac Books, pp. 1–24.

Hawkins, P. and Shohet, R. (1989) *Supervision in the Helping Professions*, Milton Keynes: Open University Press.

Hess, A. (1980) *Psychotherapy Supervision Theory, Research and Practice*, London: John Wiley and Sons.

Langs, R. (1994) *Doing Supervision and Being Supervised*, London: Karnac Books.

Martindale, B., Morner, M., Rodriguez, M. E. C. and Vidit, J.-P. (1997) *Supervision and its Vicissitudes*, London: Karnac Books.

Retford-Muir, S. (2007) 'Gender disorder in the treatment of a young person in care', in C. Case and T. Dalley (eds), *Art Therapy with Children: From Infancy to Adolescence*, London: Routledge.

Schore, A. (2001) 'The effects of early relational trauma on right brain development, affect regulation and infant mental health', *Infant Mental Health Journal, 22* (1–2): 201–269.

Sedlak, V. (1997) 'Psychoanalytic supervision of untrained therapists', in B. Martindale *et al.* (eds), *Supervision and its Vicissitudes*, London: Karnac Books, pp. 25–37.

Stern, D. (1973) *The Interpersonal World of the Infant*, London: Basic Books.

Winnicott, D. W. (1971) *Playing and Reality*, London: Tavistock Publications.

# Chapter 5

# Supervisory responses to child art therapy

## Assessment, intervention and outcome

*David Henley*

### Introduction: Case 1

During a co-led art therapy session, a ten-year-old child suffering a mood disorder attempted to draw a cat and ended up with a stereotyped cartoon version that he erased over and over again. Frustrated, he expressed to his intern (a student on placement) a wish to create a picture of the cat, which it turned out was recently deceased. The intern began by having the child describe his cat in detail as a kind of meditation prior to art making. This guided imagery-type exercise went well until it was time to draw. Try as he might the child found his own drawing to be 'like a baby's': so cartoonish and immature that he put his pencil down in despair. A skilled and gifted artist, the intern drew a sketch of a cat based upon the child's description, though in a very realistic, anatomically correct style in a dynamic pose. The child took one look at this masterful drawing and dropped his head into his hands, giving up altogether. Some moments later she reported that her supervisor at the placement, who was co-leading the group, intervened by creating another image in profile as per the child's request. This drawing recalled the style of a ten-year-old who was still childish and stereotypical in form, yet it possessed the essential characteristics and proportions of a cat. The art therapist left the details of the face just faintly sketched and without expression – a kind of *tabla rasa* cat that could be adopted by the child and refitted according to his own memory of his cherished pet. The child did indeed take up this sketch and began to superimpose his own concept of a cat on top of the art therapist's form. As it turned out, the outcome was a cat that seemed to evoke more *person* than pet – its face simple and child-like, yet also realistic (Figure 5.1). Whilst the cat may seem somewhat stereotyped, he was enormously pleased with it – proudly stating that this picture '*is just like my cat*'. In discussing this session with her supervisor, the student was distressed that her therapeutic intervention had foundered. They had a long-standing trusting relationship at this site, which enabled her to reflect upon her intervention as a constructive learning experience rather than construe it as a personal attack. Later, at the university in

*Figure 5.1* Drawn by a boy grieving for his cat, the art therapy supervisor intervened by providing some light sketches in the style of a ten-year-old, which he was free to make use of or ignore. Because the therapist's style was developmentally accessible he was able to incorporate her suggestions into his own work, thus contributing to a therapeutic victory.

supervision with this author, she was able to expand upon her reflections in a more academic setting.

## Assessment, intervention and outcomes

During supervision at the university the task turned to deconstructing the session described above. As a means of breaking down the dynamics, we approached the session with regard to each 'assessment/intervention/ outcome' that transpired during the student's work with this child. The author has developed this model for analysing cases in art therapy, whether for supervision, thesis research or for studying case material from the literature. Whatever the case, the art therapist must begin by assessing client need. We might assess that the child would benefit most from simply listening to their ideas, thoughts or problems, or they might respond to some verbal dialogue, or require adjustments in the media, or, as in this case, benefit by direct assistance with their art process. The approach might be cognitive, behavioural or developmental in nature. Whatever the assessment, the art therapist must then decide upon a course of intervention. This includes overt interventions of saying or doing, as well as when the therapist decides *not* to act – each still constitutes a therapeutic intervention that must hold up to scrutiny either during supervision or when being read by the art therapist's tutor or supervisor. With any intervention there is an outcome. This may take the form of a therapeutic outcome, or it may be aesthetic, educational or any of the above, in combination. With these three components under analysis, the art therapist undergoing supervision might be able to better tease apart the dynamics of any given clinical interaction, and thus defend their actions with greater articulation and insight.

As assessment was our initial task, we began by first identifying and applying the appropriate theory that might inform our interventions. In this case, it was developmental theory that seemed to drive the intervention by the student's supervisor. She must have assessed that this child could not make creative or therapeutic use of the student's drawing of a realistic cat, but instead needed one that was schematically or conceptually rather than perceptually conceived. As the child was located between the latency and pre-adolescent stages of drawing development (Lowenfeld 1953), his cat would have been somewhat media-influenced (cartoon stereotype), yet would also have elements of dawning realism and anthropomorphic expression.

Attachment and object relations theory was also a factor given the intense bond the child had with his subject. The child's intent, conscious or otherwise, seemed to focus upon recalling the image of a lost love object. This entailed not only conjuring the animal's physical appearance, but also creating a symbolic equivalent that captured their intimate relationship – one that was now in a state of distress through loss and grief. Each of these factors seemed theoretically sound as points of departure from which the art therapy intern could defend and analyse her therapeutic interventions.

The spirit of these interventions is partly based upon the 'art as therapy' model as conceived by art therapy pioneer Edith Kramer. Kramer's approach recognises the restorative potential of a successful *art process* as being inherently therapeutic and ego-building (1971). This approach to intervention emphasises the eliciting of strong aesthetic and therapeutic outcomes that might then be built further upon when verbally free-associating to the image (Naumburg 1973). In this case, the art therapist was attuned to the child's intentionality, his developmental level, as well as those emotions that coloured the work with evocative feeling. Staying with the image implies a supervision style that recognises the primacy of art (which includes the process) as a major therapeutic outcome. Working with the child's metaphors through their art is seen as having a larger meaning and relationship within the child's behaviour at-large.

This case has exemplified a working model of the assessment/intervention/outcome method. The rest of the chapter will look at its historical roots, illustrated with clinical vignettes based upon the author's work with children and interns in a range of therapeutic settings. The three case anecdotes will hopefully bring to life the many therapeutic and aesthetic outcomes possible with this approach to art therapy supervision and training.

## Literature survey of theoretical constructs

### Edward Adamson and the 'enabling space'

A studio-approach to art therapy was most notably pioneered by Edward Adamson who, in the 1940s, created a therapeutic studio for traumatised World War II British veterans and others with mental illness. Adamson's form of art therapy minimised overt interventions that might intrude upon or influence the artist-patients under his care. As a 'passive facilitator' his studio served as an oasis or sanctuary, where 'quiet concentration' allowed for a 'permissive atmosphere' of exploration (1990). The studio space was itself deemed an enabling space, *conducive* to the creation of art, and thus qualifies as an important intervention in its own right.

The emphasis upon creating an 'enabling' studio space can be applied to the psychoanalytic ideas of D. W. Winnicott (1965). Winnicott's concept of 'transitional space' becomes a meeting ground between the artist's inner and external experience. Here a client can safely and creatively explore inner memories, thoughts and feelings without being judged or criticised. The atmosphere also permits a safe and controlled regression to primary process material that is potentially destructive, but is deemed in the service of replenishing and strengthening the ego (Kris 1952). Adamson's 'persona' also figured prominently in the 'potential' of this space, as his quiet yet reassuring presence in the studio recalls Mahler's (1968) concept of the emotionally available yet 'benign' mother. Such a maternal-type presence gently and lovingly encourages creative exploration, yet reserves expectations, judgment or the impulse to rescue. The mother-figure is available for 'emotional refuelling' should the client's explorative energies begin to diminish, with interventions that stand ready to help the process along without being heavy-handed or intrusive. In this way, Adamson limited his function to an 'auxiliary ego', one who remains emotionally and artistically available to his studio participants for moral support, guidance and empathic attention.

Adamson's 'minimal' intervention model has evolved into a contemporary approach to art therapy. Studio-oriented art therapists embrace Adamson's pioneering work as part of the 'Art Brut' aesthetic developed by Jean Dubuffet (1986). A modern-day example of such an Adamsonian programme is 'The Living Museum', in New York, which is a studio programme led by psychologist/artist Dr Janos Marton. Influenced by the work of noted artist/philosopher Joseph Beuys, Marton maintains a large-scale open-studio and gallery spaces for individuals with acute psychiatric disturbances. It is housed in a mammoth discarded building on the grounds of a state psychiatric hospital. Within this 'Art Brut' programme, Marton's enabling space gives rise to artworks that prize raw honesty more than any overt therapeutic outcome.

### Edith Kramer and the Third Hand

In the 1950s, the naturalised New Yorker Edith Kramer drew upon a Freudian psychodynamic approach to art therapy analysis and intervention. Kramer's pioneering efforts in the field of art therapy were centred on facilitating the productive discharge and displacement of drive energy, resulting in outcomes that ideally culminate in sublimation (1971). She views the function of the art therapist as one who helps this process along by lending the art therapist's own artistic competencies and imagination. Interventions of this kind are more encompassing than Adamson's minimum intervention model. While Kramer also emphasises the creation of a therapeutic space, she also includes interventions that might suggest to the patient several media or technical modifications in the form or content of their art that encourage enhanced aesthetic outcomes. Kramer termed this model the 'Third Hand' (1987), which was taken from Theodore Reik's concept of empathically attending to the patient's utterances in therapy with an analytically minded 'Third Ear'.

As applied by Kramer, Third Hand interventions might take the form of adapting media to meet the client's needs: from offering the correct size brush to paint delicate facial features on a portrait to providing the right consistency of paint so that dripping or messing can be minimised. She might suggest changes in scale, dimension or technique, again depending upon the client's need. Interventions can also be content oriented such as introducing visual aides, art productions or art historical materials that might spark increased interest and investment in the process. These are not art teaching interventions per se, as they are not concerned with skill acquisition. They are more 'pictorial dialogues' aimed at providing the structure and tools to help the child form fully elaborated images. Studio-oriented interventions seek images that can stand on their own, engaging and challenging the viewer as does any strong work of art.

Kramer is exceedingly cautious however when administering such interventions, requiring that all interventions be unobtrusive, and do not distort the artist's intent or impose pictorial ideas or preferences that are developmentally or culturally foreign (1987). Third Hand interventions seek to promote the art process with the recognition that fully formed images can stand metaphorically for the child's issues in therapy.

### Viktor Lowenfeld and the provision of a 'stimulus'

In the late 1930s Austrian art educator Viktor Lowenfeld (1953) developed an intervention that pre-dates and parallels Kramer's model. His focus was upon facilitating sensory experiences during the art process aimed at intensifying the child's awareness of their environments, bodies, relationships and imaginations. Lowenfeld's position was 'child-centred', meaning that outcomes were developmentally oriented rather than mimetic or academic in form or content. As a refugee from Nazi Europe, Lowenfeld was concerned with liberating the child artist from any dictatorial adult influences or preferences. As early as the 1960s, Lowenfeld railed about the impoverishment and atrophy of children's imaginations due to the influence and the saturation of technological media. He eerily predicted that children would be increasingly assaulted by media that could negatively affect creativity and even preclude the need for a child's imagination. Thus, Lowenfeld's interventions attempted to rekindle the imaginations of children and thus infuse the art process with stimulation exercises that would intensify their personal and individual expression. For instance he might intervene by guiding a child through a strawberry-picking experience with eyes-closed or have them feel the topography of their own faces prior to sculpting self-portraits. Thus Lowenfeld's relevance is as fresh and meaningful today as when his methods were first conceived.

## Integrating theorists

In the opening vignette, the art therapists utilised a combination of the aforementioned practitioners' interventions, as a means of helping this child arrive at a viable therapeutic outcome. The process began by cultivating an atmosphere where the artist can work with quality materials in a studio space conducive to serious artistic endeavour. The initial drawing attempted by this child was a stereotype co-opted from a television character. This effort distressed him to the extent that he momentarily gave up on the process. The intern recognised this and encouraged the child to go within and *imagine* what this cat looked like. By having the child attempt to *visualise* his cat to his intern, Lowenfeld's concept of intensifying sensory awareness was stimulated, though with limited success given the complex state of transition of this child's drawing development. When this proved to be too limited a stimulus, the supervising art therapist intervened by using a drawing aide via the Kramerian 'Third Hand'. As a potentially intrusive intervention, it was critical that the therapist's drawing not overpower the child's fragile ego, but instead bolster it. Thus he was provided with just a *suggestion* of a cat – one that he was free to ignore, or build upon, or embellish to his liking. In all of the above interventions, care was taken to minimise intrusion and respect defences, while attempting to stay true to the child artist's intentions. The art therapist remained the benign mother-figure, there to model productive and caring behaviours. She gently exhorted the child to press on, rescuing only when necessary, essentially promoting the child's autonomy. Thus all three theorists can be drawn upon for their measured and unobtrusive interventions that celebrate the process of art. With these constructs in mind we will now turn to two other case vignettes that examine assessments, interventions and artistic outcomes in a variety of scenarios.

## Case 2: issues with therapeutic space

Issues related to our theorists' interest in creating a 'therapeutic environment' were put to the test, concerning a 16-year-old boy who suffered early onset psychosis. This boy displayed a fetishistic attachment with certain objects in his possession. As a means of making creative use of these objects, and to assist the boy to adjust to his dorm room at a therapeutic school, a graduate intern (under my supervision as senior art therapist) suggested allowing him to personalise his space. As an art therapy intervention, she proposed using his collection as a 'stimulus' to engage this difficult child and to perhaps win his trust. Upon implementing this process, it soon took on a life of its own as the boy began to create peculiar 'installations' in his room that were regarded by the school's therapeutic team as being too reflective of his psychosis (Henley 1995). Around the door he wove countless cigarette filters into a string of holiday lights. Broken appliances slowly took up residence, which he would embellish with found objects or decorate – painting faces on one hulking electric motor with stolen red lipstick and eyeshadow. Stacks of newspapers were collected and wrapped like Christmas presents. In keeping with his autistic sensibility, this odd collection of elements seemed more like his personal friends than objects of possession.

During on-site supervision we addressed the concerns of the dorm counsellors that this 'sanctuary' was becoming increasingly pathologised and, given its clutter, was now deemed unsafe. In defence of her intervention the intern voiced a strong identification with Adamson's laissez-faire model and Dubuffet's 'outsider art' aesthetic. She argued that despite the school's increasing unease, this was indeed a 'living museum' akin to that of Janos Marton's. She assessed that accepting this space as an accommodation would meet the therapeutic and expressive needs of the child, as well as open a 'door' to his world to which others could gain entry. I concurred with this assessment, but suggested however, in the spirit of compromise, that she might begin to 'wean' him from much of the clutter once she was accepted into this world, and then we might set about working with the collection as a point of departure (Lowenfeld 1953).

After two more weeks of accommodating these bizarre constructions as a living museum, the intern began to make interventions directly in his dormroom space. Gradually, the more disturbing tableaus were 'edited' and extraneous debris was removed from his room. The intern began work by 'formalising' these materials as a personal art form, rather than permitting them to remain autistic-like personal relationships. For instance, she helped him create borders and frames around the chaotic collages that spread wildly across his walls. She offered him choices as to which limited number of 'special' objects could remain in his collection and these she placed on small plywood cubes for display. The intern then added new works, which the child had created in the art therapy studio, that could be exhibited appropriately in a semi-public space (his dorm room and hallway).

The intern's interventions in this vignette were initially Adamsonian and reflective of the 'Art Brut' aesthetic. She backed up her Art Brut-minded intervention by citing the work of Henry Darger, the shut-in, outsider artist whose thousand-page novels, voluminous weather diaries and enormous fold-out paintings were created in a cluttered apartment not unlike the space of our patient's. She argued that just as Darger's unspoiled art deserved respect, so too did she attempt to meet this patient 'where he was'. My own assessment attempted to accept the Art Brut position but also to introduce the Lowenfeldian model as well, so as to accept the bizarre work but then attempt to extend the patient's 'frame of reference' beyond the compulsive, towards greater flexibility.

Supervision in this case worked towards integrating the two agendas. The first intervention entailed sending the intern into work *with* his collections. Using both aesthetic and object relations models she was to help organise and formalise the objects within this transitional space. She assessed the need to mediate between this artist's inner and outer experience as a form of 'therapeutic bridge' (Mahler 1968). She also assessed the need to 'move' the boy beyond his obsessive, fetishistic expressions towards a more expansive direction. This entailed accepting and yet managing his often intense and chaotic artistic discharges that were indicative of raw displacement. Kramer's concept of sublimation requires that the raw displacement of primary process material be *transformed* in ways that serve both the child's need for inner satisfaction along with more ego-related accomplishments. The transformation of these psychic processes seemed, in this case, to be in the earliest formative stages of development.

Because the intern identified so strongly with the Art Brut aesthetic, we discussed the need to by-pass her own strong agenda in favour of cultivating what Kris (1952) termed the conflict-free-sphere: Interventions should be implemented with the child's best interests in mind, not the aesthetician's. Our goal, then, was not to encourage the child to create more and more bizarre tableaus. We sought to balance the child's 'Wildman' artistic persona, while also cautiously working to extend his experience beyond his autistic orbit, through measured Third Hand interventions. Taking care not to introduce ideas too traumatic or inaccessible to the boy, we sought to oust him from his magical comfort zone, towards greater communication and relatedness with both his community and peers. Over six months these efforts began to bear fruit. Rather than just *collecting* and arranging his fetishistic objects, he began to *portray* them in drawings and

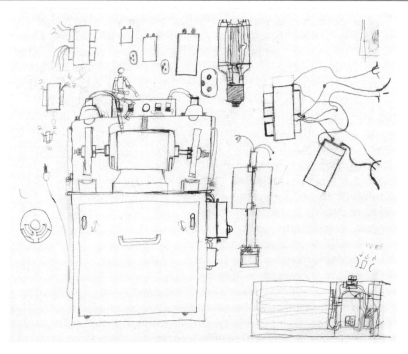

*Figure 5.2* The line between artistic license and pathology was explored by an art therapy intern in the work of a gifted autistic boy obsessed with inanimate objects. The art therapist functioned as a therapeutic 'bridge', by broadening his inner world of machines, that led eventually to the inclusion of human relationships as part of the scope of his work.

sculptures (Figure 5.2). In this complex and carefully rendered study of mechanical objects, a small yet conspicuous figure has been added to the composition. Made of wood and articulated for posing in different positions for life drawing exercises, it is shown perched nonchalantly upon the buffing machine table. While not fully human, its inclusion bespeaks of the 'potential' for figurative work that, in time, might develop into more sentient forms of expression. This transition constitutes a huge developmental advance, one that required the complex act of symbolisation rather than acting out in obsessive–compulsive hoarding. However, critical to this development was the intern's empathic understanding of the boy's unique world-view. She could see that this strange world of fetishistic collecting contained the seeds for later artistic and developmental growth.

## Case 3: successes and failures

The next case involves the supervision between the author as art therapist and his supervisor, a paediatric psychiatrist. In this complex and difficult case, an adopted nine-year-old girl diagnosed with reactive attachment disorder was seen by the author in one-to-one art therapy (Henley 2005). This is a condition in which early maternal abuse or neglect may result in the child's incapacity to bond with the mother and later to develop normal relationships or intimacy with others. Symptoms might include attention deficits, mood lability, aggressiveness and even autistic-like functioning. The child had been adopted by loving parents but, as is frequently the case, she often displayed intense rage reactions and verbal abuse, especially towards her adoptive mother.

In the art therapy session, developing a rapport with this child was immediately eased by her love of art. Although she was uncomfortable sharing the small studio with her therapist, once she saw the table full of polymer-coloured clay, acrylic paint and pastels she was entranced. Her work style was guarded at first. She created somewhat empty landscapes that conspicuously omitted people. I was essentially ignored during this process, as I was associated only as the 'supplier of the art materials'. As such I was tolerated as a necessary addition to the studio where we remained in an uneasy co-existence for almost two months. Slowly however, a cautious alliance formed amidst this small studio sanctuary and the work began to flourish.

Our studio routine began with a period of free material experimentation, then formal art-making, and ended with some limited verbal discussion. The mother would then visit us in the session, which in itself was a major intervention. This assessment recognised the necessity for encouraging therapeutic, mutual maternal interaction that could be facilitated in a positive supportive environment. The child tolerated her in the session without complaint and after each session seemed genuinely excited to show her art to her mother. However, as our mother/child dyadic work progressed I began to detect a change in the mother's demeanour. Usually the mother greeted her daughter's works with a genuine delight. Eventually as the child's affects were loosened during therapy, images began to appear that were somewhat disturbing. Despite being prepared for this possibility, the mother was noticeably taken aback. The child's usual drab, stereotyped landscapes of farm fields now began to include the occasional isolated figure in more intensely painted scenes. Figure 5.3 depicts one such image as an intense yellow and blue polar landscape that contains at the far end what the child identified as a 'penguin lost on the pack ice'. I assessed that the reference to this figure, no matter how bleak, constituted a therapeutic victory for this traumatised child. We now had the first tentative self-references, set within intensely coloured pictorial fields.

Despite my pointing out the increases in relatedness and expressivity, the mother was not impressed. She voiced her discomfort and questioned whether art therapy was 'working'. It did not help that during this period of emotional disclosure the child was also edging closer in her therapeutic

*Figure 5.3* Reactive attachment issues in a nine-year-old girl are given elegant form in a painting that depicts a single penguin floating alone on an ice flow. Despite such powerful aesthetic and therapeutic outcomes, therapy was discontinued because of the author's own transferential blunders in working with the mother as part of the therapeutic process.

alliance with me. It did not go unnoticed by the mother that the child at one point refused to share her pictures with her mother during a visit to the therapy room, stating 'Only David can see them'. During our usual post-session meeting the mother made a passing comment about how I seemed to be 'giving in to her whims and over-indulging' her daughter.

In supervision, the psychiatrist felt we were at a critical juncture and needed to make an interpretation and a strategic plan. His assessment was that, in my fervent attempts to form a therapeutic alliance with the child, I had perhaps overcompensated and worked 'too hard at winning the child's favour'. Instead of maintaining Mahler's role of the benign mother figure – one who is emotionally available but not too emotionally invested – he proposed that unconsciously it was I who was now 'cheering the child on to create the more emotional pictures'. Perhaps too I was enjoying the child's new acceptance of me and, again unconsciously, fed into and perhaps even prolonged the symbiotic phase of the attachment cycle.

While we both agreed that following attachment theory was a sound approach, the case was not playing out to satisfaction. I reasserted the theoretical position that, to form a therapeutic attachment, the child required a secure sanctuary supported by an unrushed period of permissive symbiosis. Therapy with this child must accommodate the often unruly up-rush of previously repressed affect, though such a discharge can be unsettling for the child, parents and therapists alike. He agreed with this argument but reminded me that therapists do not always have the luxury of plotting the therapeutic course of treatment, especially when the child's gains included periodic regressions that were experienced so negatively by the parent. He pointed out how painful it must be for the mother to witness how the child took such pleasure in our sessions, while her own relationship still seemed strained. Threatened by the new weirdly painted figurative works and by our relational progress, the mother perhaps felt, consciously or unconsciously, that I was stealing her child's affections – that we had unwittingly become competitors. Armed with art materials and a thera-peutic presence that placed few demands on the child, I had created an unfair advantage.

Given this assessment, my supervisor counselled that perhaps I should slowly and gently begin to place more demands upon the child in therapy. This was a theoretically sound intervention, since it would mirror the normal expectations and stresses placed upon a young child by her mother during the trials of the separation phase of development. I began by emphasising more cleanliness during painting-time and including new clean-up rituals as part of the session. I limited certain indulgences, such as using unlimited polymer clay (which is relatively expensive) or sprinkling expensive glitter on her paintings whenever she liked. In keeping with my supervision goals I sought to mirror this next developmental phase of growth – separation. Separation included having the child cope with the frustrations that a normal baby experiences when mother is 'busy' or says 'no to a mess' and so on. Essentially we were to move on from symbiosis, whether the child was deemed ready or not, ushering her as gently as possible into the next phase of rapproachment. I attempted then to cautiously integrate these demands into our positive attachment and alliance.

It was Bowlby's (1969) ideas on attachment and loss that predicted that if a reactive-type child perceives abandonment, they will mount a fierce 'protest'. This my patient did, for as soon as these first small limits were placed upon her she blew up in anger, stating 'You're just like my mother!'. She then proceeded to tip over the waste-water jar, all the while laughing hysterically. This regressed behaviour appeared to be in line with Bowlby's 'protest', which was probably in reaction to my abandonment of her during such a vulnerable time. By identifying me with the 'bad' parts of her mother, the child acted out with particularly vehement anger. In a later phone call, the mother implied that I was now losing control and 'upsetting' her daughter more than helping. In response to the mother's displeasure, the next session I wavered with regard to limit-setting. This 'easing-up' did little to dampen the flames – on the contrary, the child seemed confused, given my own inconsistency. Later that week the mother ended it all, leaving a message that it would no longer be productive to continue treatment.

Losing a patient is a difficult experience for any therapist after all the invested physical and emotional energy. During de-briefing with my supervisor I attempted to analyse each assessment, intervention and outcome, but it was difficult to stay focused, given the emotional drain. We discussed the intricacies of attachment theories as they were put into place, and felt on the whole that the approach was sound. We were particularly impressed with how successfully the child's compositions had begun to show signs of life, and these could be interpreted as being indicative of greater self-awareness and the maturational process at-large. We also recounted the moments early on, when mother and child displayed new evidence of bonding. Together, they would revel in the many art works that were shown at home and in the waiting room, much to their mutual pride.

While the art had provided the focus of the therapeutic work, it was inevitable however that much libidinal and aggressive energy would be cathected towards myself during the bonding process. Given the intractability of reactive attachment disorder (RAD), it was perhaps too much to expect that such primary process forces could be contained and sublimated through the art process alone. Whether intended or not, I was caught up in a powerful transference, one that was unexpected and that I felt ill-prepared to deal with.

## Conclusion

These three cases have provided enough material for exploring the intricate nature of analytically oriented supervision as part of the art therapy processes. Using the assessment, intervention and outcome model, the author has sought to systematise the analysis of art therapy theory and practice. This model has been applied to three very different clinical experiences: that of a university intern in the field taking a supervision course with the author, an art therapy intern under the author's supervision in a clinical setting and the author's own work with his supervising psychiatrist. In each case, supervision was conducted under the guise of mutual support and guidance. Analysing these outcomes was a team effort. It required the art therapist and supervisor to maintain an atmosphere of a conflict-free sphere that recognised countertransference as being part of the supervisory process. By approaching issues in a 'problem-solving way', supervision became a source of learning, which benefited everyone including the supervisor, therapist and clients alike.

Assessment laid the ground-work in each of these supervision experiences. In the case of the boy drawing the cat, it became clear that the developmental stages of drawing as conceived by Lowenfeld held the key to devising a workable intervention. Kramer's Third Hand intervention, of lightly sketching while the child described his cat, worked effectively in so far as it kept the child motivated and assisted him in giving form to his ideas. However, Adamsonian art therapists might consider the intervention too heavy handed, in that the resulting image was without the element of struggle that one might expect, given the child's turbulent feelings. It could be argued that the cat in profile seems Egyptian-like, flat and oddly neutral, without any evidence of grief or anger, or any other evocative feeling registering upon its face. Therefore, a full measure of sublimation might not have been achieved in this instance. Perhaps the art therapist's intervention might have unnecessarily rescued the child from latent emotions. Yet perhaps this was the most we could expect as an intervention and for a child dissatisfied over his own drawing efforts and the grief that was potentially overwhelming.

In the case of the boy obsessively collecting and assembling fetishistic elements into installations, a debate arose over the nature of psychotic art. Again a conflict-free assessment involved teasing apart the intern's fascination with such fantastic imagery from clinical considerations. The issue of how to accommodate the child's pathology becomes problematic whenever the forces of psychosis are unleashed (Henley 1994). By directly or indirectly 'cheering on' the psychotic client to produce works that, it could be argued, are extraordinary expressions of an alternative reality, we cease to function as the therapeutic benign maternal figure from a conflict-free position and instead acquiesce to becoming simply aficionados of 'Art Brut'.

Exhibiting these works poses yet another challenge for supervision, particularly if we consider the audience who may be fragile in their own right. They certainly have rights *not* to be confronted with such disturbing images in their environment (Henley 1997a, 1997b, 2004). Yet in Adamson's mould, we must take care not to sanitise or dilute any artist's expressions, which can skirt dangerously close to censorship issues. The Art Brut aesthetic exists in response to any actions that tamper with the artist's intent and integrity. However, these children were not professional artists intentionally creating like a Francis Bacon or Dali, but children who suffered in pain. Thus our assessments and interventions chart a course to relieve their suffering rather than satisfying the art-world's appetite for outsider art.

In the final case, we experienced art therapy as it adapts to the family system, in this case the complex dynamic between child, mother and therapist. In order to fully treat the child, the parents would have needed to have been extraordinarily patient, trusting and secure within themselves. To have reached this challenging child, therapeutic and creative risks needed to have been taken, which might have taken years and in the end might have proven ineffective. However, the initial therapeutic interventions yielded some promising outcomes. The child was able to engage in the art process with a formal beauty and passion that bordered on sublimation. The passion and intensity of the later images were clearly beyond the autistic or symbiotic stages, but seemed fully formed and alive (Kramer 1971). During her most productive sessions her marks were bold, strokes of colour virtually cut into the fiber of the paper, suggesting tremendous displacement of drive energy. Without romanticising or sentiment, we witnessed the artist working at her best – struggling with material, emotion and conflict, and emerging exhausted yet strengthened by her ordeals. But this process is not for the faint of heart – for artist, patient or therapist.

## References

Adamson, A. (1990). *Art as Healing*, London: Coventure.

Bowby, J. (1969) *Attachment and Loss*, vol. 1, New York: Basic Books.

Dubuffet, J. (1986) *Asphyxiating Culture*, New York: Four Windows Four Walls Press.

Henley, D. (1994) 'Art of annihilation', *American Journal of Art Therapy*, *32*: 99–107.

Henley, D. (1995) 'A consideration of the studio as therapeutic intervention', *Art Therapy: Journal of the American Art Therapy Association*, *12*: 188–190.

Henley, D. (1997a) 'Expressive arts therapy as alternative education: devising a therapeutic curriculum', *Art Therapy: Journal of the American Art Therapy Association*, *14*: 15–22.

Henley, D. (1997b) 'Art of disturbation: provocation and censorship in art education', *Art Education: Journal of the National Art Education Association*, *50*: 39–45.

Henley, D. (2004) 'The meaningful critique: responding to art from preschool to post-modernism', *Art Therapy: Journal of the American Art Therapy Association*, *21*: 79–87.

Henley, D. (2005) 'Attachment disorders in post-institutionalized adopted children: art therapy approaches to reactivity and detachment', *The Arts in Psychotherapy*, *32*: 29–46.

Kramer, E. (1971) *Art as Therapy with Children*, New York: Schocken Press.

Kramer, E. (1987) 'The art therapist's third hand: reflections on art, art therapy, and society at-large', *American Journal of Art Therapy*, *24*: 71–86.

Kris, E. (1952) *Psychoanalytic Expressions in Art*, New York: Schocken Press.

Lowenfeld, V. (1953) *Creative and Mental Growth*, New York: Macmillan.

Mahler, M. (1968) *On Human Symbiosis and the Vicissitudes of Individuation*, New York: International Universities Press.

Naumburg, M. (1973) *An Introduction to Art Therapy: Studies on Free Art Expression on Behavior Problem Children and Adolescents as a Means of Diagnosis and Therapy*, New York: Teachers College Press.

Winnicott, D. W. (1965) *The Maturational Processes and the Facilitating Environment*, New York: International Universities Press.

# Chapter 6

# Imagery in supervision

## The non-verbal narrative of knowing

*Caroline Case*

## Introduction

In thinking about supervision, my particular interest is in the part that images play in the process of reflecting on the clinical work presented. In order to explore this I am going to approach it from the two points of view of what I experience when I am a supervisee in supervision, and what I experience when I give supervision as a supervisor. Good supervision can leave me feeling excited, my mind buzzing with ideas and a sense of satisfaction at having got to the bottom of something; fired with enthusiasm to go back to the client, feeling renewed in some way. The next session with the client has usually got a different quality reflecting a shift in understanding when one has been stuck and a freeing up of thought that is non-verbally communicated to the client. Supervision that is not successful can leave one with feelings of restriction, misunderstood and rather despairing about one's lack of ability to practise. I think that this can happen with a didactic approach where there is one perceived way of working that is being taught, rather than an exploration of the dynamics of the situation, together with a consideration of possible approaches. Pedder (1986) discusses the jug, potter and gardener models of supervision: the jug is where information is poured into a passive recipient; the potter is where the supervisee is fashioned after one's own image; and the gardener provides, prunes and trusts in the innate processes of growth and development. It may not be possible to get everything that is needed from a particular supervisor, which may lead to a sense of emptiness rather than having been fed in some way. Possibly one has to be realistic about what chemistry one relationship produces. The whole process of supervision needs to be able to breathe. We need a containing space to play in, which has many similarities to the therapeutic space.

In supervision, I ask supervisees to bring art objects made in the session under discussion, if any, but I also work with a written account of the session that I prefer supervisees to bring, because the process of writing and setting space aside starts a process of reflection. When the supervisee enters the consulting room another process starts adding other equally useful images. There are those that had formed in the mind of the therapist and are brought to supervision and the images formed mentally, recalled or made as we are working together; it is this aspect of supervision that I have taken for my focus, as I think it is in these additional images that our understanding of the client hovers on the edge of awareness. In a previous paper I discussed the making of the therapist's own artwork, outside the sessions, as a 'reflective counter-transference' (Case 1994). Scaife (2001) suggests using other creative approaches in supervision, but much can be gained from being receptive to these inner images, whether or not they are actually made.

The possibility of bringing an object created in the session by the client is unique to art therapy. Kris (1953), writing about the artist and image magic, discusses the power that images have over memory. 'Gestures must be seen when they are made; words must be heard when they are spoken. Pictures can be read in aftertime. They persist, control time, and overcome its passage. In this very fact there is magic' (Kris 1953: 50). The artist is able to preserve that which vanishes. Henzell (1997) calls this an 'inscription' of the session but another way that the session is recreated is in the parallel process that may take place between supervisor and supervisee, the transference of aspects of the original session, variously described in the literature as the reflection process (Searles 1995), parallel process (Ekstein and Wallerstein 1972), mirroring (Doehrman 1976), paralleling (Wilmot and Shohet 1985) and reciprocity (Astor 2000). There is not space to discuss the differences in these concepts in this chapter.

## Images and memory

In supervision, we rely on memory of the client, the session and ourselves, usually a verbal narrative. It is the narrative beneath this surface narrative, (one that emerges in mental and felt images) and the way this enters the session that is the focus of this chapter. Damasio (2000) argues that the foundation of consciousness is the presence of a consistent non-verbal, imaged narrative to which we secondarily give words, 'the non-verbal narrative of knowing' (Damasio 2000: 186).

In Suzanne Langer's (1963) study of symbolism, *Philosophy in a New Key*, she looks at various impractical, apparently unbiological activities of man (i.e. religion, art, magic, dreaming) as languages arising from a basic human need to symbolise and communicate. Langer discusses discursive and presentational forms of symbolism. The symbolism of the secondary process is discursive; conscious rational thinking is symbolised through words that have a linear, discrete successive order. The symbolism of the primary process is non-discursive, expressed in visual and auditory imagery rather than words. It presents its constituents simultaneously, not successively; it operates imaginatively but cannot generalise. Therefore complexity is not limited by what the mind can retain from the beginning of an apperceptive act to the end.

Language is the only means of articulating thought; in this picture she draws of the mind, everything that is not speakable thought is feeling. She describes this as the inexpressible world of feeling. 'Not symbols of thought but symptoms of inner life' (Langer 1963: 85). In defining 'a picture' as an example of 'non-discursive symbolism' she describes it as having units that do not have independent meanings like a language, i.e. the vocabulary. There is no fixed meaning apart from content. 'It is first and foremost a direct *presentation* of an individual object' (Langer 1963: 96).

In responding to presentational symbolism the mind reads in a flash and preserves in a disposition or attitude. 'Feelings have definite forms which become progressively articulated.' Or, in the words of Adrian Stokes, '. . . the insistence by its form that distinguishes the communications of art from other embodiments of phantasy or of imagination' (Stokes 1978: 266).

Thinking of therapy as forming a bridge between inner and outer worlds, between imagination and reality, it is helpful to be able to move between these two ways of working. The research of neurobiologists into the making of memory, images and how images are created, as well as how they affect the mind and body, adds a different perspective to that of the philosopher.

Damasio (1994), a neurobiologist, writes that our mind responds to imagery that we imagine in the same way that it responds to imagery that we see. In supervision we create a narrative of the past through writing up the session, bringing the art objects and the parallel process between us; we reflect on this history that is formed and try to understand the relationship with the client and the effect it has on the supervisee (transference and countertransference), considering technique and future action. All kinds of images are really helpful in this process. Research findings into left and right hemispheres have shown activity on both sides of the brain when mental images and art making are taking place, although originally the right brain has been associated with intuition and creativity. Western thinking about the mind and body has been dominated by the Descartian split, which separates thinking from feeling. Damasio's work with patients with neurological damage to parts of the brain has enabled him to reassess this division. What he has found is that emotion and feeling assist us in 'predicting an uncertain future and planning out actions accordingly' (Damasio 1994: xv). He sees feelings as a continuously updated image of the structure and state of our body. In this way feelings serve as 'internal guides'.

Damasio found a close bond between a collection of brain regions to do with processes of reasoning and decision making, personal and social decision making, and the processing of emotions. Emotion and feeling are part of the neural machinery for biological regulation that is to do with survival. He posits that a large part of knowledge is recalled in the form of images, from many sites in the brain. We retrieve images and translate them into language form, hold them in our attention. We need to have them actively in mind and have a high order working memory. Our brain has the capacity to 'display images internally and to order those images in a process called thought', which in turn influences our behaviour in the future. Essentially we reconstruct memory from dispositional representations that are made up of past experiences. These combine with perceptual images and recalled images of the past and an imagined future. Damasio suggests that emotions and feelings are a central part of biological regulation and 'provide a bridge between rational and non-rational processes between cortical and non-cortical structures' (Damasio 1994: 128). He argues persuasively that intuition may be based on imperceptible body changes that help us make a decision based on past experience. Creativity rests 'on a merging of reason and intuition' as quoted by Jonas Salk in Damasio (1994). In our 'mind landscape' images correspond to a myriad of options for actions and outcomes. Basically the body provides a ground reference for the mind.

## A model of supervision

In over thirty years of working as an art therapist and child psychotherapist I have been a supervisee with various models of practice in supervision: peer group supervision without an external supervisor, group supervision with a supervisor, individual supervision and whole project supervision thinking about organisational dynamics. At the moment I have pair supervision of two individual cases with two different colleagues, one for private work and one for NHS work. In the NHS I also have supervision that is more to do with case management and family work. There are times when one may want image-centred supervision, or emphasis on inter-personal/intra-pyschic dynamics, managerial issues or institutional dynamics. All may affect the making of an image in therapy and do in fact contribute to the way it is made and the form that it takes.

The model of supervision that I find most useful is to ask the supervisee to bring one session written up in detail with any art objects made, if possible. If the session is detailed then I think that the process of self-supervision has already begun. I ask people to write the session like a film in their head from the first moment of contact with the client. In the session they will usually tell me any update on the client, if needed. Then, placing the things made between us, I ask the supervisee to read the session while I also have a copy of the script and they can fill in any pieces they suddenly remember, and we can think together about why they may have been forgotten. I find that I can then get a clear picture of the unfolding inter-personal dynamics between supervisee and client, the pattern of the session and see how the picture-making process is part of this dynamic. When does it start to be made and what is being said or not said? What is going into the picture, is being said or is being communicated in a different non-verbal way? In this last I think the non-verbal communication between supervisor and supervisee and their whole stance and attitude to me will be an emotional base to the whole session and will inform in terms of parallel process. After the supervisee has read the session we go through it from the beginning, but will consider it part by part, trying to elucidate the transference and countertransference by taking into account the feelings I find myself having and those of the supervisee, discussing what has been made. However, some supervisees prefer a free-floating discussion and I can adapt to that method of working but find it important to focus on one case in depth as a scattering of attention over many clients may dissipate what work can be done.

I would describe what I do as working with the whole image, what is made, how people present, the images formed within me to them, their words and non-verbal communication. Damasio (1994) describes how our primary emotions, which are innate and pre-organised, are used as scaffolding for our secondary emotions, which are learnt from experience. Our feelings are our awareness of body changes, what he calls somatic markers, in response to emotion. When we reason or make a decision, for instance when we are thinking and working in supervision, we call on past knowledge that is stored in the mind in the form of images. These are retrieved and translated into language and are used together with our response in the immediate situation, whether to pictures brought to therapy or attention to the interpersonal relationship. In this way, recalled images, present images, body changes and feelings are all interconnected in a process of thinking (Figure 6.1):

- The conscious account, or first appearance of the session.
- Theoretical knowledge that we bring to bear on the case.
- Body feelings that re-present aspects of the therapy relationship.
- Conscious reflection in the supervision session.
- Reverie and play, created between supervisor and supervisee.
- Unconscious reflection in the form of intuition and insight, which may lead to change in the therapist's understanding and approach.

## Myself in supervision

One of the reasons that I might take a case to supervision is to work on trying to understand any puzzles left at the end of a session. When we work with severely disturbed clients, where there are profoundly defended areas of the psyche, the processes of projective identification (Klien 1952; Rosenfeld 1952; Bion 1959) and intrusive identification (Meltzer 1986) are very powerful and may inhibit our ability to withdraw from the client to

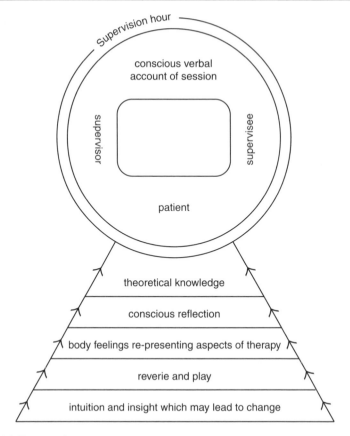

*Figure 6.1* Diagram: Imagery in supervision.

think to ourselves in the session. We may be very affected emotionally or left with disturbing images that we cannot elucidate, not being able to gain a third perspective on something that has been projected into us.

In the supervision material to be described Jane had come to a first session after the summer holiday. She is a child who had been severely sexually abused and suffered neglect and deprivation. She was now twelve but had the physical size of a nine-year-old, although she had recently reached puberty. As I met her at the door I was struck by the incongruous image she presented. Her head was at first bowed so that I could not see her face. She was dressed all in yellow, which was an unusual colour for her to wear. She had copper auburn hair, and as she looked up I saw that she was wearing heavily applied make-up. Her cheeks were a bright pink, and she had heavy blue eye shadow and bright red lips. Everything combined to attract attention to her. Momentarily, I had an image of a sort of dwarf western geisha, something very disturbing from the film *Don't Look Now*. I had not been able to get this image out of my head and had also felt very confused in the middle of the session, so for these two reasons I took this session to supervision.

## Supervision material

In supervision, we discussed that I had noticed that the self-mutilation on her arms and legs had healed over the summer break, and that there were no new sores or abrasions, potentially a good sign. As she came in she had stumbled at the stairs and taken my hand, holding it all the way to the therapy room. My supervisor talked about this oscillation between little girl and pseudo grown-up. I agreed, it was partly right, but it had not reached something in the way she presented. She is a child who is a long way from making a traditional image. She makes magic potions with materials and concretely uses the surface of her body, painting her hands, arms and face, and moves in and out of psychotic thinking. We talked about the way she had come back and how there was to be little acknowledgement of loss at the summer break, the pseudo grown-up presentation suggesting that she no longer needed grown ups.

She began to talk about a ghastly sounding film called *Shame* and had I seen it? It was a film where a girl got raped and then murdered at the end. There was a tough cookie stance to the way she spoke, she was not frightened and it was really good. I was finding it quite difficult to listen. Various questions were in my mind about what I was being made to listen to and also the fact that she was in foster care. Was what she was talking about fact or fantasy and had it happened in the past while with abusive parents or in the present? A challenge was thrown out to me, letting me know it was an eighteen certified film and she had seen it and, what is more, she was going to see it again. Was I an adult who would take care of her and set boundaries on what she could watch? I found it quite hard to reply clearly enough to this; she was lost in feelings of the shame of the abuse that had happened to her, which led to my wondering if she was ashamed, not only of being a victim of abuse but also of the soft feelings of having missed me during the break. I had tried to talk to her about the film but not very well and she was scornful. My supervisor was very helpful in talking about Jane's sexual anxiety, the attraction to boys and the possible danger. She thought I could usefully make a general comment about what can happen to a girl as she is a girl. I had not thought of this while in the session.

She had moved to play with the sand and made a potentially erotic comment on my eyes, with a seductive look, saying that they were like Aladdin's. I swiftly grounded this, linking it to my suntan and her noticing of changes since before the break. My supervisor was very positive about my response and I have included this because it is important to confirm people in what they are getting right. Then, there followed a very tricky interaction. She had got hold of a soft ball and asked me to hold it while she cut a piece out of it. I said that I would not do this because I thought she was going to spoil what made it a ball. If she did that, it would not be able to bounce or roll. She did it anyway, very cross with me, and then there developed one of her magic mixtures of pieces of ball, water and old dry flowers that she had brought in before the summer. She became more and more controlling and destructive and started to deliberately wet herself with the water down her front. In retrospect, I can see that she was attacking the ball/breast and that the mixture was a magic way of trying to manage feelings aroused by the break.

During the session I had a strong feeling of confusion over what she was doing with the water, ball and scissors. Should I assist her when she asked for help in responding to the little child who had held my hand at the beginning of the session or would I be responding to a seduction to take part and collude with something destructive. My supervisor is very good at working with the psychotic process and has a way of getting hold of hatred and destructive impulses that I feel I need with this very tricky girl. In supervision we talked about the perversion of changing good clean dry clothes into a wet uncomfortable experience and the countertransference of my confusion over whether she is making or destroying. The countertransference was a parallel experience to her not being able to discriminate between what is good and what is bad or between creation and destruction.

I had a sudden insight into the image she presented on arrival. She was offering herself up to be abused. The play at make-up plays along with the internalised abuser who helps to recreate situations where she might be abused again. It was more deeply destructive than a pseudo adult presentation. You could say that she wants to play dangerously with the boys, a tough cookie, but it could end like the film *Shame*.

Good supervision can help one to think about what one does not understand but may be on the verge of consciousness: the latent image of what one knows but has not yet articulated. I find that this knowledge is quite often held in an image and if there is a fruitfulness of interchange it can emerge as an insight. A supervisee is then helped to inhabit their professional self. In similar situations with sexually abused children I find it hard to speak to destructiveness unless I am certain; it has to be fully in the room. I wonder if this is harder for artists because they enter into destruction as part of creation quite readily in their own work. The dynamics around this work are very powerful. One can be so aware of what has been done to children that it can be hard to think about their own aggression and destructiveness that is contributing to a situation. One can also feel shame that there is sexual abuse in our society, of which we are a part. In this supervisor, I appreciated a certain clarity of technique and reflection on psychotic thinking that I needed with this case.

## Playing with the image that is presented

A space to play is needed in supervision and I have in mind Winnicott's (1971) thinking about play in psychotherapy. Ogden (1995) suggests that the most mundane thoughts that pass through the therapist's mind during a session can provide clues to the inter-subjective relationship that is unfolding. One needs trust to be able to play in this way. Maclagan (2001) discusses trying to 'imaginatively inhabit a picture'.

A colleague and I in a Child and Adolescent Mental Health Service (CAMHS) have peer supervision with the intention of following a case each, taking it in turns to present. I am bringing a new piece of work with a child who was four when I started, now five. At the beginning she was a puzzling child with several symptoms causing some speculation that she could be on the autistic spectrum. She had communication difficulties, language delay and disorder, at times not seeming to hear, and speech that was very difficult to understand. She seemed to be in a world of her own. She was hard to reach and only needed an hour or two of sleep a night, which was a huge strain on her parents. Her mother, who had learning difficulties, had been in a violent relationship and had only been able to extricate herself by a determination that Linda would not be hurt, managing to escape to a women's refuge. They lived a chaotic life for the first two years. She is now in a stable situation with mother, stepfather and new siblings.

At the beginning of therapy she was chaotic, darting about from one activity to another, with very little focus or eye contact. There is an angry whiny part of her that says 'can't do it' and collapses, that seems to be anti-growing up and wants to be the baby. In an early session she wanted to draw a house but wanted me to do it, and collapsed, after angrily scribbling, and I said 'you have made an angry scribble'. She said 'It's a spider!' She then made her first three-dimensional image of a spider. The spider was made from plasticene with pencils stuck in it for legs. As she finished she whined 'can't do it' at me and I said in fact she could do it and had finished. She said she was frightened of spiders and began to pretend-chase me with it. This was the first of many such spiders that have come into many sessions.

In supervision we have played over and used free association to try to elicit the changing meanings and significance of the various spider makings. In my colleague I have appreciated the capacity to play with me in thinking about the imagery in plasticene and later drawings on paper. In this reciprocal relationship, it is not as formal as some other supervision relationships, although we do keep to the task. At first the spider seems to be to do with her anger 'the angry scribble'. She says that he is scary, and she is frightened of him. She makes and breaks him up many times in a session; sometimes the breaking is set off by hearing a noise, which could be in the building or in the distance outside. Then he is thrown, so that the pencil legs come out, or he is deliberately cut up with scissors, only to be made again. She struggles with a need for a container for frightening feelings and a fear of it becoming a container of persecutory forces (Foster 1997). Sometimes he is drowned in water in the sink or stuck with glue to paper or put under a cover with 'he's sleeping now'. On her folder in a session a few weeks into therapy she drew a 'scary face' and a shape with some letters from her name. I thought that this might be a picture of mother and daughter (Figure 6.2).

*Figure 6.2* Linda: folder cover.

It was helpful to discuss with my colleague that Linda is at a developmental stage where a drawing can have a rapid succession of meanings. Keats, in his idea of 'negative capability', drew our attention to the way that the adult in us searches for *the* meaning as if there is only one truth, which is very different from the child's fluidity of changing meanings. The following drawing was a house, then hair was added and it was her half sister, older, then hair changed and it was her best friend, a boy, then hair changed and it was her baby half sister (Figure 6.3). While talking with my colleague about the extraordinary way that one picture can change and be named as different things at this age, I had a memory of a spider experience. A lot of people are afraid of spiders. I can pick up small ones but not large ones and I feel happier with them in the garden but not in the house. One day while gardening I felt a tickle on my chest but did not find anything there, I was wearing a v-neck. Much later that day while changing I felt another tickle and found a spider curled up in my bra in the space between my breasts. Strangely, instead of being horrified I had the sense that if you could nurture what you were afraid of then it was no longer frightening. I linked this experience with a firmer realisation that Linda was playing with different fears and getting to know them. The spiders originally had a very terrifying element but gradually could be put to bed, that is, nurtured, both literally and metaphorically.

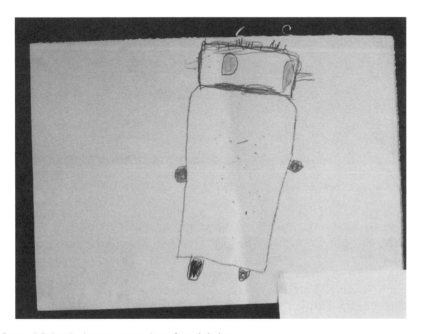

*Figure 6.3* Linda: house, sister, best friend, baby.

This memory allowed me to think about Linda's mother with my colleague, and the fear that Linda experienced in the situation of domestic violence, and whether it was her mother's fear that was frightening, also making it difficult to manage her own fears and anger. Could this be part of the scary picture and be preventing Linda from sleeping? She had a capacity to be 'on guard and alert' at night, when she could play literally all night, only occasionally falling asleep for twelve hours from utter exhaustion but then not sleeping again for several days. I thought that Linda's feelings about the new baby also came into the picture, clearly part of the 'can't do it' is a wish to be the looked after baby. The spider play developed so that at times they are scary and at times they are looked after. Sometimes there are lots of 'baby spiders', in the form of tiny marks on paper (Figure 6.4).

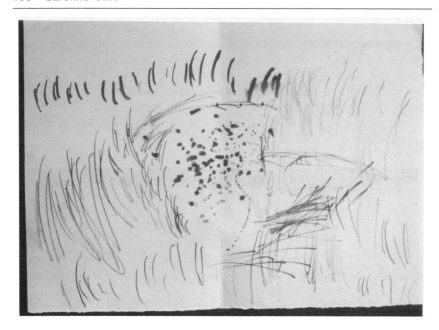

*Figure 6.4* Linda: baby spiders.

She would want to be chased by 'the plasticene spider', but eventually play centred on being 'at night', when she is asleep. She wants me to play the good mother who says 'goodnight' and the spider who comes in the night to 'eat her'. During one of these sessions she drew 'mummy in a circle, mummy is dying' (Figure 6.5). This picture became the spider's nest or web. Progress came with the spider being made a web (a home) and then he became not so scary (Figure 6.6). 'She is not scared of this spider' but she is scared of real spiders because they eat butterflies; she had seen one caught in a web. The next phase was that he was fooled by Linda and teased, and at this point it felt as if her fear had been contained. She now had a transitional toy and was sleeping between three to five hours every night. At this point in the therapy a new animal made an appearance, 'Alien Dog', who comes down to earth from space and is looked after by a lady, and the spider play ended (Case 2005).

I wanted to link the way that in the session Linda and I were able to play with the spider images from plasticene and pictures so that they moved into being more humanised emotion: loving and scaring became part of a dual human characteristic in the therapist/mother. In the supervision we were able to link present and past spider images, child development, anger and fear both in mother and in Linda and think about how this might be affecting her sleeping, which was one of her major symptoms. This illustrates Damasio's ideas about how we use past experiences, mental images

*Figure 6.5* Linda: mummy in a circle, mummy is dying.

*Figure 6.6* Linda: spiders web.

and body feelings (somatic markers) in order to help us in decision making and thinking. Obviously I have many spider memories, but what I recalled was helpful in my thinking with my colleague about the many meanings that the spider took on – anger, fear, potential threatening 'other babies', her mother's fear, her siblings when he was teased with presents he could not have – and how through this play these aspects of her inner life become known and, eventually, not frightening.

## Parallel process in supervision, with myself as supervisor

One of the ways that we usefully work in supervision is to be aware of 'parallel process' or the mirroring in supervision of the dynamic between therapist and patient that may be re-played between supervisor and super- visee, which has been variously described by different writers.

A newly qualified art therapist arrived for her first session of supervision anxious to describe her client. She described his painful history of mental illness, and upper middle class social status that was higher than the majority of patients at the hospital. He was someone who would not usually communicate with members of the team but very delicately she had invited him to do art therapy and he had begun to come. She described him as so sensitive that she could not possibly comment on his paintings at all. She had put a painting of a landscape on the floor between us and as she was talking about him she gradually slipped onto the floor beside me, showing me the painting, until she was literally kneeling at my feet. She was clearly waiting for me to speak about the picture to her. I began to feel very uncomfortable. It was her first supervision session with me and I was aware that she was in awe of me and had a strong transference to me as a potential mentor. I asked her if she had any thoughts about the picture and she did, but felt she could not possibly say them to him, nor could she attempt to draw him out about his own thoughts. This felt very sensitive. Was I going to impinge on the process between patient and therapist if I suggested that she might either speak her own thoughts or encourage his? I also felt that if I did not speak then we here, as well as therapist and patient, might remain in a situation of waiting for each other, so I drew out as many thoughts from her as I could about the picture to try to give her confidence in her perceptions and understanding of her patient. I began to talk to her of some possible idealisation of her client and the picture- making process that was hindering her using her own response. The process needs to be respected but not idealised. I felt that in idealising the process, both here and there, she was not working with what she knew. Therefore, her client could be feeling left out of her attention and rather lonely, based on my own sense of a lack of reciprocity in our interactions together. Permission to think, speak and have thoughts needed to be given all round.

Employed on a short-term contract with slippage money she had been successful in making this into a six month project to test the viability or efficacy of art therapy with the possibility of permanent funding in the future. She desperately wanted it to succeed and was delighted to have a client drawing in an important and meaningful way, but she was idealising the process of art therapy in her client as she idealised me. In both situations she was not thinking herself but waiting for her client/me to speak, anxious not to impinge on us, but leaving us potentially isolated. I did not point out to her what she was doing by kneeling on the floor, because it was her first session, but it was interesting that as she started to think for herself she gradually drew back till she was sitting on her own chair, and we immediately felt on a level footing.

It is an enormous responsibility to be the recipient of such idealised transference. It is illustrative of the power relations and how one can fall into the trap of 'imparting the knowledge' as a supervisor. Because one is at a distance and not the participator in the immediate dynamics it is possible to think with the supervisee of what might have been said; it can be experimented or played with once someone feels some mutual trust. To a less experienced art therapist it can appear that you have *super*vision. When working with a more robust therapist who is established I would have talked directly about the image she presented at my feet and used it. Parallel process can happen with the supervisee unconsciously re-presenting the client with the supervisor as therapist or, as in the case above, the supervisee as herself and the supervisor as client.

An experienced art therapist came to supervision talking about her frustration with a member of an adolescent group who was not making any images but was verbally dominating every session. This is a very difficult client group to work with in a secure setting. She was furious with him and described the wrestling match she was having volubly to me. Part of her anger is that he had been in a group before and had not been able to paint, but he had made a request to her to be part of this next group. They both knew what it was he needed to work on after he had made one very speaking image, of his abusive childhood, in the first group and then no more. He was quite verbally abusive in the group. As she talked it was apparent that they were engaged in a fight. The art therapist wanted him to do art therapy and he both did and did not want to. He was terrified of what the image had aroused but also had to maintain the hard man image in the group.

I discussed this in terms of the transference. She was playing one part of him, the part that wanted to come and work in therapy, and he was embodying the other that was resisting the potential relationship. Technically should she stand further back to allow him some space? Possibly a therapist centred response such as 'you really feel therapy is hopeless' or 'you cannot see what use a therapist could be' would allow him to have a thought about it not being so bad. In her annoyance she was really responding to every provocative comment he made like a terrier. At the end of the session in describing another group of adolescents she mentioned two members, one who was volatile and one who was pedantic, and how because of this no work could be done. I was able to use this to say: 'look you have described yourself and your other client!' She was able to laugh about this, recognising the way work was being inhibited by the positions they had taken up. This led us to thinking about the possibility of individual work for her client who had to maintain a hard man stance in the group, because of keeping his place in the hierarchy outside the group in ordinary institutional life. We were able to think productively about this and the way that they *were* engaged in a relationship.

## Working with the picture

In this example the picture leads the way, or in Henzell's (1997) words 'pictorial works may supplement the accustomed dependence on words'. He writes about paying close attention to the picture as a crucial part of supervision. 'The patient's image is a statement, it embodies meaning, intention and subjectivity'.

An art therapist who works in a CAMHS arrived for supervision saying that she wanted to talk about one child but she was feeling anxious about something else and did I remember Luke whom we had talked about before the summer? Her anxiety was that the consultant wanted to show the pictures to the paediatrician, in the city hospital, who had originally referred him and she was worried about confidentiality. Part of the difficulty was that the pictures were so amazing and he had made an extraordinary recovery and everybody on the team, the nurses on the ward, was feeling pleased with this success. This led us to talking about how usually so many cases ended much less well with worries about whether situations would hold together. She communicated a lot of high excitement saying that it was good for art therapy that people were attributing such a change to the work with her as well as other inpatient treatment. I suggested that we look at a session with Luke and one of his paintings that she had brought to show me and we would look at the other child next time.

She unrolled a delicate drawing with a figure at the centre with gold iridescent wings that really caught the eye. I remembered that when she had spoken of him before, Luke was a child of eight, with jet black hair and heavy build. He had been referred to child and family psychiatry because he had stopped being able to walk but there was no organic damage. He was an only child, of high intelligence and high achieving but without friends. He had a rather worrying relationship with his father who had some depression or breakdown before Luke was born. He seemed to be devoting his whole life to Luke.

There had been a question as to whether this was chronic fatigue syndrome or illness behaviour. Luke had been admitted accompanied by his father, who resented the ministration of the nurses. Mother worked in a professional job and seemed a shadowy figure, uninvolved in Luke's care and unknown to the staff team. In art therapy, Luke had drawn two images where a figure emerged from being trapped. Then, he had amazed the art therapist by walking to the next session, not using a wheelchair, and had worked on the picture she had brought over two sessions. It felt like the miracle child who had lifted up his mat and walked and all the staff had been delighted. Father had described Luke as a gifted sensitive child too special to play with other children, saying that only he can interpret his every need. Was this child fulfilling this role for the hospital staff in the transference? The art therapist and I discussed how we would also like success (in art therapy); could we be enacting the father's role and where does mother fit into this? On the one hand there seemed to be a general picture of health, Luke was walking and he was playing with other children on the ward almost despite father. He was talking about wanting to go back to school and was going to be discharged. What seemed to be missing was any understanding about what had happened to him or exploration of family dynamics. Everyone seemed caught up with idealisation of this child. Luke described the centre figure in the picture as 'coming out'. We decided to look at the picture closely. I asked her to describe it being made.

The first week he had drawn the figure, which looks like a mythical knight or hero, and he had spent a very long time on the wings (of the knight), which were cut delicately from gold iridescent paper. The clue to me was that they caught the eye so completely and it was almost difficult to see the rest of the picture. The phrase 'flight into health' came into my mind. I had a great worry that this child would be discharged without the rest of the clinical picture being seen, that is, both the family work and the consolidation of Luke's coming out. He seemed to carry a burden of speciality. The figure knight carries a sword with lines of power coming from it: like Star Wars, 'the force be with you'. She drew my attention to a force line that had gone wrong and said a wrong line was so worrying for him that she had gone to get typex from the office for him. To leave him alone in the therapy room was out of character, so we discussed this. She said that there is something about him that makes one want to treat him specially, i.e. the transference had been enacted rather than exploring with him what it felt like or might mean to make a wrong line.

The figure is rising from 'some exotic foliage', with the exotic suggesting the special. On one side is a dragon, lines of force attack it, and we noticed some rather strange lines of fire or force coming from the dragon to the figure but they might be blocking the dragon's mouth, it was not clear. It is part of the effect of the shiny wings that one does not see the details. The other side of the picture is empty, not yet finished, but the composition suggested that there would be another element. It was possible that the space represented the other (missing) parent. The picture communicated 'the hero fighting to be free'. We thought about him fighting to win free to his peer group. The last interesting element is the face of the figure. I had to hold the picture very close to my eyes to see this clearly. I could not really make it out and she explained that he had tried and failed to give a face to the knight and had put a mask on it. This confirmed for me that the child's true self is still hidden and that probably the miracle child is a false self that has grown to fit the need of the father.

In the case described the supervisee knows that something is wrong and brings this worry. There was a question around confidentiality, as to whether Luke's pictures should be shown to a professional outside the immediate CAMHS team, but during discussion it emerged that she was under terrific pressure to show the pictures to Luke's father who asked intrusive questions around every session. It was clear that Luke was emerging, coming out from something. He had been able to express a wish to go to school and be back with his peer group. This was a healthy move forward but the family dynamics that were contributing to his situation were obfuscated by the attention this 'miracle cure' received. In such a situation the work with the whole family needs to be consolidated for a successful outcome. A flight into health could seriously threaten the therapy as, although Luke was coming regularly to therapy in the hospital, his parents would be relied upon to bring him once he was discharged and became an outpatient. Unless both parents were engaged in work as a family at the hospital I thought it possible that once Luke was home his father would try to sabotage the therapy because he found it unbearable to be left out. It was clear that long-term work with Luke and with the parental couple would need to be done. In order to protect Luke's privacy and confidentiality we discussed ways of communicating with the small team the art therapist works with, but also how it might be possible to meet with the paediatrician and talk about the work while keeping the pictures confidential.

In summary, the picture beautifully encapsulated the total dynamics around this child and his struggles with internal figures. Supervisees really give you clues if you like, of what needs your attention, as in the way she drew my attention to the use of typex that I would have missed. Confidentiality and issues around it were wider than we at first realised; in a sense this child struggles to have a private life at all of his own and she was struggling to keep their work together private. Following supervision it was clear that the need for ongoing family work was indicated and that art therapy had had a role in highlighting that need. This was therefore addressed by the team and the family were able to engage to some extent.

## A note on idealisation

It was only as I finished writing that I realised I had chosen two examples for this chapter, where I was working with different presentations of idealisation as a supervisor. In the earlier example, a situation was discussed where the supervisor was idealised, as well as the client, by a newly qualified art therapist. This may occur as a result of anxiety about failure. Intense anxiety may cause splitting of aspects of the object as a defence. The client was idealised so that the anxieties about the outcome of the case and the whole situation at the workplace and whether art therapy would be proved to be successful could be managed. The supervisor is kept as an idealised 'perfect object' and bad aspects of the supervisor split off onto another person. The supervisee then does not have to manage feelings of ambivalence towards the supervisor and the anxieties that these may arouse. It can be such a struggle to get art therapy established that this is sometimes a danger and in these cases supervision can provide a necessary grounding to experience. In the second example, Luke's father idealised his son but in such a way that he had become a vehicle for the father's needs, which was such a powerful dynamic that it was in danger of being enacted by the staff group. Idealisation will always involve the splitting off of ambivalent feelings, and can be a defence against envy or painful anxieties. To see the good and bad in someone we care for needs a certain maturity and bearing of the anxieties of the depressive position; at times of great stress we may slip back to splitting as a defence.

## Conclusion

In this chapter I have wanted to give attention to the particular part that is played by mental images and memory in the mind of therapist and supervisor, parallel process, and paying close attention to the image that is made in art therapy and brought to supervision. In order to do this I have used examples from myself in supervision and myself as supervisor. In Figure 6.1 I have made an attempt to map the interplaying dynamics between: the conscious verbal account/written account; theoretical knowledge that we both bring; body feelings as somatic markers, re-presenting some aspect of the therapy session; conscious reflection in the session; reverie and play between supervisor and supervisee; and the creation of a space for unconscious reflection in the form of intuition and insight. These all contribute and feed back into understanding the image at the centre of the relationship in art therapy and may lead to change in the therapist's conceptualisation and approach. My interest has been in the way that images encapsulate understanding that hovers on the edge of awareness and how, following the ideas of Damasio, we can uncover this 'non-verbal narrative of knowing' lying beneath the presented verbal account of a session.

## References

Astor, J. (2000) 'Some reflections on empathy and reciprocity in the use of counter-transference between supervisor and supervisee', *Journal of Analytical Psychology*, *45*: 367–383.

Bion, W. R. (1959) 'Attacks on linking', *International Journal of Psychoanalysis*, *40*: 308–315.

Case, C. (1994) 'Art therapy in analysis: advance/retreat in the belly of the spider', *Inscape*, *1*: 3–10.

Case, C. (2005) *Imagining Animals: Art, Psychotherapy and Primitive States of Mind*, London: Routledge.

Damasio, A. (1994) *Descartes' Error: Emotion, Reason and the Human Brain*, New York: Putnam.

Damasio, A. (2000) *The Feeling of What Happens: Body, Emotion and the Making of Consciousness*, London: Vintage.

Doehrman, M. J. G. (1976) 'Parallel processes in supervision and psychotherapy', *Bulletin of the Menninger Clinic*, *40*: 9–104.

Ekstein, R. and Wallerstein, R. S. (1972) *The Teaching and Learning of Psychotherapy*, New York: International Universities Press.

Foster, F. (1997) 'Fear of three-dimensionality: clay and plasticene as experimental bodies', in K. Killick and J. Schaverien (eds), *Art, Psychotherapy and Psychosis*, London: Routledge, pp. 52–71.

Henzell, J. (1997) 'The image's supervision', in G. Shipton (ed.), *Supervision of Psychotherapy and Counselling: Making a Place to Think*, Buckingham: Oxford University Press, pp. 71–79.

Klein, M. (1952) 'Some theoretical conclusions regarding the emotional life of the infant', in M. Masud and R. Kahn (eds), *Envy and Gratitude and Other Works 1946–1963*, The Writings of Melanie Klein Vol 3, London: Hogarth Press and the Institute of Psychoanalysis, pp. 61–93.

Kris, E. (1953) *Psychoanalytic Explorations in Art*, London: Allen and Unwin.

Langer, S. (1963) *Philosophy in a New Key*, Cambridge, MA: Harvard University Press.

Maclagan, D. (2001) *Psychological Aesthetics: Painting, Feeling and Making Sense*, London: Jessica Kingsley.

Meltzer, D. (1986) *Studies in Extended Metapsychology: Clinical Applications of Bion's Ideas*, Strath Tay: Clunie Press.

Ogden, T. (1995) 'Analysing forms of aliveness and deadness of the transference and countertransference', *International Journal of Psycho-Analysis*, *76*: 695–709.

Pedder, J. (1986) 'Reflections on the theory and practice of supervision', *Psychoanalytic Psychotherapy*, *2* (1): 1–12.

Rosenfeld, H. (1952) 'Notes on the psycho-analysis of the super-ego conflict in an acute schizophrenic patient', *International Journal of Psychoanalysis*, *33*: 111–131.

Scaife, J. (2001) 'Creative approaches', in J. Scaife (ed.), *Supervision in the Mental Health Professions: A Practitioner's Guide*, Hove: Brunner-Routledge, pp. 173–188.

Searles, H. (1995) 'The informational value of the supervisor's emotional experiences', *Psychiatry*, *18*: 146.

Stokes, A. (1972) 'The invitation in art', in R. Wohhelm (ed.), *The Image in Form, Selected Writings of Adrian Stokes*, Harmondsworth: Penguin, pp. 101–115.

Wilmot, J. and Shohet, R. (1985) 'Paralleling in the supervision process', *Self and Society: European Journal of Humanistic Psychology*, *XIII* (2): 86–92.

Winnicott, D. W. (1971) *Playing and Reality*, Harmondsworth: Penguin.

Part II

# Theoretical innovations in group supervision

# Chapter 7

# Image consultation

## Supporting the work of art therapists

*Riitta Laine*

## Introduction

This chapter is a contribution to the discourse on the role and use of images in the supervision of art therapists. How can images sufficiently and creatively be taken into account in the supervision setting? In this chapter I shall propose a method that may offer one answer to this question.

In Finland, art therapists are usually supervised by psychotherapists or psychoanalysts but we also have peer groups known as 'image consultancy groups'. In my view, such a group can function as an important – perhaps even as a crucial – complement to psychotherapeutic one-on-one supervision. 'The image consultancy group' concentrates on observing visual creations made by the clients of group members.

In this chapter I use the words 'picture' or 'work' to stand for all the visual creations that clients produce in the therapy setting. I also use the term 'art therapist' (or simply therapist) even though, considering my training in Finland, the title of visual art therapist would most closely correspond to the title of analytical art psychotherapist used in England. I refer to the therapist receiving consultation as the supervisee.

The idea in image consultation is to try to understand the client's experiential world specifically through the pictures. Pictures made in art therapy express and structure what can live and resonate in the interaction between the therapist and client. In the consultation setting, the group concentrates on observing and understanding this. To facilitate these observations, I shall propose some methods that I consider to be noteworthy and useful. These are *intuition, mobility, amodality, amplification* and *lightness*.

I will discuss the pitfalls of groups working without a leader, but also the potential for such groups to support the work and advance the art therapist's understanding. A group can help therapists be touched by their clients and their pictures in a new way. The therapist's relationship to the client's unconscious is revitalised, deepened and reshaped. This in turn influences the course of therapy. The group challenges its members to reflect upon their habitual ways of viewing and relating to images in the psychotherapeutic framework. Series of images, perhaps created over several years, can challenge the art therapist to observe the progress (or lack of it) and to understand where important changes have taken place, possibly even to discover something essential for the therapy.

In considering this I propose the following:

1   It is important to approach the client through the expressive medium they use to tell about themselves. In art therapy, this primary medium is the picture. Since expertise in this medium is the art therapist's speciality, this needs to be taken into account in supervision as well.

2   An image consultation group helps art therapists view their client or client group in a multi-dimensional and revitalising way.

3   The group challenges its members to explore and become aware of their own conventions of looking. It helps them to develop professionally and to deepen their expertise.

4   The group strengthens the professional identity and solidarity of the participants.

5   The group's ability to observe is based on members being able to commit to working together.

## A brief history of image consultation

The way image consultation groups have functioned at different times gives some indication of what the professional community has required from them and what has been found useful. Thus, at different times they seem to have played different roles.

A group that was assembled in 1984 seemed primarily to function to reinforce professional collegiality and bonding. A second group assembled in the late 1980s emphasised the need for art therapy to be acknowledged as a legitimate psychotherapeutic profession. There was also a shared, fervent desire to understand the use of images in therapeutic work more deeply. The consultation group allowed therapists to discuss their own professional burdens and share feelings about the images they were encountering. A third group met for the past few years. This group functioned alongside and complemented the individual psychotherapeutic supervision of each member. What seemed to be important for most members was to be able to see other therapists' cases and to compare their own experiences with these. In this chapter I present some of the comments of group members (in tinted boxes) that I have collected through a questionnaire.

## The task of the image consultation group

The task of the group is to observe and comment upon clients' works presented in turn by each art therapist. According to a mutually agreed

*Figure 7.1* Chandelier.

schedule, each participant takes a turn as a supervisee, while the rest of the group act as consultants. The size of the group may vary, but optimally consists of 5–9 individuals.

Supervisees select works (or a single work) by a client or client group on which they wish to hear other art therapists' thoughts. Group members endeavour to express verbally everything they experience while viewing these works, with the aim of reaching the countertransferences evoked by the image(s). Participants communicate their own feelings and thoughts to others, though the goal is not really to have a proper discussion but no attempts are made to quell discussion. The task consists of association as well as dialogue. The focus, as well as the starting point, is always the client's work, to which the group's attention continually returns.

The group can perhaps best be compared to a chandelier: like a group of lights emanating from a single hub, the members share a connection. In this case, the connection is the images: the hub of the chandelier (Figure 7.1) is the centre around which the group has gathered. The atmosphere of the group's work and thinking is dependent on the hub, but at the same time the group is also structuring and working through that hub with new perspectives. Image consultation works through permissiveness, which allows imprecise expression, apparent illogicality, humour and stammering; such permissiveness acts as a counterforce both to petrification and chaos in the group (Blackwell 1998).

The group's effectiveness can paradoxically be seen as arising from its potential to be inefficient. By this, I do not mean irresponsibility or apathy, but rather the freedom not to direct contributions towards attaining goals external to the group's work. Nor is the aim to help the supervisee as much as possible, to produce plenty of associations to understand the client. This is because actively striving to have an influence and be effective can easily become an obstacle to *being*; and *being* in the face of these images is of primary importance. The group adopts an unhurried attitude; participants accept that they can observe slowly and tentatively, that they are groping in the dark.

### Supervision and image consultation

As it attempts to support therapists in their work, image consultation fulfils the objective set for supervision. In practice, however, image consultation seems to complement individual supervision rather than supersede it. The group corresponds to the supervision model described by David Edwards (1994), where the emphasis is not so much on education as on listening to the transference–countertransference dynamics of the therapy process. Image consultation differs from traditional psychotherapy supervision. Firstly, sessions last longer. The group can meet for 1.5–3 hours at a time. This enables it to focus on extensive series of images, so that it is possible to get a better grasp of the whole. In regular supervision there is seldom opportunity to spend extensive amounts of time looking at many images.

Little information about the client's life history is given, and may, upon mutual agreement, be completely withheld. Indeed, the group may well be able to take advantage of this lack of comprehensive background information (cf. intuition and amplification). Also missing will be a follow-up of the therapy. The group usually meets on a monthly basis, so depending on the size of the group one may have to wait for one's turn for a rather long time. Naturally, a group that meets this infrequently does not provide sufficient support for intensive therapies.

Normal supervision does not generally provide ready-made answers and guidelines for action but image consultation groups usually leave much more for the supervisee to digest. The group is not responsible for guiding therapy, but could be thought of as a one-off intensive event. Thus, supervisees must organise what they have heard and structure the contribution of the group in a way that they can use. This is the case particularly when the group has presented a lot of conflicting comments, impressions, thought fragments and bodily sensations that seem mutually incompatible.

Image consultation may provide support by reinforcing the therapist's previous understanding, but it may also shake their views and potential points of fixation. However, this takes place in the spirit of reinforcing the therapist's many-sidedness and psychic mobility.

### Balint groups and image consultation

In their own way, everyone was an expert on what they themselves saw, experienced and were able to take in. The client emerged as the most important person, as the protagonist.

There is a resemblance between Balint groups and image consultation. In both groups there is an emphasis on trying to listen to and recognise one's feelings and associations in relation to the presented case; however, in image consultation the case consists primarily of the client's pictures. While a Balint group attempts to get away from an illness-centred towards a patient-centred approach (Trenkel 1994), one might say that image consultation is image-centred when compared to typical supervision, which is client-centred and at times focuses actively on discussing therapeutic interventions. In both groups the idea is to utilise the group as 'an organ for understanding' (Trenkel 1994: 28).

Like Balint groups, image consultation groups work qualitatively differently at different times. In Balint supervision, the fundamental idea is that everything that happens within the group is connected to the patient (Balint 1986). Likewise, in image consultation we can explore the changes in the group's working as a reflection of the client case. Image consultation does not, however, define structures (such as outer and inner circle, which would regulate the group and thus ensure staying on task). (In Balint groups there is a small circle of members surrounded by a larger circle of people.) The group does not have a specific leader who is responsible for what happens at any given meeting, but rather each participant is responsible for furthering the work. This places certain demands on participants, a topic I shall return to below.

Therapists presenting their clients' pictures may also ask: why am I presenting this person? Formulating the question structures and maps the problem and provides supervisees with an opportunity to explore their relationship with the client and the client's images. The answer may also point to the relationship between the supervisee and the peer group.

## Meeting, 12 April 2003, Part I

In one image consultation group meeting, I presented pictures by a client with whom I had been somewhat at a loss for some time. At every therapy session the client made a picture as we talked, but once the picture was finished she would relate to it unenthusiastically and rejectingly. In her therapy, the pictures seemed to have two conflicting meanings: she found it necessary to make them, but once they were finished she felt them to be worthless. She was competent in expressing herself verbally, and talked about her issues and feelings while painting. In fact, she felt that she could not talk unless she painted at the same time.

The work seemed to be created as a kind of by-product of verbal interaction. Mostly, it looked as if she simply coloured the paper, seeming to select her colours and change to another colour at random. The pictures looked like layers or streams of colour, and the client usually had no associations linked to them. Viewing them felt oppressive and embarrassing to her, since she felt that she 'did not understand them at all'. Therapy seemed to be helpful to the client, however, and during the first year her anxiety diminished markedly.

I asked the consultation group what purpose the pictures were serving in this therapy (besides the client feeling that she could only talk while painting). I was in a way asking whether it was permissible for me to be this confused and unable to understand my client's works, whether I could justify my work as an art therapist with this particular client. (In fact, this was the same question that permeated my client's entire being, but this, and all of its ramifications, I only understood later.) In the consultation, I felt an urge to simply give the pictures to the group, thinking that they could do what they wanted with them, that I did not care. I realised how frustrated I was when I was presenting the case. I recognised shame, guilt and anger in myself. Thus I also asked myself what I was unintentionally and unknowingly allying myself with, what I was carrying and what I was blind to.

In the image consultation group, the pictures first of all evoked many varied physical sensations in the viewers. The group spoke about intensities and their amodal sensations that they felt these works were evoking. They sensed the client's fear of being in a one-on-one relationship. The group discussed how pictures can be used to regulate distance and contain anxiety. They wondered about whether the issues talked about and the picture created, during this discussion, were related to each other at all or if they were two separate communications.

The group also belittled the pictures; feelings of worthlessness and insignificance could begin to live and become more conscious. Meaninglessness was beginning to have meaning. The shame (my client's: 'stupid works'; mine: 'I am helpless') and guilt (mine: 'I don't understand these pictures'; my client's: 'I have made something lousy') lessened. My anger was transformed into interest. I was able to accept the works as a way of regulating distance. I shall return to this case in part II, but turn now to a more detailed discussion of images in therapy.

### The image in therapy

I will next briefly discuss some of my views concerning a picture produced in a therapy setting. I understand the picture as a view into the invisible that lives between the therapist and the client and is mainly unconscious. The work is formed within the therapist–client relationship and reflects this space. It consists of what clients are able to experience in the therapeutic relationship at that point, and what they can bear. Since the picture has been made in the therapy setting, it is formed through these dynamics and interprets them visually. In other words, the client's picture reflects and works through the transference in the wide meaning of the word. Naturally the picture also influences the therapist–client relationship.

Joy Schaverien (1992) has made an important contribution to this discussion, explaining that, 'the unconscious of the client and that of the therapist may meet and mingle within the framed area of the picture' (p. 119). The picture is not made without a particular viewer in mind. Clients are conscious for whom they are making the picture, and this influences the outcome. A picture created in group art therapy forms part of the series of images produced by the whole group. Here, the picture reflects the experience of being in a relationship – that which is live but invisible in-between the group members.

Pictures present the nature and quality of their maker's experience and reveal how they relate to that experience. A picture indicates how clients live their emotions, what sorts of physical–psychological sensations they experience. The individual characteristics of a personal experience are visible and observable. The unique significance of a picture is not that it 'tells' the viewer about joy, but that it expresses the personal experience of joy of this very client: how joy feels, its softness, lightness, bubbliness, and so on (or the softness, rigidity, severity, heaviness, impermeability, fragility or suffocating power of sorrow).

A picture is always a great gift to the therapy process: it is an achievement and a creation; it cannot be taken for granted. No matter how elusive it is the picture evokes thoughts, and talking about these creates a space for shared viewing and awareness. This means that there is an opportunity to seek more potential interpretations. Creating pictures is a psychic and physiological state that enables creators to process and communicate their own mind. The primary meaning of the picture is not how it could be put into words; rather, it already has an absolute and unique meaning as it is, in its visual form. A completed work should always be approached with appreciation and respect.

### Taking in the picture

Pictures always bring to view something new and previously unseen. After all, we do not ask clients to paint what they already know, but to paint something they have not yet seen. In their unfamiliarity, the pictures create a disturbance and usually work against the order and established ideas cultivated by the conscious mind.

The therapist's experience is dependent on the client's experience, which is manifested in the picture s/he has created. The therapist's experience, when facing the picture, is their countertransference feelings to the work (Schaverien 1992). Viewing the picture thus entails that countertransferences become vivid and can be identified. Schaverien also uses the concept of an 'aesthetic countertransference' (cf. p. 120). Art therapists must be touched by the clients' pictures, in order to understand them and to be able to work through them, in their own mind. David Sedgwick (2000), basing his discussion on Jung, wrote about countertransference and how it draws on the analyst's openness to the experience of being psychologically wounded. This always tests the limits of therapists' capacity to look, what they are able to take in from the picture, what they can identify, tolerate and digest in their mind, as well as what they cannot. Jung (1961) considered it important that the client and therapist 'become a problem to each other' (p. 143). A picture poses a challenge and is a problem already through its novelty and unfamiliarity. The art therapist needs to have both the willingness and the courage to grapple with this problem.

When we are working with pictures we are always working with a countertransference orientation. Sedgwick (2000: 146) describes the dangers inherent in this kind of work, since 'a countertransference orientation is inherently an area of uncertainty, lack of clarity, and subject/object confusion' (p. 148). In the area of the shadow of the countertransference, or the unconscious, the therapist's own fears and desires might get mixed up with the client's treatment. The therapist might see incorrectly and use the client's works to satisfy his or her own needs: the need to be all-knowing, a liberator, a problem-solver, a magnificent and wise ruler. Awareness of this places a responsibility on us, as viewers, to reflect upon our own state of being in relation to the picture. It is necessary to work through obstacles we encounter in this, both in supervision and in our own psychotherapy.

It is also important for art therapists to question their ways of relating to pictures. How does the therapist, unconsciously, evaluate the pictures created in therapy; is there a specific allure of specific pictures? What is the therapist's relationship with his or her own artistic work, etc.? It is questions like these that help shed light on the therapist's beliefs, needs and values that form the foundation upon which the therapist relates to clients and their visual creations.

### To see more and better

Seeing is a skill that can be improved with practice. I shall next describe some tools that can be used as a basis for making observations about pictures in the image consultation group. These tools, among others, can in my view support us in the challenging task of viewing. Calvino (1998: 17) quotes Henry James:

> It was as if these depths, constantly bridged over by a structure that was firm enough in spite of its lightness and of its occasional oscillation in the somewhat vertiginous air, invited on occasion, in the interest of their nerves, a dropping of the plummet and a measurement of the abyss.

## Intuitiveness, permeability

It was valuable to be able to be open in an open space.

The mind is capable of instinctive knowledge. Intuitive observation largely happens instantaneously and without rational deliberation – unconsciously. The origins of such knowledge may thus be difficult to trace, and its nature is not always easy to define or to describe to others. The nature and dynamics of intuition could perhaps be illustrated by the experience of 'being on a journey' where one's trust in the guidance of one's bodily sensations, emotions and mental images is essential. Wilfred Bion (1984a, 1984b) draws a parallel between intuition and our other senses: hearing, vision, taste, smell, touch. He speaks of intuition as the potential for sensing and identifying emotional states, e.g. anxiety, that lack the characteristics needed for other types of sensing: no smell, no taste.

In art therapy, anxiety can become visible to the eye through the client's pictures. However, anxiety does not have its own visual set of codes that the eye might read. A prerequisite for viewing is to have as unimpeded sensory contact with the work as possible.

Bion (1962) discusses obstacles to intuition, calling them 'opacities' (p. 315; Calvino 1998: 14). He considers this to be a state permeated by memory, desire and understanding. He calls the opposite of this state 'transparency', where the therapist's ability to record to memory and retrieve from memory is functioning but her mind is not overcrowded with memories. The therapist's mind has room to take in the atmosphere of the client's pictures. The tendency to hold onto theoretical views, interpretive formulas or the client's life history can easily obstruct intuition if these become the starting points for looking and the therapist begins to use the pictures as evidence for what is already known.

Desire is linked to the future in much the same way as memory is linked to the past. If therapists have a predetermined and predictive view of a client's work, this prevents them from seeing the images here and now. Therapists may have a fixed understanding of their clients, may have hopes and expectations for them, while clients might feel constrained to conform to these expectations. By contrast, by surrendering oneself to pure sensory perception, one agrees to confront the unpredictable and incomprehensible.

## Mobility, renewal

In the group I could share my wonder with others . . .

Viewing pictures is always about reaching for something new in the infinite space of possible interpretations. In the receptive stance of art therapy, one repeatedly positions oneself to view differently. This stance includes the imperative of viewing without a need to dominate or to be right. What one has seen previously must, in a way, be lost from consciousness in order to be able to view with new eyes. The notion that one has hit the mark (seen the picture as it 'should be seen') feels satisfying. But the fallacy of being right locks in place and terminates the act of viewing. Therapists may then mistakenly believe that they possess the truth about the picture.

Letting go of one's own insights, one's own singular and precise observation, is part of the viewing process. Indeed, the eyes must close intermittently in order for the lachrymal fluid to maintain their ability to see. If the eyes stay open, we are not looking but staring, and our sight gradually glazes over and extinguishes, no longer illuminating the work but becoming blind to it. What we need, then, is at least a blink of the eye, which momentarily takes away our ability to see what we just saw. In the same way, the precise and analytical gaze of consciousness must continuously step aside and yield space for the new and as yet unclear and unrecognised to enter our view. The mind must be able to swing between grasping and losing. Marion Milner (1988) talks about perception as a creative process, which is based on a continual oscillation of the mind between the states of merging and separation. After achieving a sense of separate existence, i.e. that things are perceived as having their own separate, finite and perceivable existence, it is '. . . necessary to be continually undoing it again, in a cyclic oscillation, if psychic sterility is to be avoided' (p. 204). Thus, at issue is the therapist's capacity for renewal.

When looking at pictures, it is important to be able to agree to return time and again to uncertainty and non-understanding. We must sacrifice the interpretation we have reached in order to make room for a new perspective.

## Amodality

> My viewing was (at times) more physical. The picture caused my 'eyes' to move into my fingers and then along some kind of track, to 'experiential viewing'.

A picture's essence can be recognised in the effect it has on the viewer's mind as well as on her body. An art therapist takes in the pictures through multiple senses, amodally. This translates to a holistic perception, bringing together various sensory modalities (cf. Stern 1985; Kristeva 1989). In addition to using the sense of vision, one 'listens' to the work via one's bodily sensations and attempts to feel their qualities: how the paint has been applied, how the process of creation is visible in the completed work, how the artist has treated his subject, etc. The process of taking in the qualities mediated by the material in the picture happens, as it were, as a physical roaming within the picture, with one's gaze acting as the guide. What one looks at also evokes an olfactory sensation. The loudness and quietness of the picture, its heaviness and lightness, movement and stillness, its temperature and taste may be experienced as auditory: taste, scent and tactile impressions and combinations of them. The viewer lives the picture rather than observing it from a distance. The form and content of the work, which cannot be separated from one another, can be identified in the resonance that takes place within the sensory totality of the viewer.

In Ogden's (2002) words, '. . . the unconscious is not imagined to reside *behind* the reveries or at the end of a chain of reverie associations, but as coming to life in the movement of feeling, thought, imagery, and language of the reverie experience itself' (p. 107). Ogden describes beautifully how this relates to language. Taking in a poem is saying it out loud: the timbre of the words, their meaning and how they feel in our mouth when we utter them. The task of the reader '. . . is to marvel at how a poem works – what the language is doing as opposed to what it is saying (what it "means")' (p. 61). The question is: *how* is this picture, what is it like? Not so much: *what* is that? The art therapist does not face the pictures in a state of relaxed passivity but rather opens her sensitivity in the direction of active reception.

## Amplification

> . . . one could give time to the infinite meanings of the picture.

Instead of free association, Jung describes a somewhat different approach to the exploration and interpretation of his clients' dreams or visual

symbols. This approach he calls amplification. Compared to free association, amplification is a more narrowly defined, more controlled and more
focused type of association where one attempts to search for analogies that
would expand upon the symbol in question. Amplification is drawing
parallels, finding correlation in myths, legends and other fields of science:
ethnology, anthropology, history of religion, biology.

Amplification does not aim to explain a symbol. Rather, the objective is
to circle around the symbol, to enrich it with new parallels and perspectives,
using these to stay close to the meaning without being fixed on any
particular interpretation too soon (Jacobi 1942; Jung 1961). It concerns
changing the point of reference, changing the language of thought and the
area of focus, whereby one distances oneself and finds something new by
using new metaphors. Parallels enrich one's view and help one perceive
similarities and differences between things.

In amplification the work is temporarily separated from its primary
references, i.e. from the therapy setting. The situation in which the work
was created and the history of the therapy are not considered at this point,
but the work is viewed as it is, without a history. An individual pictorial
symbol is likewise temporarily taken out of context or the background of
the picture as a whole. Looking at it separately like this helps one focus
one's attention, frees one from the requirement of being therapeutic and
makes space for new ways to talk and find meaning.

### Lightness

I was struck by the seriousness with which we concentrated on the task.

By lightness I am firstly referring to the lightness of the image consultation's structure. The group very simply rests upon three substructures: the
task, the presentation prepared by the supervisee and time limits.

Italo Calvino (1998) writes about lightness in his book *Six Memos for
the Next Millennium*. He sees lightness as the opposite of immobility and
being extinguished, and notes: '. . . there is such a thing as a lightness of
thoughtfulness, just as we all know that there is a lightness of frivolity. In
fact, thoughtful lightness can make frivolity seem dull and heavy' (p. 10).
Calvino uses the myth of Perseus to describe the power of lightness.
Perseus, 'who flies with winged sandals' (p. 4), cuts off Medusa's head. He
avoids Medusa's petrifying stare by looking at her reflection in a mirror
that he lifts against the lightness of the sky (cf. also amplification; looking
via something else). The beheading of the monster gives birth to Pegasus.

Heaviness and petrification are transformed into a winged horse taking flight. But Perseus, the vanquisher of the monster, also must have great delicacy: he gently places Medusa's heavy head, face down, on a bed of leaves and branches of sea plants. A miracle then follows: the seaweed turns into coral. '. . . the fine grace of the coral touches the savage horror of the Gorgon . . .' (p. 6). I understand that the therapist is acting like Perseus when dealing with the heavy scenes the client provides: tenderly, respectfully, with an ability to metamorphose them into something else.

Humour likewise emerges from lightness while also creating it. This is a way of being and seeing that illuminates the work in question, which allows one to see it in a different way, even the opposite way from that of the first viewing. Humour and play require precision and concentration in order to be effective. In fact, lightness requires serious commitment and determination to stay with the task.

Following the gaze of another group member requires an agility of the eye and of the mind. The movement of one's gaze must yield to variation and changes of rhythm, and if it is dragging and heavy it cannot succeed. Being sensitive and concentrated is not the same as having one's thought move slowly and heavily. At best, the dialogue within one's own mind and between the group members is effortless and flexible.

Calvino also brings up the world's infinitely light particle nature that sustains us, as well as how trains of thought and sequences of events reflect that 'subtle and imperceptible elements are at work' (p. 17). I think this can also clearly be seen in how the group members' observations can sometimes sound clumsy and totally unrelated to each other. They may seem as if they are floating in the air in isolation, making no sense and lacking interconnectedness. Nevertheless even the fragmentary thoughts that have emerged in the group's mind are always (freely) tied to each other within the matrix of the group as a whole (Foulkes 1986).

## The group

> What someone found moving in a picture could irritate someone else immensely.

Members of the group live in a continuous motion of connecting to each other and separating from each other. Joining a group always means that to some extent one becomes part of a group unity and identifies with the group, from which an individual then develops towards their own identity via the route of dependency (Neumann 1970; Foulkes 1973; Skaife 1990).

With the help of the group, an individual separates from others, finding her own unique qualities. Art therapists need a group to which they can belong and in which they can develop further even after they have completed their education and entered professional life.

The desire and need to join a group are in conflict with the fear of fusing. Bion talks about humans as group animals, who are at 'constant war with their groupishness' (Brown 2003: 154). Sharing the same mindset and being in agreement can feel both desirable and dangerous to individuality. Disagreeing with the group means that one is left alone, but it also reinforces one's identity. In a group, similar observations, thoughts and interpretations alternate with conflicting interpretations. This continuous movement is a counterforce to stagnation and weakness.

### Pitfalls and opportunities

An image consultation group can be liberating, inspiring, envious, dismissive, demanding, pushy, safe.

Morris Nitsun (1996) talks about 'Anti-Group' phenomena as the ever-present potential for destructiveness that shadows creative group processes. This can be manifested as possessiveness when concerns over losing control grow too great. This can be seen for instance in the need to dominate the group's space, and can lead to rejecting and dismissing the comments of others. The group becomes exhausted and fails to provide anything worthwhile. Leadership rivalry is linked to an inclination to create hierarchies and assume roles when their lack is seen as a threat.

Making comparisons in turn stems from the misconception that there are right or wrong, good or bad, observations that can be brought up in the group. One result of powerful envy is often an effort to defeat the other in an attempt to rid oneself of one's experiences of worthlessness and incompetence. Nitsun (1996) also talks about envy directed at the group itself. The group is experienced as being rich and fertile, but is not allowed to provide assistance. Naturally, the group may also be envious of the competence, experience and merits of the therapist presenting his client case.

At worst, this kind of a situation can lead to poor attendance, silence, accusations and dismissal. The stronger these sentiments towards the group are, and the more they seem to vary from one client case to the other, the more certain we can be that they are also manifestations of countertransference. It is good for group members to be aware of their vulnerabilities, including the threat brought by fears of being exposed. However, exposing oneself can also be an opportunity to be accepted into the community, to be appreciated, sustained, acknowledged and respected for one's unique qualities.

> Is an image consultation group less structured than group supervision; is it more playful, experimental, readier to take risks and more demanding?

A group with such a loose structure requires its members to:

- trust that the group can make a valuable contribution and be willing to do their own part in this;
- value both their own experience and that of others;
- be able to take risks and participate without vying for power or a need to show off their own competence;
- be able to bear uncertainty and groping in the dark;
- be able to be carried away by group associations and to detach themselves from them (have an ability to play together);
- be able to tolerate conflicts (between their own neediness and what the group has to give) and solitude (when the group does not understand them).

This type of work calls for what M. Pines (1981) termed a 'mature group'. A mature group strives for coherence instead of cohesion. It is more important that the members are in a mutual relationship than for the group to be highly solid. We may speak of an integrated group where members retain their own, differing views and yet feel that they belong to the group. Working in the group requires one to create and maintain a private space for looking, while still staying in contact with others. Here group members are permeable, as it were, but still within their own boundaries. It is always possible to learn to look at images even better. In image consultation, our teacher is the other person's way of looking. Here we travel the picture's landscape according to the other's observations, using the other as a guide. With their different observations, each member challenges the viewing conventions of the others, the limitations of their seeing or the possible one-sidedness of their perspectives.

The group progresses through a dialogue that it does not consciously strive to have. The interaction consists of exchanging bits of observation, digesting them and processing them. Exchange of ideas can bring forth a new, shared creation: one without clear boundaries, in motion and constantly being shaped emerging from many different countertransferences and mental images. This functions as an interpretative suggestion for the supervisee, who in turn tries to feel how useful it is. Schaverien (2003) discusses the interrelatedness between seeing and interpreting, and observes how 'a picture which we have made, consciously intending to show one thing, is transformed by our perception into something else as well. This has the effect of an interpretation' (p. 11). Viewing pictures produces words and trains of thought that the group continually moulds together. This discussion in turn enriches the therapist's ability to articulate and understand her task with the client. As one group member put it: 'In the group I also learned to talk about the pictures in a new way to myself'.

## Meeting, 12 April 2003, Part II

The comments of my colleagues in this particular consultation gave me space to think about the multiple uses of a visual orientation in therapy. I could increasingly see the pictures as expressing the tensions caused by our interaction. They clearly functioned as the stage for the fear and anxiety my client felt in the situation.

Afterwards I thought about the fate of each individual picture during the client's sessions. She always judged them harshly and felt them to be inadequate. Indeed, she dismissed them as soon as they were created. Right away, something happened, which Schaverien (1992) calls 'disposal'. The client seemed to be painting only to get rid of her feelings. The life of the picture was greeted as harshly as possible: she did not wish to look at it. The 'scapegoat transference' (Schaverien 1992), where the non-desired part of the self is projected into the picture, was working powerfully and its resolution remained incomplete. The picture was not allowed to live. My client closed her eyes to it and did not want to build a relationship with it.

I gradually understood that by relating to the pictures in this way my client was revealing over and over again her own difficult abandonment experiences in infancy. The group, by contrast, was creating and reinforcing a relationship with the pictures, thus providing a counterbalance to this abandonment. For me as a viewer, the group also made it possible to take the necessary distance from these pictures. I looked at them through the eyes of the group; I listened to my own and my client's point of view through the filter of the group. It relieved me to hear comments like, 'I don't get these at all!' I was not alone in being confused and frustrated. The group looked at the pictures like the client and like me, but also differently. The very presentation helped structure my feelings of frustration and confusion. The opportunity to question my own work in front of my colleagues felt liberating and gave me more space.

## The image consultation code

The image consultation group is a work group that has an agreed task: to study pictures, not itself. However, it is useful for the group to be sensitive to its own ways of working. How a group carries out its task always also reflects both its own developmental level and the group members' own personal processes that resonate with it (Foulkes 1964; McNeilly 1990). As its starting point, the group tries to get in touch with what it sees in the picture itself, not what is behind it. The process of looking is a process of becoming aware. This process is a continuous and always regenerating event and thus involves a continuous return to the picture's surprises – indeed, to its reality – without knowledge or words. Group members can mirror their own way of looking, their difficulties in seeing and their way of working with others. The therapist's relationship to her client or group of clients can be supported and questioned; it can elicit new questions and thoughts on how to proceed in therapy.

Another contribution of the group is to reduce the fatigue – a kind of 'snow blindness' – caused by the abundance of pictures. But as the semiotician and art historian Altti Kuusamo notes: 'an open way of looking at things is, paradoxically, always a result of great effort' (Kuusamo 1984: 17), since we approach the pictures from our own symbolical system. We easily tend to see in a way guided by our conventions and wishes. However, Kuusamo notes that: '*An art exhibition code* tunes us into a state of intensive attention during which our expectation threshold is lowered and we make unanticipated observations' (p. 17). As I see it, a setting where one is not required to be effective can likewise bring forth and reinforce an attitude where reverie and the mind's agile but apparently purposeless wandering in the client's images help to build a new connection with them. The inner vivacity of the group members can increase, and their readiness to see with fresh eyes is reinforced. At best, the group can together discover something missing or essential in the client–therapist relationship. The supervisee can also present a series of pictures made by the client. This allows the works made at different times to engage in an important dialogue. Through the meetings, the working of the group can mature so it becomes capable of tolerating and acknowledging ever more complex and even conflicting comments. Thus the group grows stronger.

This kind of a supervision setting can and should be developed further, varied and focused according to need. One possible line of development for image consultation would be to choose a consultant or supervisor for the group. This consultant would be responsible for managing the group's time, for bringing in quieter members of the group if necessary and for attempting to sum up the group's observations. Each group member could take a turn at this, thus getting practice and gaining competence in observing the group's working. Rotating the position of authority would prevent the group from always turning to the most experienced member for these observations. On the other hand, the very lack of leadership in the present system gives every member the opportunity to summarise and, at times, to act with the whole group in mind.

## Epilogue

If I call a greyish-black blotch in a painting a rock, I am interpreting this trace of paint. But if I am conscious of my attempt to use this brief word to describe the grey area's impermeability, heaviness and hardness, the spirit of the situation is different. I could also say a 'lump' or a 'piece of metal', but a piece of metal would feel like it lacks the three-dimensionality of a lump, and a lump would seem to refer to something too soft. So rock might be the best way to characterise the blotch. But it should not be allowed to remain the only word, thus becoming a truth and locking the blotch into this as its only meaning. A 'blotch' in turn refers more to the way in which the grey paint has been brushed or transported onto the paper. A 'rock' is a nickname, a working title and an interpretative hypothesis. It is part of the poem evoked by the picture. It is a metaphor through which one can talk about that element, a verbalisation to communicate the mental image evoked by that trace of paint. 'Rock' guides our thought process along; it opens vistas to places where there are rocks: on the shore, at a stone breaking plant, on a mountain, in a forest, etc. The words 'blotch', 'heap', 'area' or 'island' do not evoke these vistas, although they evoke others instead.

### Editorial note

Riitta Laine explains that in Finland there are differences between their practices and those in other parts of the world. Riitta Laine's professional title is visual art therapist/registered psychotherapist. In order to earn this qualification, Riitta Laine completed a four-year training course organised by the Training Centre at the University of Art and Design Helsinki. The prerequisites for entering the programme are either a basic degree in art plus suitability for the field, or alternately a degree in health care with at least two years of full-time art studies. The objective is to integrate psychotherapy with practical understanding and theoretical knowledge of the creative process. The programme consists of theoretical studies in psychotherapy and art, practical training where the student carries out individual as well as group therapy lasting a minimum of two years, as well as personal psychotherapy (either group or individual). For the training therapies, two different supervisors are needed: an art therapist and a psychotherapist or psychoanalyst. One of them supervises the individual therapy, the other supervises the group therapy for a minimum of two years. Supervision takes place weekly. This training model is the oldest of its kind in Finland (since 1974), and graduates are entitled to join the Association for Art Therapists in Finland. Since 1996, the state has registered those who have completed this training in the professional registry of health care professionals under the title 'psychotherapist'. This registration allows art therapists to work as private professionals. A two-year art therapy supervisor and teacher training programme began in 2003. In contrast to 'visual art therapist', the title of 'art psychotherapist' is used in Finland by psychotherapists or analysts who have completed a two-year programme in the use of art in psychotherapy. This training programme began in 1990. The titles of visual art therapist and art therapist are not protected professional titles in Finland, so these titles are commonly used by graduates of other training programmes in the country as well.

# References

Balint, M. (1986) *The Doctor, his Patient and the Illness*, Edinburgh: Churchill Livingstone.

Bion, W. R. (1962) *Learning from Experience*, New York: Basic Books.

Bion, W. R. (1984a) *Attention and Interpretation*, London: Karnac Books.

Bion, W. R. (1984b) *Transformations*, London: Karnac Books.

Blackwell, D. (1998) 'Bounded instability, group analysis and the matrix: organisations under stress', *Group Analysis, 31* (4): 153–180.

Brown, D. (2003) 'Pairing Bion and Foulkes, towards a metapsychosociology', in R. M. Lipgar and M. Pines (eds), *Building on Bion: Roots*, London: Jessica Kingsley.

Calvino, I. (1998) *Six Memos for the Next Millenium*, Massachusetts: Harvard University Press.

Edwards, D. (1994) 'On reflection: a note on supervision', *Inscape, 1*: 23–27.

Foulkes, S. H. (1964) *Therapeutic Group Analysis*, London: Unwin Brothers.

Foulkes, S. H. (1973) *Selected Papers*, London: Karnac Books.

Foulkes, S. H. (1986) *Group Analytic Psychotherapy*, London: Karnac Books.

Jacobi, J. (1942) *The Psychology of C.G. Jung*, London: Routledge.

Jung, C. G. (1961) *Memories, Dreams, Reflections*, New York: Collins Fount Paperbacks.

Kristeva, J. (1989) *Black Sun*, New York: Columbia University Press.

Kuusamo, A. (1984) 'Kohti epäpuhdasta havaitsemista', *Synteesi 4*: 9–19.

McNeilly, G. (1990) 'Group analysis and art therapy: a personal perspective', *Group Analysis, 23*: 215–224.

Milner, M. (1988) *Suppressed Madness of Sane Men*, London: Routledge.

Neumann, A. (1970) *The Origins and History of Consciousness*, Princeton, NJ: Princeton University Press.

Nitsun, M. (1996) *The Anti-Group: Destructive Forces in the Group and their Creative Potential*, London: Routledge.

Ogden, T. H. (2002) *Conversations at the Frontier of Dreaming*, London: Karnac Books.

Pines, M. (1981) 'The frame of reference of group psychotherapy', *International Journal of Group Psychotherapy, 31* (3): 275–285.

Schaverien, J. (1992) *Revealing Image, Analytical Art Psychotherapy in Theory and Practice*, London: Routledge.

Schaverien, J. (2003) 'Inaugural Lecture, University of Sheffield, The eye of the beholder: Eros and art in psychotherapy', *Inscape, 8* (1): 2–16.

Sedgwick, D. (2000) *The Wounded Healer, Countertransference from a Jungian Perspective*, Hove: Brunner-Routledge.

Skaife, S. (1990) 'Self-determination in group analytic art therapy', *Group Analysis, 23* (3): 237–244.

Stern, D. (1985) *The Interpersonal World of the Infant*, New York: Basic Books.

Trenkel, A. (1994) 'Rhymän ohjaajan ahdistes', in R. Rinne and J. Rekola (eds), *Ryhmä kohtaa sairauden* [The Group Meets Illness], Helsinki: SMS, pp. 27–35.

# Chapter 8

# Working in black and white

## An art therapy supervision group

*Sally Skaife*

## Introduction

This chapter explores issues arising from a supervision group that took place in the mid-1990s in the context of art therapy training. The group material illustrates the complexity of exploring difference in art therapy supervision groups, but also a potential there that might be particular to art therapy. The chapter explores the difference of perspective between the positions of black and white, and relates these to differences between verbal articulation and art making. Both sets of differences are understood as both artificially constructed and at the same time materially inhabited, a paradox that can allow for a creative outcome if the movement generated is harnessed. A paradox explored in this chapter is that it might only be through silence that one can speak, or in empty space that there is art.

I will first of all discuss the background theoretical ideas, then go on to present the group and follow this with a discussion of the issues arising from it that brings together responses to questions asked of the group participants sometime after the group ended, and the literature on race and art therapy, groups and supervision.

## Binaries and paradoxes

Living in multi-cultural Britain in the 21st century and working in the 'helping professions', developing racial awareness is imperative but in practice it is often very difficult. As a tutor on art psychotherapy training I often hear requests for more teaching on race and culture, however, my experience is that whilst specially focused teaching sessions on areas of difference are immensely valuable, entrenched unconscious ways of relating and thinking about racial difference are difficult to tackle; they take time and the endurance of painful feelings to reach the open. Added to this, it is often difficult to address race because of the predominance of single culture trainees (something I will come back to). The example described in this chapter may reflect its time, the 1990s, before three major books that address race and culture and art therapy had been published (Dokter 1998; Hiscox and Calisch 1998; Campbell *et al.* 1999), and when black and white race issues dominated compared to current conflicts in the West, such as those that have resulted since 9/11 or through changes in the countries of origin of recent immigrants. It may also show up racisms that we are all now more aware of. However, I believe it still has relevance for art therapy supervision, as it illustrates the difficulty that this chapter hopes to come some way to addressing, that in looking head on at race we face the history of racism, identify as either victims or perpetrators and get caught up in double binds and paradoxes. The first of these paradoxes is black and white as racial difference itself.

The group analyst Dalal (2002) discusses how race, and colour as attached to race, are artificial modes of difference socially constructed for political ends. Dalal reminds us that white is all the colours shining at once, and true black cannot be seen at all, it is an absence of light and therefore colour. The relationship of black and white to the multiple shades and reflections of skin colours is then only tenuous. Black and white over the years have come to have associations attached to them: white with all things positive, and black with the negative. There has then been a slippage whereby dark skins have become black and light skins, white. It is only since the 16th and 17th centuries that difficult emotions have come to be coloured black, and Dalal thinks that this coincided with European imperialism. Dalal's argument is that language has been used by those in power to inculcate, at an unconscious level, a sense that black is negative and inferior; and the reason for this is to create a division between 'the haves, and must not haves' (Dalal 2002: 210). The result of this is that people's identity gets colour coded, and they are put into a double bind. To identify as black means to accept an identity forced on one; to reject the category, however, means to have no way to combat the racism, a paradox turned around by black activists of the 1970s in the celebration of 'black' culture, as described by several black art therapists (Annoual 1998; Hiscox 1998; Lumpkin 1998; Brookes 1999).

A parallel binary in art therapy is the artificially constructed division between talk and art, or words and non-verbal communication. Similar to the history of the terms white and black, the distinction between talk and art has a hierarchical history in which logical, verbal articulation associated with the mind and thought has been privileged over the tactile, sensual, bodily, feeling and art. This division is on the one hand false, in that words can be art and art productions can be cognitive. On the other hand there is a distinction between artworks as irreducible to anything other than themselves, and the search for meaning in the words of logical argument. Within art there is another binary whereby financial encouragement for making images is only given to those few adding to the art market, whilst images abound in advertising influencing our buying habits. The powerful potential of art is active but unacknowledged, owned by business but not by ordinary people. This hierarchy has left art therapy struggling on the fringe of mainstream therapeutic input, or in more recent times joining the mainstream by sidelining the non-verbal sensual side of the activity in order to fit into a culture regulated by the cognitive.

It is interesting to note that in terms of character, the literature written by white art therapists (with some exceptions, e.g. Liebmann 1999) appears to be more theoretical and as standing at a distance from the writing. The literature written by black art therapists appears more embodied, written from a personal viewpoint. Hiscox (1998) refers to the paradox described by the black scholar and feminist writer hooks (1989), of getting through to people by talking from a personal viewpoint, but then being in danger of being regarded as anti-intellectual, intellectually weak and unprofessional, fitting an anti-black stereotype. This paradox seems to mirror the privileging of the mind over body, or talk over art.

Rather than reverse the binary, i.e. promote the black students' experience over the whites', or forefront art over words, we need to upset the stability of the binaries. We need to give equal attention to both sides of the binary, which will show up the paradoxes within them as has been described. Thus, we cannot look at what white and black have in common in the fight against racism until we have recognised the different experience that is had when in the skin that has been designated either white or black, painful though this difference might be. Similarly, until we recognise that logical verbal language and art as irreducible to language both have a part to play in art therapy, though they do not sit comfortably together, we cannot utilise what is unique to the profession. Cross-cultural art therapy supervision then needs to embrace paradox. The paradox relevant to this chapter is the admonition by all writers on therapy and race that we need to learn to articulate our positions in relation to race in order to avoid embedding in supervision, and therefore the clinical practice of the supervisee, racist or colour blind practices. Where does this leave art therapists, who in supervision might possibly be making art (Brown *et al.* 2003) and then not have much time to talk about it? I argue that talking is not the only way, and the example I describe shows how it was a lack of words that brought something important out into the open.

I will now go on to describe the context of the supervision group, and then the group itself.

## Context

The group took place on two year full-time/three year part-time art psychotherapy training. The training programme is based on a tri-partite structure of supervised clinical practice, experiential learning and theoretical studies. The students take part in a series of interlinked groups and learn the basic tenets of art psychotherapy practice – the therapeutic effect of art making and looking within boundaried psychodynamic relationships through reflection upon their experiences in differently focused groups that operate reflexively with learning from clinical placements and from the written elements.

What is particular about the training of art therapists is that rather than learn about work with particular client groups (e.g. children or adults) or in particular settings (e.g. the NHS or schools) or one-to-one or in groups, they learn about the art therapy process, which then has to be applied in a particular way to the unique combination of circumstances that the client or clients present. This means that supervision groups are complex. There may be students on placement in a school, in a hospice, on a psychiatric ward, in a Child and Family clinic or working with groups and individuals all in the same supervision group. Added to this is the dimension of different mediums of communication: as well as the words that are spoken in therapy sessions there is the artwork made, and the way in which the client has used the materials and the space of the therapy studio, that form the material that is to be examined in supervision. There may also be the student's own artwork made in response to the clinical work (Brown *et al.* 2003).

It is important in the following vignette to realise that college supervision groups are not the only place where the students receive supervision of their clinical work. There was also supervision taking place on a one-to-one basis at the placement. The group that is to be described was a third year group of students studying on the part-time option. It was thus the third, year long supervision group that they had been in on the training (though in the first one they would not have had clinical work from art therapy placements to present). In the third year the students did not have experiential groups or theoretical lectures. They only came to college for group supervision and tutorials.

## The supervision group

There were six women in this supervision group, two were black and four were white, and I was the white supervisor. The episode in the group life that I am about to describe happened, as far as I remember, before the mid-point, and began with a white student bringing a dilemma from placement. This was, that she was wondering about the make-up of a children's art therapy group that she was to run in a school. There were to be four children, three black and one white (as I remember). She was concerned that the one white child would be a singleton, and the literature on group psychotherapy consistently suggests that it is not ideal to have a 'one' of any type in a group. It seemed appropriate to throw this open for discussion in the group, as there was experience of being in a minority in the group, black students being a minority on the training and in the profession at large. If the minority was white, as was the case at the school, would the issues be different?

From this point on, the group seemed propelled into a very difficult and painful space. The white students entered into some lively discussion but the black students remained silent. The gulf between black and white seemed to open up. I think the white students and myself were rather bewildered that the black students seemed not to want to share their experience with us, and did not want to contribute to the discussion. The white students continued to debate the issue without them, but the silence could not be ignored. As they tried harder and harder to find ways to engage the black students and to try to understand their position, I felt myself very torn. As a white person I identified with the things that the white students said they felt and the sort of comments they were making about the situation, but as a supervisor I needed to identify with all the students.

I am not sure how many weeks we remained stuck in this stalemate, but in my felt memory it was a long time, it felt very painful and I had no map for the territory. I was concerned that the clients who the students were working with were not getting discussed in the group. However, the issue had arisen in this group in relation to client work. I was also aware that we were engaged in something very important and I felt that if we could stay with it we might learn something meaningful. For this reason I did not direct the students away from the discussion to their placements. I felt that the white students might feel that I had sided with the silence of the black students against the hard work that the white students really were putting into trying to understand the dilemma.

After some time the black students explained their situation. They felt angry that they were always the ones to have to explain to others what it felt like to be discriminated against, or to be in a minority. Why should this be their responsibility? There followed some angry and difficult exchanges. The stalemate seemed to be: the frustration of the white students that the group could not move the issue on through discussion, and the feeling of the black students that it was impossible to communicate something to us, or for us to understand something. There was no resolution within the life of the group. I think we decided that we had to get on with thinking about the work with clients and accept that there were strong feelings between people, different experiences and a lack of understanding that could not be easily overcome.

In retrospect, I have always felt that this group marked the beginning of my understanding some of the real issues in thinking about race and culture that are beyond what often seem like token gestures towards acknowledging it. What I learnt was that we have to recognise history as well as the feelings engendered by present-day discrimination, but that one supervision group is not going to find solutions for worldwide and historical abuse of one race toward another. One could argue that because of this it would have been better to leave the issue alone and focus on the client work. I considered at the time that it was important to enter what was, for me, uncharted water, as a unique opportunity had arisen in which the whole supervision group might learn something about working with difference and in particular about issues of race. In retrospect I felt that the group achieved something quite important in staying with the feelings. I had learnt about the paradoxical feelings that black students have about having to speak about their experience, and I felt that I now had begun to find my voice on race.

I wondered though what the students felt in retrospect about this supervision group experience. Did they feel that they learned anything worthwhile? If so, what was this, and was the pain and frustration worth it? Did they go away with a feeling of having had a bad experience or a worthwhile one? Did their feelings vary from one another? I felt that the black students may have felt that at last space had been given to their experience, but that the white students may have felt in some way betrayed by me.

I got back three out of six of the questionnaires I sent to them. I was doubtful that all had reached the students due to the lapse in time. Two white and one black member responded. The black member said she could no longer remember the group. The key things that came across from the questionnaires were about the silences, and about feelings of fear. The not remembering could also be understood as communicating silence.

There are two themes that I wish to discuss and I will relate them to the literature on art therapy and race, supervision and groups:

1   How appropriate is it in supervision groups to spend time away from a direct focus on client work to look at issues about race?
2   How should one understand the silence in the supervision group – as resistant or as transformative?

### Focus of supervision

The literature on supervision points to the importance of some reflection on 'here and now' dynamics. Shipton (1997) warns that without reflection on issues of difference, supervision could be a 'microcosmic space where matters that are unregulated may also determine therapeutic work with patients: issues of discrimination or lack of recognition and respect for difference may be reproduced or amplified . . . The supervisory relationship can then be seen as a crucible in which impurities are melded into the very fabric of therapeutic practice' (p. 144).

Driver (2002) describes the supervisor as walking 'a precarious tightrope between group conductor and supervisor while maintaining the focus on the work of supervision'. Pines (1995) talks of the group experience acting as an amplifier, 'increasing the range and intensity of the supervisee's response' (p. 2). Hearst and Brown (1995: 93) distinguish between the personal internal, and the institutional and sociological external. In supervision the personal is hidden but is drawn on to understand the dynamics. It is left to the supervisee to make the links between the internal and the external. In the questionnaires, group members expressed uncertainty about where the difficulties in the group lay. One student felt that the experiences of the black students were 'maybe not always the experiences of "black" people at large – but maybe were reflective of their personal experiences within their families'. Another student related strong feelings to the strong personalities of people in the group, and to group members going through 'great personal difficulties'.

Looking at the individual, the institutional and the sociological inter-subjectively, one sees that each one of them is present within the other, so an individual black or white member's personal development will have been determined by the power relations of these designated races in history, as will their clients' development. The culture of the institutional setting in relation to race will affect the way client work is brought to supervision, and the way this is then thought about will affect the social world, as in the clinical work and in the writing of this chapter. The different parts cannot be separated then and none or all will be the starting point. How then is race to be addressed in art therapy supervision groups?

The group, and me as supervisor, were faced with a paradox. Our focus was the client work, but the subject of the client work, the white singleton in the group, could not be discussed without revealing a conflict: that is, that the black and white students could not but have different positions in relation to the issue. It was impossible for these different positions to be exposed without conflict. If I think now to the choices facing the supervision group, there was no way we could not stay with the group dynamic on race, unless we had acknowledged that it was too difficult to handle, and then left it alone. In this case we would have been avoiding a focus on client work. If focusing on the client work meant facing the black/white difference in the group, then the next question was how this was going to be possible: was the group going to be safe enough to confront what is usually hidden? The paradox in this dilemma may have been felt differently by black and white members.

Miche Lewin (1990) quotes from the poet Pat Archer who said 'First forget I'm black, second never forget I'm black'. The black art therapist

Brookes (1999), talking of training experiences, describes being pleased in lectures when racism was discussed, but then also uncomfortable because in these situations she became conspicuous; this reminded her of a history lesson in school in which slavery had been fleetingly talked about, and she had felt humiliated. On placement she was unsure whether being referred black clients meant the institution recognised the clients' needs for a therapist who understood their experience of racism, or whether assumptions were being made about which clients a black therapist could work with. Across the Atlantic, Annoual (1998) describes being pleased that her blackness was seen as positive on her training course in terms of the contribution it could make to art therapists and their clients, professionally, but felt that her personal skills then were hidden.

Blackwell (1994) reflects these concerns in his work as a white group analyst. He describes how it is very difficult to tackle racism when there is only one black person in a group, and two or even three black members of a group may not be enough. The single black person will be absorbed into the group in a beneficent denial of their difference. This 'colour blindness' is then actually a blindness to the particularity of this person, which is difficult for her to challenge without being regarded as having a chip on her shoulder. If the conductor challenges the white members' colour blindness, he isolates the black member from the rest of the group. If the group do accept the black members' blackness, the black member may feel they are expected to speak for black people generally, and her individuality is ignored. She also may be covertly if not overtly given the power to grant absolution to alleviate guilt of the white members.

The white group members' responses to the questionnaires revolved around the safety of the group for opening up issues of difference. One member commented that 'the freedom and responsibility (and maturity as a group?)' that came with being third year students enabled them 'to start exploring some of the areas which had remained taboo or too dangerous during the previous 2 years'. She said that members 'seemed less inhibited by fears about damaging other people, of experiencing defensive blocking in response to looking at sensitive areas'. Another member 'felt the group was very insecure at times', and without me present as happened on one occasion, 'felt unsafe'.

These fears are supported by the literature. Hawkins and Shohet (2000) describe mixed race supervision as 'fraught with difficult and even violent feelings' (p. 97). Margaret Green (1987), who ran workshops for 'unlearning racism', discusses the difficulty of exploring racism without replaying it. She describes the roles of victim and persecutor as roles that can get dangerously played out in groups, and for this reason she ran separate white and black groups. The idea was for white people to find where in their lives they had learnt to imbibe racist notions that were now embedded in their relationships with others at an unconscious level. White-only groups were important as, she says, 'a white person's acquired racist conditioning is a black person's oppression. Safety is not enhanced by repeating racist situations as they exist in society. There is a point in informing each other but only when people have dealt with their feelings separately, sufficiently to be able to listen' (p. 184). She describes even the white-only groups as having issues around safety.

She talks about white people coming to the workshops because of guilt and because they are in some way hurt by racism. This guilt is echoed in the questionnaires. One student says 'I felt guilty about being part of a majority group when the students with a different skin colour to me talked of how attacked and rejected they felt in society (and for some on the course) because they were not white'. Brookes (1999), following a lecture on race, describes feeling the weight of the white students' guilt. Green (1987) talks interestingly about telling people they are not personally guilty, which often allows for stories of rage with black people for having confronted them at some time about being racist. This feeling of being attacked then reverberates with other situations of oppression where they may have felt helpless because of a feeling of having colluded with the debasement. She describes roles of oppressor and oppressed in which we can identify with both. Work on either role 'undermines the fulcrum and eventually the whole structure will collapse'. This conceptualisation sounds very useful for upsetting stuck binaries in groups, however it relies on verbal analysis and there are times when it seems words do not come easily; silence may be a paralysis in the face of guilt, used as a means to oppress, a projection of feelings or as a means to express something unspeakable. How it is understood may depend on who is receiving it and who is delivering it.

## Silence

One of the group members thinks that there was a 'collective failure to challenge the "silent" members of the group', but also wished that as a supervisor I had challenged the silence 'both as a version of avoidance and at times as a form of aggression'. (I am reminded by this that it was not only the black students who were silent; some of the white students also spoke minimally, and not all returned their questionnaires.) The oppressor/oppressed dynamic could describe what was happening in the supervision group. The silence could be understood as a persecution of the white students and myself, or as an attack on the work of the group. This might then have been construed as retribution for what we stood for as whites (the history of slavery and present-day racism) or for our blindness to the here and now experience of the black students. Perhaps my not challenging the black students was a fear of becoming a persecutor in the group, with the result that I might then get persecuted. However, an opposing way of thinking about it, as the black students' went on to say, was their refusal to take on what rightly belonged to the group as a whole. It forced a lot of discomfort into the white students and led them to deal with an issue that had been left traditionally, and on the course perhaps, for black students to deal with. It was thus not only a step towards greater articulation of the experience of racial difference, but also an expression of the unspeakable, the gulf of difference of perspective between black and white that makes it difficult to understand one another, but that needs to be addressed before it is possible to move on. I have found whilst writing this chapter that it has been difficult to hold onto these two perspectives at the same time.

I am now going to explore this dualism further by considering the paradox of silence as an emptiness that has materiality and as an absence that allows something to speak powerfully. Both can be either positive or negative, creative or destructive.

Blackwell talks about how racism is often enacted 'silently' rather than spoken, leaving the racially abused person with no evidence to support their suspicion or certainty that they have been victimised for their colour: for example, being stopped by the police, or not being given a room when on the phone the landlord sounded happy to accept them. Lumpkin (1998) describes the black art therapy students as finding it difficult to provide evidence of their feeling of being discriminated against by college tutors. Hiscox (1998) says that 'the insensitivity of white peers is evidenced in the "do nothing, say nothing" attitude that allows the perpetuation of racist ideology' (p. 281).

Blackwell (1994) describes a silence/verbal analysis opposite in his description of an analytical group of trainees who had three black members and five white. A discussion about migration and cultural difference is sparked off in the group by a joke made by the conductor that only English people may have understood; when the conductor insists on looking at black and whiteness despite the mixed nationalities in the group, out come the black students' stories of racist abuse. As each one tells their story, another of the black trainees makes positive remarks about being in Britain. Blackwell speculates that they were protecting the whites, forestalling an attack or avoiding victim status or the group polarising. The whites, including the conductor, are at a loss for words; eventually one white student remarks that he feels ashamed and helpless, but it stops there. 'The experience of the white members in relation to the black members could not be articulated' (p. 207) he says. Blackwell thinks that white 'autism' in regard to race must be analysed much as oedipal issues, dependency or sexuality. He counts himself as the conductor amongst those who were autistic. He also says that it is the therapist's responsibility to raise the issue of race. This call to the articulation of experience is made by other authors (Mollon 1997; Shipton 1997; Hawkins and Shohet 2000).

The silence involved in racist acts uses the non-verbal in its capacity to speak volumes. In silent omissions that allow racism to continue, the silence is stuck as in the example Blackwell gives where his white students became 'autistic' in the face of guilt. This dynamic between stuckness and communication, silence and speech, can also be understood in artwork, as is described by Case (1995).

I was interested to note that very few of the chapters written by art therapists about race include discussion of art or images, and where they do this is given very little attention. Lumpkin (1998) reflects on the fact that the black art therapy students she invited to send in images for her research (about the experience of being black art therapy trainees) did not do so, and this she says 'created a very loud silence' (p. 226). She suggests their reluctance may have been due to: 'an inability to reconcile ideals or articulate the message; or their inability to balance the concept of high visibility due to skin color, as opposed to invisibility to society; or a desire to remain anonymous in this study' (p. 226). This chapter is similar in that there are no images to discuss from the supervision group.

Interestingly, the following comment from the questionnaires on memories of artwork in the supervision group relates to silence in response to an artwork: 'I remember an occasion (earlier in the course – on an occasion when every one had presented artwork) when the only piece of art work with explicitly race-related subject matter was left undiscussed, apparently because time ran out . . .'.

Another student remembers an enactment of feelings about race: 'I remember a student talking about her client in a mother and baby unit who used to cover her dark skin with white powder or cream and dress in white to express the difficulties in her life around her skin colour.'

Blackwell's discussion of the autism in his group made me think of Sarra's (1998) discussion of the autistic image – the blank piece of paper, the crumpled up or torn piece of paper. Sarra relates the autistic image to Foulkes' idea of the symptom as autistic, mumbling away to itself, hoping to be overheard. He sees the autistic image as struggling 'to communicate to exist; but it is hated and rejected by the maker for its propensity for integration and change'; Sarra is contrasting this image with one that does communicate and help integration and processing. He thinks the art therapist must accept the autistic image for in it is the potential, the hope of communication.

The autistic image described by Sarra could be mutative because although it communicated nothing (a blank piece of paper), its existence as a material thing meant that it said something. In the same way the black student who returned her questionnaire stating no memory, brought the silence back as a 'thing'. This way of looking at the silence in the group suggests that rather than it being autistic in the sense of stuck or as waiting to be put into words, it could be understood as a communication, a something in itself in the space of the group. In this way it was like John Cage's 'Two minutes silence', a piece of music that is silence within a boundary of time – a work of art. As a work of art it was irreducible to words. It was a felt sensual experience putting us in touch with the depth of feeling that was involved in what we were addressing. This does not mean there should not be words, because these followed, but they were not necessarily the words of the silence, and although they went somewhere in helping learning they, in themselves, were not the complete answer anyway.

If we think of art as an aesthetic, a sense of a thing, be it visual, sound or something tangible, then in the supervision group we can allow this some space to speak for the unspeakable. This means us tolerating the pain of the sounds of anger, fear or frustration but not necessarily attempting to solve them. In allowing the group to experience this together, whilst also attempting to find words, then some movement may be possible. It is not then that the silence is just the precursor of words, rather it opens a space in which something other than the verbal is communicated, just as art does. The supervision group, I felt, through the experiencing of the pain of difference enabled something creative to happen that continued to outlive the life of the group. One group member said of the supervision group: 'I'm aware that I am still learning things from it after all these years'.

Whether images are made or not, respecting that there are two different modes of communication in art therapy brings difference into the heart of the group, making it possible for difference of all sorts to be addressed. One of the students remarks: 'I found the group a useful and inspiring place to be . . . when I talked about how I had grown up in an all white working class environment and on coming to London as a young adult experienced different cultures and colours with trepidation and curiousity, I felt relief that this was accepted as okay feelings'.

## Conclusion

Race awareness is very complex as it is not only very painful to be in touch with the humiliation embedded in one's own persecution, but it is also extremely uncomfortable to be in touch with oneself as unintentionally being a persecutor. People deal with these feelings by projecting them out and groups can become stuck in polarisations and thus move off the subject, or never get into it, particularly if there is only one black student in a group. In a supervision group where the focus is client work it is even more likely that race issues will be either dealt with using a light touch or avoided altogether. The supervisor is then unlikely to build up skills to work with the issue. This results in the continued disadvantaging of black students/clients.

In exploring a supervision group in which there had been racial conflict and attempting to understand this in relation to relevant literature and the benefit of hindsight and the responses to questionnaires from the students in the group, I discovered the potency of paradox. Already engaged in thinking about the paradoxes involved in art therapy between art and verbal analysis I found the ambiguity of materiality and social construction that make up art useful also for thinking about the difference in embodied perspective of those in either 'white' or 'black' skins. This thinking meant that understanding a silence in the supervision group as possibly having opposing meanings offered the potential for movement. This then reflected my experience in the supervision group of it being both creative and also very difficult.

Shifting dualities around so that they do not get stuck in either persecutor or victim, silence or speech, art or talk, with a hierarchy of good and bad, seems to me both the way forward for race awareness and for thinking about the potential of art therapy and art therapy supervision.

## Acknowledgements

I am grateful to the members of the Goldsmiths Supervision Group for their contributions to the chapter and to Caroline Case, Andrea Gilroy, David Kirby and Joy Schaverien for their comments on the draft.

## References

Annoual, P. (1998) 'Art therapy and the concept of blackness', in A. Hiscox and A. Calisch (eds), *Tapestry of Cultural Issues in Art Therapy*, London: Jessica Kingsley, pp. 13–23.

Blackwell, D. (1994) 'Racism in group analysis', *Group Analysis*, vol. 27, London: Sage Publications, pp. 197–210.

Brookes, F. (1999) 'A black perspective on art therapy training', in J. Campbell, M. Liebmann, F. Brooks, J. Jones and C. Ward (eds), *Art Therapy, Race and Culture*, London: Jessica Kingsley, pp. 275–286.

Brown, C., Rhyda, J. and Merclowitz, J. (2003) 'Thinking with image making in supervision', *Inscape*, 8 (2): 71–78.

Campbell, J., Liebmann, M., Brooks, F., Jones J. and Ward, C. (1999) *Art Therapy, Race and Culture*, London: Jessica Kingsley.

Case, C. (1995) 'Silence in progress: on being dumb, empty or silent in therapy', *Inscape 1*: 26–31.

Dalal, F. (2002) *Race, Colour and the Processes of Racialization: New Perspectives from Group Analysis, Psychoanalysis and Sociology*, Hove: Brunner-Routledge.

Dokter, D. (1998) *Arts Therapists, Refugees and Migrants: Reaching Across Borders*, London: Jessica Kingsley.

Driver, C. (2002) 'The geography and popography of supervision in a group setting', in C. Driver and E. Martin (eds), *Supervising Psychotherapy: Psychoanalytic and Psychodynamic Perspectives*, London: Sage Publications.

Green, M. (1987) 'Women in the oppressor role: white racism', in S. Ernst and M. Maguire (eds), *Living with the Sphinx, Papers from the Women's Therapy Centre*, London: The Women's Press, pp. 178–212.

Hawkins, P. and Shohet, R. (2000) *Supervising in the Helping Professions* (2nd edn), Buckingham: Oxford University Press.

Hearst, L. and Brown, R. (1995) 'Simultaneous supervision and personal analysis', in M. Sharpe (ed.), *The Third Eye: Supervision of Analytic Groups*, London: Routledge, pp. 25–30.

Hiscox, A. (1998) 'Cultural diversity and implications for art therapy pedagogy', in A. Hiscox and A. Calisch (eds), *Tapestry of Cultural Issues in Art Therapy*, London: Jessica Kingsley Publishers.

Hiscox, A. and Calisch, A. (1998) *Tapestry of Cultural Issues in Art Therapy*, London: Jessica Kingsley Publishers.

hooks, b. (1989) *Talking Back: Thinking Feminist, Thinking Black*, Boston: South End Press.

Lewin, M. (1990) 'Transcultural issues in art therapy: considerations on language, power and racism', *Inscape*, Summer: 10–16.

Liebmann, M. (1999) 'Being white: engaging with a changing world', in J. Campbell, M. Liebmann, F. Brooks, J. Jones and C. Ward (eds), *Art Therapy, Race and Culture*, London: Jessica Kingsley Publishers.

Lumpkin, C. (1998) 'We wear the masks: a study of black art therapy students', in A. Hiscox and A. Calisch (eds), *Tapestry of Cultural Issues in Art Therapy* London: Jessica Kingsley Publishers, pp. 219–228.

Mollon, P. (1997) 'Supervision as a space for thinking', in G. Shipton (ed.), *Supervision of Psychotherapy and Counselling, Making a Place to Think*, Buckingham: Oxford University Press, pp. 24–34.

Pines, M. (1995) 'Introduction', in *The Third Eye: Supervision in Analytic Groups*, London: Routledge, pp. 1–2.

Sarra, N. (1998) 'Connection and disconnection in the art therapy group: working with forensic patients in acute states on a locked ward', in S. Skaife and V. Huet (eds), *Art Psychotherapy Groups: Between Pictures and Words*, London: Routledge, pp. 69–87.

Shipton, G. (ed.) (1997) *Supervision of Psychotherapy and Counselling, Making a Place to Think*, Buckingham: Oxford University Press.

# Chapter 9

# The art of supervision

*Arthur Robbins*

This chapter represents the compilation of over half a century of work in the mental health field. In this period of time I wore many hats, which were associated with the tri-disciplines psychology, psychiatry and social work, as well as the broad range of expressive arts therapies. In 1970 I was instrumental in creating one of the first pioneering graduate art therapy training programmes in the United States. In the interim I have been a part-time sculptor and associated with one of the first post-masters expressive therapy training programmes in the country. The first part of this chapter emphasises work with students, which takes place at Pratt Institute, located in Brooklyn, New York. The chapter then deals with supervision that takes place in a private practice setting. I will first offer a framework that has gradually evolved over this period of time.

Supervision is an art form taking place within a professional relationship. The psychic artistry contains the dimensions of time, space and form. In the supervisory relationship a living breathing space evolves between both members of the dialogue, containing a dynamic play of energy and polarities. Ideally, the atmosphere is free and disciplined, aesthetic and creative and, above all else, strives towards making the interaction a mind/body experience. The concentration of work deals with the inner affective experience of the practitioner. Because this work is very personal, a very clear boundary needs to be drawn between the differences between dynamic supervision and therapy. As with the psychotherapist, the art therapy supervisor calls upon his/her knowledge of a discipline based upon defences, developmental levels and a range of projective transferences that are assimilated into an approach to the interaction with the supervisee. These therapeutic skills and the artistic materials become woven into the fabric of this very intimate process. A discipline frames the supervisory dialogue. Yet, as an art form, the magic and mystery persist in spite of our clinical knowledge and expertise. The incongruities of reactions by both parties to a particular supervisory session are worth noting. How often do we hear from the supervisee/therapist that a particular session has been fulfilling, when as a supervisor it was viewed as a 'washout?' The reverse is also true. Another interesting phenomenon is the psychic presence of the patient in a super-visory dialogue. Often changes in patient treatment will occur before the supervisee/therapist has had a chance to benefit from the recommendations that arise from the supervisory session.

## The work of the art therapist

More often than not, art therapists who work in institutional settings face a wide scope of demanding and challenging patients, ranging from borderline conditions, psychotic states, bipolar pathology, to severe primitive mental states. To add to this complexity, transference and countertransference reactions precipitated in treatment not only spill over into the supervisory relationship but are also re-enacted towards the institution. There is simply too much stimulation and, indeed, therapeutic material of a chaotic nature often overwhelms the practitioner's defences. The net result of this state of affairs often creates therapeutic burnout. Trauma occurs in a wide number of patient cases and the supervisee's exposure to traumatic material can be both overwhelming and disturbing. Defences are built up against any further stimulation, and as a result this particular problem becomes a central issue for the supervisor to deal with. The ability of the supervisee/therapist to nourish a pre-conscious accessibility to affects of rage, pro-jections and over-eroticisation is all part of discovering their emotional availability to do the work.

Art therapists who work in the private sector often encounter more opportunity to work with patients who have intact egos. However, trans-ferences are still there, and often spill over from the artwork into the relationship. Intermixed with all of these issues, the supervisee's existential concerns about survival often come into play. Feelings of being trapped in a job or being caught in an overwhelming family situation may have a profound impact on the supervisee's capacity to work effectively. Problems of financial stability become interfused with this most complex and demand-ing role. Consequently, the supervisor develops a sensitive attunement to a wide range of psychic material that is presented on their supervisory con-ferences. Quite often supervisees/therapists identify with traumatic patients and present themselves in supervision either as a victim or a victimiser. In addition, therapists are often the receptacle of a good deal of rage, which can threaten the most secure individuals. For many, the life circumstances of their patients do not resonate with their own life histories. The notion that projections can be contained in the art material is both naïve and misleading. Conflictual material leaks into the relationship with a force and violence that potentially can overwhelm the practitioner. As a response to these most difficult professional circumstances, the supervisor offers a non-judgmental holding relationship where there is ample room to express feelings of shame, guilt and despair.

This description of the role of the supervisor is an ideal one that few supervisors can realise 100% of the time. In reality, they too are often overwhelmed and burdened and simply do not have enough patience to listen. One of the antidotes to this very difficult circumstance is for supervisors to participate in their own continuous supervision. Their problems often are intense and complex and require very senior people to offer opportunities for processing and empathy.

In light of what I have described as the work of the art therapist, the first order of business in supervision is one of helping the supervisee/therapist to become grounded, centred and focused. Retreating to a level of intellectualisation on the part of the supervisee, or, worse still, defending his/herself in a discursive or dissociative manner is to be attended to, if at all possible. Often, stopping to take a deep breath, learning some good grounding exercises and clarifying one's intentionality can be useful. In the best of cases a good deal of trust, safety and holding develops between supervisor and supervisee. When the supervisor also has an administrative responsibility to the institution in which the supervisee works, the limits of confidentiality and boundaries should be clear and direct. In this atmosphere, connections are safely made between body experiences, symbolic representations and interpersonal relationships.

## Process

What underlies both psychotherapy and supervision is the sensitive awareness to process. Let me define what I mean by process. In this open, dynamic field, feelings, attitudes and insights move in and out of consciousness. Clarity blurs into nebulousness. A breakthrough occurs and the case takes on a new perspective. Affects of mastery, helplessness and excitement often accompany this process. Various levels of a virtual alchemical mix take place within both participants, and sensory motor connections fluidly transform into images and symbolic thinking.

To complicate matters, the supervisee in the supervisory session also describes his or her visceral contact with the patient. Thus we have, at least, two relationships percolating in this mix. We also can include both the supervisor's and supervisee's relationship to the institution. When we also add the personal aspirations, values and artistic biases of both parties we have quite a complicated relationship. Transference and countertransference reactions often erupt in the supervisory relationship, mirroring some of the problems that the supervisee confronts with his or her patients; also, transferences often colour supervisory connections ranging from idealisation to devaluation, competition, fear and authority issues that are associated with power, feeding and sexuality. In short, there are numerous levels of contact creating a sense of excitement and creativity or, by contrast, feelings of deadness and depletion.

## Mind/body connection

My work as a supervisor encompasses a number of overriding principles. Supervision is a visceral interaction. Therapy is not an intellectual process but a mind/body experience. Brain research supports the very basic premise of art therapy (Cozolino 2002: 147). We initially make contact through a sensory motor process that ultimately filters up into a cognitive framework. Obviously, defences from both parties can distort or interfere with this process. Hopefully, the supervisor has developed a more sophisticated understanding of his/her defences than the supervisee. I might add that this is not always the case. What seems to be most important is an awareness of the life-giving process in the relationship. When the interaction feels dead it is a fairly good assumption that defences have built up around a particular affect or group of attitudes that interfere with an oscillating flow of form and formlessness. Again, making the distinction between psychotherapy and supervision can be tricky.

In psychotherapy a wide variety of engagements can occur, ranging from confrontation and mirroring to empathy. When the psychotherapist becomes pointed the patient can certainly bring into the process negative and angry reactions. No one likes to have his/her defences challenged. The hostility that is manifested becomes grist for the mill and can facilitate a good deal of growth. In supervision, how the supervisor deals with the supervisee's defences is a delicate affair. For purposes of clarification I refer to the term 'student' as someone who is part of a training programme. If the student/supervisee is in his/her own personal therapy there may be considerable room to examine what interferes with the flow of the material. In the case of relatively young students who have little or no therapy behind them, and are relatively naïve, the situation becomes a perilous one. If the student is very walled off, you certainly refer them to an appropriate psychotherapist. However, from a legal point of view, in the USA, the programme cannot require a student to undergo personal therapy. Yet, worth mentioning, by the end of the first term, nearly all students voluntarily elect to enter therapy. Please note: I do not believe any practitioner can do this work without personal therapy. Nevertheless, the supervisor is often confronted with a student who is psychologically naïve and threatened. Working on an art level where the supervisee draws a variety of pictures relating to the therapeutic problem at hand can certainly help. It can sometimes lessen the student's implicit sense of shame or guilt if the supervisor shares his/her own fears or conflicts that took place at the beginning stages of his/her career. I hold in my supervisory storehouse a variety of stories about my own early struggles as a therapist. These stories reduce the student's projection that I am omnipotent or omniscient. What is most important to emphasise is that I attempt to keep the relationship fairly positive and supportive.

Supervision is not a good place to work out negative transferences. There is simply not enough room to work with resistances, negative projections and all the attendant progressions and regressions that occur in therapy. More important, a respect for the students' boundaries and the concomitant baggage they come with in entering this profession cannot be over-emphasised. If the supervisor also has a position of authority, particularly in an academic training programme, it is utterly unfair to students to draw them into a quasi-therapeutic relationship. The supervisor holds too many cards in terms of power, grades and his or her responsibilities to the institution. Yet, I wish to emphasise, given enough trust, safety and holding, supervision can be a very lively exchange that is both emotional and intellectual.

## Resistances

There are some exceptions to the governing principle of minimising negative transferences in supervision. When the supervisory frame has been challenged there is a need for immediate intervention, otherwise the entire relationship becomes unclear and insecure. Lateness to appointments, forgetting notes and absences are often disguised communications that require attention and investigation. A clear structure regarding time and responsibilities often helps. The management issues that occur in supervision are often the very problems that a student neglects with his/her patients. In addition, the supervisee's character structure often looms like the tip of an iceberg in the relationship. Here the old adage that different folks need different strokes is very applicable. Whenever a supervisee acts out, the problems of internal and external authority immediately come into focus. These issues call for in depth exploration in supervision.

What I have discussed in the above paragraph are important management issues. The resistances to discuss primitive affects that are stimulated in the therapeutic relationship as well as the artwork are common phenomena. Supervisees encounter in their patients trauma, fears of abandonment, chaotic panic attacks that underlie fragmentation, over-eroticisation and fears of fusion and victimisation. Often this material occurs on a very pre-conscious and non-verbal level. A very careful and sensitive attunement to what the supervisee/therapist can tolerate must be assessed. Sometimes using the art form can help unravel some difficult projections while at the same time offering safety. Thus, in any supervisory connection, there is a focused attention to when the flow of the dialogue is over-organised or lacking structure. In either instance, these are signs that the learning process has gone askew and an intervention on the part of the supervisor to rebalance the communication is in order. In contrast, the communication can be formless or fragmented. Here, the supervisor provides a balance to help create a more orderly flow of material. Offering an articulation as to the content in the therapeutic process can relieve anxiety, or on the other hand it can overwhelm the supervisee and create feelings of inadequacy. Thus, the supervisor is constantly accessing the ego resources of the student in order to make the most appropriate intervention to facilitate the flow of supervisory material.

## Energy

The oscillation from form to formlessness in the supervisory dialogue sets the stage for a transformation of energy. For instance, both parties may dwell upon primitive archaic imagery of the patient's art form and then shift to an articulated and verbal translation of the structure of the case. Ideally, there are permeable boundaries that exist in both parties, permitting an exchange of different levels of consciousness. Consequently, if one or both parties are attempting to keep a tight control of fantasy or imagery there is likelihood of a rather sterile dialogue. In this mix there is a good deal of inter-subjective relatedness that keeps on shifting in terms of the form and content level of the supervisory session. Often flatness in the supervisory process covers over powerful affects and formidable defences. In the mix are also transference and countertransference projections, which can completely put a damper on the energy exchange. It is a common supervisory phenomenon for one or both parties to try harder to make something happen, but the underlying causes are avoided to the neglect of the life of the process.

The use of one's aesthetic eyes facilitates an attunement to energy. I invite the supervisee to follow his or her eyes in viewing a particular art form. Ideally an art piece contains a centre that moves deeply into the soul of the art. Holding this centre can be a frame. Here the eyes travel to the outside that surrounds the centre. The particular nature of the observer's eye movement tells the story of how the soul of the patient has been held or resonated with.

The word 'soul' has been used in many different contexts. The phrase 'soul mate' implies a relationship that lasts beyond the bodily existence of the two parties. Soul has often been associated with light or transcendence. When there is an absence of 'soul' in supervisory sessions there is often a lack of resonance or authenticity in the interaction. How the supervisee's soul resonates with his/her personal past history may well set the stage for their future work experiences. For example, some supervisees have an uncanny way of repeating work experiences that are either abusive or rejecting. This may require intervention and exploration by the supervisor.

There is also a particular rhythm to the quality of the supervisee's form of contact in supervision. Some supervisees organise their reporting of a particular case by first going to their inner emotional experience and then give it a more objective articulation. We also can note instances where supervisees never include their inner experiences in discussing a client. The rhythm of sessions can be characterised as either cohesive or fragmented. The reported material can fly all over the place and lack a ground, while others can be characterised by a heaviness framed by ponderous responsibilities and judgment. In all these examples the supervisor, supervisee/therapist and his/her patient attempt to rebalance the field to permit a greater flow of energy to facilitate an attention to the essence of the case. From an energetic perspective, the patient seems present in this supervisory conference. Let me clarify what I mean. The psychic image of the patient becomes sharpened through discussion and role-playing. Sometimes it feels like the patient is sitting in on the session and benefits from the work even before the therapist sees the patient in their next context. This all seems very mystical, but these changes have been reported often by a variety of therapists.

## Transference/countertransference communication

When the supervisor or supervisee loses his/her centre or ground we have evidence of transference material interfering with the process of treatment. Under this definition, one or both parties are not communicating in an authentic manner. This is similar to an art piece in which the soul of the artist is either evaded or lost in the creation. Likewise, there is an absence of a centre to the supervisory discussion. By contrast, the material can be so convoluted and symbolic that it loses all inter-personal relatedness. With this definition, it is quite possible to contain strong feelings regarding a particular case and still maintain relatedness to the patient.

A problem arises as to what to do when supervision is so clouded by projections that the supervisory process bogs down in repetition or acting out. If the supervisee brings to supervision a good deal of past treatment, many of these projections are not unfamiliar and are workable in the here and now of the present interaction. The problems occur, however, when the student presents little or no personal therapy and maintains defences surrounding the projections. A gentle opening up of the topic of transference for the supervisee to explore may facilitate the process. Referral for personal therapy may help in the long run. In the short run, offering various possible interventions may be the only recourse. There is, however, a good deal of frustration and need for both tolerance and a limiting of expectations.

Occasionally, working with the art form opens up the eyes of the supervisee. The request that they draw the patient, move like the patient or vocalise the quality of the patient may offer some insight. In some instances I may ask the supervisee to do the same exercises with members of their own family. Again, I wish to emphasise the issue of intent that underlies such personal work. The exercise becomes a stimulus for discussion that relates to resistance and principles that relate to aesthetic dynamic expression. The student becomes emotionally involved in this work, but the structure holds very tightly to the goal of learning what it feels like to be a patient and allows for the exploration of a variety of interventions that are appropriate to the work at hand. I sometimes use this option when I believe the student is ready to at least recognise the parallels between past relationships and the present one. The goal here is to develop the capacity to contain the past rather than being disconnected from its power. However, if too much anxiety and negative projections are stirred up, such an exploration is counter-indicated. Negative transferences are stimulated by open-ended questions regarding conflictual personal material and are more appropriate for therapy than supervision.

## Attributes of good supervision

Every supervisor has a particular bias and training in a specific therapeutic model. Most likely, this bias will permeate the type of supervision that is offered to a supervisee. We do know, however, that different supervisees possess a temperamental and cognitive sensitivity to one model or another. In the most ideal of circumstances the supervisor creates an atmosphere that fosters a tolerance for ambiguity, an avoidance of premature closure and a permissiveness to shift back and forth from reality to fantasy. Being centred and grounded enhances the ability to maintain this creative state.

At this point, an overall synthesis may prove helpful even if some of these issues contain elements of repetition. Good supervision creates opportunities for openness and communication, and the development of a holding, safe and trusting relationship. The atmosphere is non-judgmental, grounded and yet maintains boundaries. The supervisor provides a container for primitive affects that are stirred up both in the artwork as well as in the therapeutic relationship. Characteristically, supervision encompasses an understanding of the many varieties of support that a particular student can utilise. Some need an active mirroring of their struggle to understand a particular concept. Others easily flower when there is a quiet space for reflection. Others are hungry for stimulation and feel fed in an atmosphere of active engagement.

New students are often overwhelmed, particularly when they first embark into the field of art therapy. Given an education that is often so overwhelming, my goal for neophyte students is one of survival. New students are inundated with affects arising from multiple levels of consciousness. In a safe relationship the student can unwind and share some of their most forbidden fears and thoughts regarding their patients. Many students are relieved when they share their ambivalence regarding the choice of their profession. Others feel ashamed by their own stimulation regarding erotic material. Some are very frightened and avoid hostile affects. In short, new students wonder whether they have signed up for more than they have bargained for. A supervisor–supervisee relationship provides room for laughter and relaxation, trust, stimulation and structure. For some students the art therapy supervisor becomes a mentor. This shift in relationship is subtle and profound. When this occurs, there is room for the sharing of everyday problems as well as the development of one's personal and professional identity. There is a long-term commitment to this relationship and supervision provides a source for spiritual nourishment and replenishment. The supervisor becomes a resource to offer a perspective on balancing out the delicate connection between professional responsibilities and having time for relaxation and fun.

As a supervisor, I am most comfortable as a facilitator, but also recognise the need for structure and information. Ideally, knowledge of technique and the use of materials arise out of a core of self-reflection and emotional growth. Yet, there are obviously many times when introducing information is necessary to move the process along. As much as I emphasise freedom and self-exploration, I am aware that a good art therapist evolves from a foundation of knowledge, experience and a sophisticated understanding of the merger of art and psychology. The play of being open and yet grounded, accepting but not naïve, is an all-important step in becoming an art therapist. The supervisor can be an excellent role model for this development. In many respects the skills of good supervision entail an enormous range of versatility and flexibility. Central to these notions is the sensitivity to balance, for indeed as supervisors we attempt to provide the counterbalance for the forces within the supervisee that are either overused or underdeveloped. These supervisory skills are not easily acquired in this very unique balancing act of facilitator, artist and spiritual guide.

## Clinical examples

The supervisees I will discuss have considerable experience behind them, yet the issues they present are part of the ordinary happenings in a supervisor's day. I choose each supervisee on the basis of their relative comfort in having their work under such close personal scrutiny. All my groups consist of ten members, often with different professional backgrounds and training. Of note, the members of these groups attend over a long period of time. The groups meet on a weekly basis and break for the summer months. Please refer to Robbins (1998) for a more detailed description of this format for working with practitioners in the mental health field.

### Example

Joan is one of the newest members of a supervisory group that has been ongoing for eleven years. In this group are two members with psychoanalytic training, one music therapist and the remaining are practising art therapists. They are two men and eight women. Since the group began there have been a few replacements of members who have withdrawn for a variety of reasons. Joan is visibly pleased that her work had been chosen to be part of this chapter. The group feels reassured that identities have been protected and little or no discussion takes place regarding the publication of this presentation.

Joan's background includes work with acting-out adolescents and young adults who have been court mandated. After being in the supervisory group for six months she announces that she is starting a new job in a child guidance agency. The major part of her work takes place with three groups of sexually abused adolescents. Her experience level with this population is minimal and she voraciously consumes the literature regarding the clinical issues in working with this type of client. In her work she sees one group after another and there is very little pause for reflection. There is minimal supervision at the agency and she is justifiably anxious and insecure about meeting the challenges of her programme.

Joan is a plucky and aggressive woman of forty who enters the group with a good deal of enthusiasm, assertiveness and ability to spar with other group members. She also brings with her a couple of years of her own therapy. She worries about criticism from the group for she is aware that she is on very insecure ground with minimal experience with this population. In her previous work most of the clients were abusers yet she cannot readily see the transfer of her past experience to this new client caseload. Joan is very aware that she is on her own but at the same time wants to do meaningful and significant work. She realises that it could be very easy for her to offer art exercises to the group and no one would be the wiser. She makes it very clear that she sought this job to expand her knowledge and she wants to make the experience meaningful.

In her past presentations Joan referred to her mother as cold, untouchable and not very connected. She worries that this mother inside of her might unconsciously interfere with her doing good work. She then offers an example of a young adolescent in one of her groups who starts to cry. A member of this group gets up and holds the client. Joan reports that she feels inadequate for she wonders about her role as the therapist. She questions herself: 'Should she be the one who does the holding? Perhaps she should have shown more demonstrable action to indicate that she is warm and responsive'.

Up to this point the supervisory group listens with interest and support. She then makes a provocative statement to the group. She states that from her readings abuse can be painful and upsetting yet there also could be pleasure connected to the experience. Suddenly there is an eruption that contains strong political and emotional overtones. Judgments and opinions are voiced by a variety of members. One member vehemently protests that abuse is never pleasurable. Others want to talk about sex and its connection to powerlessness. Another member chimes in that sexuality and power often go together. In response, another member states, 'I don't want to hear about Freud or another male perspective'. I am aware that the explosiveness is originating from one or more identifications with either the abuser or the abused. The anxiety is of a very intense nature and does not permit much self-reflection. The presenter then shares with the group that this is exactly what she feared. There would be no grey area when it comes to sexual abuse. In fact, there was no room for her 'unpopular view'. The supervisee protests, 'Personally, sexuality is a very positive experience and we should not lose sight that it can be pleasurable'.

I remind the group that as long as they take a judgmental attacking position, any flow that could deepen the process will be curtailed. One member comments that things just get distorted. I ask her what she means. She says 'There is too much talk about Freud's point of view on sexuality. He was no authority, just a male chauvinist. But most important', she says, turning to the presenter, 'I do not want you to impose your feelings about sexuality on these kids. They have been hurt, wounded, and misused and there is no pleasure in that'.

As the group quiets down and they start to reflect about their own personal experiences regarding sexuality and abuse, I comment that a cold mother could easily have filtered into our discussion. Seductiveness as well as sadism and eroticism could be a substitute for warmth and relatedness. One of the members of the group remarks that this certainly applies to her family situation. I make this comment as a way of opening up this area to give space to the group members, as well as the presenter. Then, suddenly, another member blurts out, 'Someone in my building was murdered during a casual sexual pickup'. She adds, 'It was horrible and extremely violent'. The group continues to express feelings of helplessness, impotency, rage and accusations.

My reaction to this emotional onslaught is a pulling into myself as well as retreating to a protective disassociated state. I start to reflect as to what is going on in me and take a couple of deep breaths to permit myself to regain centre and ground. I point out to the group that all their reactions held fragments of a mirror that may well reflect the presenter's internal state. The earlier political comments, which were so passionately expressed, are not opening up the countertransference issues. The presenter needs the group to hold and contain some of these feelings until she could better digest her reactions to working with this population. This is no longer an issue about working with grey areas. The issues here are the difficulties of experiencing the repercussions of abuse as well as being able to contain them. Obviously, in going deeply into this work, there is always the real possibility of experiencing countertransference trauma that can be hidden by an eruption of accusations and judgment. I requested that all of them take a good look at the piece of this process that belongs to them and take back their projections.

After some pause and reflection the presenter starts to develop a space to discuss some of her own countertransference issues. 'I am not a hugger, but I can be intuitive'. 'Perhaps', I responded, 'the source of your intuitiveness comes from the positive mother that also lies inside of you'. I took this position for I realised that the female inside of her required support and not abandonment.

In the meantime, Pandora's box has been opened. Rage and contempt towards the men in the group are expressed by at least some of the women. All of them are associating to abuse issues of their own. The men report that they too have experienced abuse in their background. In the meantime, I am very aware that the presenter was being abandoned, as is so common with abused patients.

Some of the participants in the group verbally contribute very little and seem disassociated. Others take the role of owning impotency and rage. Many speak about the fear of being placed in a demeaning position with men. Finally, many realise that underneath the political diatribe is a cry for support by the presenter. I realise that I may well have re-enacted a personal trauma for Joan, for I participate in her abandonment by not intervening early enough in the process. She too has her role in this, for her statements certainly have a provocative tone to them. Thus, as the passion and intensity start to die down we arrive at an initial understanding of the process. During this heated dialogue I am aware that the presenter was not really in touch with her own countertransference issues regarding work with this population. The group, however, certainly offers a mirror of what it is like to undergo first hand contact with young women who are deeply damaged and abandoned.

## Case discussion

It is not uncommon for a therapist to inadvertently set off chaos and helplessness when an abused patient is presented. One of the more valuable functions a group serves is to provide a frame for containment and mirroring. In this process there can also be a good deal of re-enactment. My job as a supervisor is a difficult one. I sat in the eye of a storm attempting to live through flying fragments that were whirling around me. The exposure to intense affects not only impacted upon Joan and the group, but also impacted on my own supervisory effectiveness. The problem as to when to intervene or to allow affects of a stormy nature to build up and explode has to do with one's style and temperament. Even though I admittedly was somewhat 'out of it' in the discussion, ultimately the material, though somewhat of a resistant nature, brings the group together.

In this example, we see the pervasive impact of traumatic experiences that have multiple ramifications. In this presentation I believe there is a secondary trauma to the therapist. I also believe that there is a tertiary trauma encountered by myself in this supervisory process. These reactions are quite common and are typically part of the re-enactment process that is so present in working with traumatised patients. Helping students to live with these very diverse reactions to trauma without judgment or shame becomes part of the learning process.

## Conclusion

Supervision requires a good deal of sensitivity, empathy and the capacity to work on many levels of consciousness. The skills of supervision in working with characterological resistances, projections and transferences are as daunting as any aspect of performing the duties of a psychotherapist. From this perspective, supervision potentially can be dynamic, experiential and supportive, as well as emphasising the slow integration of mind, body and affect. Obviously, my clinical orientation has filtered through this entire chapter. My extensive background in psychoanalytic thinking and practice is a strong base for my supervision. My work as an artist has also impacted my professional orientation. Once again, I wish to emphasise that there is room for therapeutic art and, in fact, in some instances it is the treatment of choice. I leave with the reader this important reflection. The supervisor has a responsibility to acknowledge his/her strengths and biases and to avoid being caught in any one role that restricts his/her vision.

As I review this chapter, I want to highlight some of the major guidelines that run throughout. In the best of circumstances supervision combines creativity development, aesthetic form and a sound clinical framework. I realise that this orientation does not fit every practitioner's temperament or predisposition. I respect these differences. A profession that is open to different points of view offers the most fertile ground for growth. Many practitioners have different notions and articulation of creativity development. Yet the underlying message that I wish to leave is one that creativity, backed by principles of aesthetic form, is an organic part of our work. Hopefully, the reader has assimilated a message that any art form requires discipline along with freedom. Supervision can be a lifelong process even though it may come in different forms. Our colleagues, peers and teachers can have something to contribute to all of us during our professional lifetime.

We have, as a profession, come a long way in our development. My fellow colleagues and I have changed over the years in our perceptions and knowledge of the role of the art therapist. As supervisors we can carry a vision of the true potential and possibilities of the breadth of the field. We need to nourish our students, for the professional world is a difficult one, and they carry the hope and dreams for the future growth of our profession. We need to nurture our future leaders so that they can deal with the difficult realities of functioning as an art therapist without giving up their dreams and aspirations.

## References

Cozolino, L. (2002) *The Neuroscience of Psychotherapy: Building and Rebuilding the Human Brain*, New York: W.W. Norton & Company.

Robbins, A. (1989) *Between Therapists: The Processing of Transference/Countertransference Material*, London: Jessica Kingsley.

# Chapter 10

# Thinking with image making

## Supervising student art therapists

*Chris Brown, Julia Meyerowitz-Katz and Julia Ryde*

The authors describe how regular discussions about their supervision of art therapy students highlighted the role of image making in art therapy supervision. The nature of the supervision process and the role of image making in supervision are discussed with reference to the literature. The aims and composition of the supervision groups and the effects of incorporating aesthetic experience into the groups are explored. It is proposed that by using the aesthetic tools of their profession in supervision, art therapists can enhance and deepen their understanding of their clinical work.

## Introduction

- I felt I could really create a picture in my head of what was happening, which helped me to comment on the therapeutic relationship.
- It was particularly good at helping me explore feeling states.
- It brought up surprising issues that I had not thought of.
- It acted like a reference point.
- It took the space to talk away!

These are a few of the comments given in anonymous feedback by students after their experience of using image making in supervision groups. In this chapter we describe the introduction of image making into the groups. The authors are all art therapists, with backgrounds in private practice and NHS work, who facilitated weekly clinical supervision groups with final year art therapy students (Brown *et al.* 2003).

The discussions, which were originally aimed at examining the supervision process, became focused on the role of image making within that process. We shared the experience of having had predominantly verbal supervision during our art therapy training, subsequent further training and as professional art therapists. We began to formulate questions as to what the image making contributed to supervision in this context.

As far as we were aware, introducing image making into the supervision of students was a new development. Studio practice was an important part of the training on this course and the supervision groups took place in the studios where art materials and evidence of art making were visible. We were in an interesting position to observe and reflect on the effects that this would have on the learning function of the groups and the development of the professional skills of the students.

We begin by looking at the nature of the supervision process and then introduce considerations about image making and aesthetic experience in supervision. The structure and context of the groups are described and vignettes illustrate the effects of image making on some of the aspects of supervision that we identify as important. Finally we discuss the effects of image making on the supervision process.

## The supervision process

Supervision is a relationship that facilitates another relationship, that of the supervisee and the patient. It is a place for thinking and reflection (Edwards 1993; Shipton 1997). It is a creative, imaginative activity in which the supervisor and supervisee together create a picture of the patient and the therapeutic relationship. Together they assemble the fantasies, thoughts, impressions and feelings reported by the supervisee and evoked during the supervisory session (Edwards 1993; Jacobs *et al.* 1995). Bion, in writing about reports of sessions, points out how they cannot be regarded as a factual account of what happened due to the involuntary distortions of memory. He says:

> . . . therefore in any account of a session, no matter how soon it may be made after the event or by what master, memory should not be treated as more than a pictorialised communication of an emotional experience.
>
> (Bion 1967: 2)

We propose that image making is another, alternative way of formulating and communicating this emotional experience.

The shared experience of the material is akin to Winnicott's (1971) transitional phenomena where the report of the therapy is both real and not real at the same time. This enables a more playful approach to understanding and containing the material than a model which supposes that one person gives a factual report and another tells them what to do. It enables more vitality in exchanges between participants and leads to greater independence of thinking and the development of the student's own internal supervisor (Casement 1985, 1990).

The model of supervision brought to the groups was based on our experiences of our own training and subsequent supervision from a range of practitioners including psychotherapists, psychoanalysts and art therapists. This mirrors the history of art therapists having tended to rely on supervision from other professions in the absence of suitably experienced art therapists (Edwards 1993; Rees 1998). We have distilled from our past experiences, and from what we have read, a number of important qualities for the establishment of a safely boundaried supervisory relationship. It requires building of trust and respect that involves honesty on the supervisor's part, use of their own experience and struggles, confusions and not-knowing. Humour is also an important ingredient in this process, as is skilled listening, which involves listening without prejudice and listening to one's own countertransference (Gordon 1992). As well as creating a supportive atmosphere to lessen anxiety it is also important to challenge the student's approach to the work (Gordon 1992).

The dynamic relationship between transference and countertransference is an essential part of how we work and therefore an important part of supervision. The knowledge and experience of the supervisor helps the supervisee to contain the feelings evoked, and the anxieties generated, by the clinical material. The rapport between the unconscious of the therapist and the unconscious of the patient creates a pool of feelings in the room. This arises from the emotional contact on an unconscious level between both minds, which the patient uses to create and then communicate states of mind in order that they can be consciously understood. Supervisees bring these states of mind to supervision in varying degrees of awareness. Once the countertransference has been made conscious and identified in supervision, it is then possible to support their recovery. By this we mean to recover their ability to use therapeutic understanding and technique rather than being in the grip of responding to the pressure exerted on them by the patient's transference. In this way the supervisee becomes more aware of unconscious processes and is able to think about them in relation to therapy.

The processing of clinical material can be seen as a continuum, with the raw undigested material at one end and its transformation into thinking at the other. This is not an abstract intellectual activity; it is more about the connection between feeling and thinking, which Bion designates as alpha function (Bion 1962). In order for this to occur feelings must be contained, which then allows for a mental space to develop where thinking can take place. Hinshelwood writes that 'containment derives from Klein's original description of projective identification in which one person in some sense contains a part of another' (Hinshelwood 1989: 244). The work of processing occurs at different stages. It may be possible for this to occur in or straight after a session, on reflection or through image making; or it may depend on an interaction during supervision.

## Image making in supervision

The body of art therapy literature is beginning to include references to images in supervision. Henzell (1997) emphasises the importance and value of the patient's image and what it can add to the supervisory process. He writes that to have the patient's image in the room is to be in direct contact with an aspect of the patient in a way in which verbal reporting has no access. Schur (1998) describes supervision of art therapists where the patient's image is looked at and analysed, before group members are given any information about the patient. In this way the image is used as a primary source of information. Maclagan (1997) writes about using subjective qualities of fantasy and play in responding to the patient's image, as an aid in bringing the patient into the transitional area of the supervisory space. These authors refer to the role of the patient's image as it is brought into supervision, but not to the supervisee's image making in supervision.

Our understanding about the meaning of images from an art therapy perspective has been enriched by the work of Maclagan and Schaverien. Schaverien has much to say about the triangularity of art therapy relationships and the different levels of aesthetic countertransference that operate when viewing images and she makes the important distinction between diagrammatic and embodied images. She defines the embodied image as one 'which conveys a feeling state for which no other mode of expression can be substituted' (Schaverien 2000: 59). Maclagan (1995) writes about the image in terms of its ability to intuitively capture and evaluate emotional experience and he emphasises the importance of fantasy in accessing subjective qualities of experience.

Even though the role of images in art therapy supervision has been referred to, Rees (1998) suggests that very few art therapists actually use image making as part of their supervisory process. Whereas verbal supervision makes use of metaphoric and creative possibilities, Rees points out how rare it is to find a model that makes use of an overt and named space for image making in the supervisory relationship.

## The supervision groups

The central task of these groups, as required by the university, was to train student art therapists to work with a wide range of psychopathology in a variety of clinical settings. This was done in closed membership small groups that were run in a confidential and supportive setting for the exploration and presentation of the clinical placement experience and the development of therapeutic understanding.

The groups ran weekly during the academic year. Clinical material was brought in the form of formal and informal presentations. The group membership of approximately seven students was formed from full time and part time students, meeting both as a group, and with the supervisors for the first time. Students represented a mix of cultural and ethnic backgrounds, including some students from abroad.

Supervision is a learning experience for us all. In these groups we hoped that the students would be able to develop and deepen a therapeutic relationship with their patients. We aimed to foster their sensitivity to different layers of meaning in their patients' communications, which includes verbal interaction, art making process and image. By having an experience of group supervision they learned how to use the setting to reflect on each other's material and help each other to think.

The students undertook clinical practice in a setting where individual supervision was provided. This supervision ranged from professional case management from a non-clinician, to in-depth exploration of the clinical work by an experienced clinician, usually, but not always, an art therapist. Because of this, it was important for the groups to provide a setting where students' work could be thought about with their peers and the art therapy supervisors, thus paying attention to the art therapy processes. We tried to instil in the students a psychodynamic way of thinking.

The institutional aspect was multi-layered, consisting of the training course and its location within a faculty of art and design, which in turn was located within a newly constituted university. Supervision in this context involved trying to contain the movement between academic demands, including the students' understanding of theory and our role in assessing their abilities, and the raw emotion stimulated by the clinical work. Dudley, Gilroy and Skaife (1998), writing about experiential groups in training, stress the need to try to maintain this balance so that emotional material can both emerge and, through applying intellectual processes, become a learning experience.

As the supervision described here was conducted in a group setting, group dynamics inevitably operated. Some groups will be more cohesive than others. Yalom defines cohesiveness as the attraction that members have for their group and for other members and he sees it as a precondition for effective group work. He also writes: 'whether or not a group jells . . . the critical variable is some, as yet unclear, blending of the members' (Yalom 1970: 192). If cohesiveness is lacking, there may be more dependence on the supervisor to do the work and to use her thinking as a substitute for developing their own.

Part of the supervisor's task was to form a working group that was focused on the task. We postulated that there was a spectrum, at one end of which was group dynamics and at the other was the supervisory task; the groups move between the two. Transference and countertransference in the groups are characteristically multi-layered. All of this becomes part of the group matrix and may find expression in ways that either blur or clarify the focus on the patient. The idea of parallel process (Searles 1955) is one way in which understanding what is happening in the group can be used to understand what is happening between the patient and therapist. This can be seen to operate, for example, when a split along the lines contained in the clinical material occurs in the group. The role of the supervisor is to address this by using the countertransference material to focus the discussion on what is happening with the patient. This means that awareness of the group dynamics is held in mind by the supervisor but not necessarily commented on unless it is to elucidate the clinical material or to help the group to acknowledge a dynamic that is possibly obstructing the work.

## Introducing image making in the groups

In the supervision groups students, in response to their clinical work, had brought images into the space in two different ways: either in the form of patients' artwork or as images made outside the groups with patients. The students had already been encouraged to use image making to help them process the feelings evoked by difficult clinical material. It was thought that this could be integrated into the supervision setting.

In considering the historical context of how supervision developed, we discovered that the traditional model of supervision, which is based on a degree of distance between supervisee and supervisor, was not always the case. Ferenczi and the Hungarian school believed that the therapist's analyst, as the one who knows the therapist through having an intimate knowledge of his unconscious mind, is therefore the best person to supervise his work. This view did not prevail however, and during the 1930s most training institutes separated the function of supervision from that of the training analyst. One criticism of this was that something got lost from the supervisory relationship (Jacobs *et al.* 1995).

What was felt to be lost were elements of the unconscious relationship and intimate knowledge of the therapist's mind. In thinking about introducing image making in the groups our concerns were that there would not be a clear enough boundary between supervision and therapy. This was surprising considering that we were already aware of and working with these dynamics verbally. Somehow the idea of the supervisee making an image in the session was felt to bring more of this unconscious element into play. It would be an enactment of the same process that takes place with the patient and it would result in a visual record of the therapists' conscious and unconscious attitude to the work that they were doing with their patients. Rees (1998) speculates that few art therapists use image making as part of their supervisory process because it may reveal too much about the therapist and so they may be anxious about becoming over-identified with the position of the patient.

The making of the image involves a physical engagement with materials and the image then exists as a concrete object in space and time. When ego and materials engage together, the unconscious emerges through that engagement, which produces an embodied picture. Ehrenzweig writes that:

> The medium by frustrating the artist's purely conscious intentions allows him to contact more submerged parts of his personality and draw them up for contemplation. While the artist struggles with his medium, unknown to himself, he wrestles with his unconscious personality revealed by the work of art.
>
> (Ehrenzweig 1967: 72)

In considering the experience of having the image in the room, we can think about discursive and non-discursive modes of expression (Henzell 1997). In other words, language symbols can be delivered in a sequential form over time, whereas visual symbols can be presented simultaneously in the form of a picture.

Through the supervisee making an image, the unconscious relationship between them and their patient can become visual and available for discussion and thought. Art therapists, who are used to looking at images, can use the very tool in which they have a specialised skill. It was as though we had to go through the process of trusting what we already knew about how the image functions in art therapy, which is that images can contain a high degree of feeling and that instead of something being described it can be seen all at once in the image. For students to paint in the supervision session brings these elements into a live situation where they can be worked with in the service of further understanding of the patient.

## Effects of image making on the supervision process

In the supervision groups that were set aside for image making, art making occupies the first 30 minutes of a 90-minute session. When image making is undertaken in the supervision group, the students disperse from the group circle to collect their materials and then position themselves to start working. The way the students use the space, including where they place themselves in relation to the supervisor and each other, can be understood as part of a non-verbal communication.

Some students may work behind the supervisor, hidden from view; others put themselves in the supervisors' view or actually work at their feet. The forms of non-verbal communication can be acoustic such as banging, thumping, squishing, tearing. For example, one student spent 15 minutes rhythmically banging a paintbrush out of view of the supervisor. After a while, by reflecting on his emotional experience of the banging, the supervisor became aware of a potential rebelliousness in the student, which was confirmed later by discussion in the group. However, the supervisor did not communicate any of this until the rebelliousness appeared in the student's clinical work and was addressed within that context.

The circle is re-formed and the images are placed either inside or sometimes outside of the circle. This has a powerful visual impact because we are seeing all the images together. This is different from a verbal group where each student contributes by turns. Here we have the opportunity for all the students' contributions to be seen together, reflecting their individual preoccupations with the clinical work and showing how these preoccupations link and overlap in the group. The physical relationship of the images, including their overlapping and the colour relationships within the circle, can be seen as an unconscious communication of the group matrix (Foulkes 1975).

In one group a student's image of a long chute, with their patient at the end of the chute, was overlapping another student's image of a colourful emotionally imbued egg. The combination of the two read as a third image, which communicated something different and gave an impression of the experience of birth. This could then be reflected on by the group, and in relation to the patients of both students. These processes are often difficult to articulate verbally, but when they are made concretely visible in the artworks they can be realised, experienced emotionally and shared simultaneously.

One of the functions of an image is the way in which it can act as a receptacle for the individual's and the group's anxieties, and so it becomes a container. The image can help to hold anxiety so that it is no longer experienced only internally but is in part contained in the external image. Images made in the supervision groups can carry the dominant group experience. For example, during a group at the start of the academic year a student made an image of her car with the headlights on. She talked about her 80-mile journey to her placement and worried about whether her car was up to it. The car became a metaphor for the group as a container on a number of different levels and the students were able to share their own anxieties about starting their placements. This image reveals apprehension about the robustness of the group – to have its headlights on – to show them where they were going and not break down. Would they be able to get to where they wanted to go, in terms of becoming good enough art therapists? Thinking about the different levels of this metaphor led to a greater cohesiveness in the group. As well as being a preoccupation of an individual student, it also became an expression of the group's preoccupation. This experience was important in promoting the group's trust in the supervisory process. As well as being useful to the group in the process of supervision, image making is used by individuals to think about their relationships with their placements, as well as with their patients.

A clear example of a student using image making in order to gain greater understanding of a patient is seen through two images made about a female patient. The student had just started with this patient and was feeling stuck and was wondering whether it was because her other two patients were male and therefore for some reason she was finding the adjustment to a female patient disturbing. Her first image was of the figure of the patient. It was done in wax crayons. The second image was of how she, the student, was feeling when thinking about her patient. The image was dark, fluid, messy, colourful, using paint and charcoal. It was only when she put these two images side by side to look at and talk about them that the contrast became apparent. The cold blue colours of the figure and the superficiality of it contrasted with the interiority of the other image, and its darkness, warmth and messiness. Through discussion in the group the student was helped to understand that the difference in the two images related to two aspects of the patient. She therefore was able to gain insight into the fact that her stuck-ness was not about the gender issue, but about a lack of connection between the patient's internal and external worlds.

There is often resistance to looking at the countertransference. One student expressed reluctance about image making in the supervision session, saying that she had been so immersed in writing her case study that she could not face looking at the therapeutic relationship anymore. She said that she felt depleted and that it would be too draining to look at it again. The supervisor suggested that she could do an image based on feeling drained and depleted.

The image she produced was of a child's face with an adult's hand over its nose and mouth and she said that a song had been going through her head, repeating the words 'take my breath away'. The patient, who was a child, had continually tested the boundaries of sessions with difficult behaviour and the student talked in the group about feelings of control and anger. On further exploration it became clear that it was not so much a case of feeling so angry that she could kill him, but that she simply wanted him dead. This was linked to the hand over the face taking his breath away and suffocating him. If he were dead then he would not be able to do all these nasty things to her, which she could not tolerate anymore.

The acknowledgement of her countertransference was not only a relief to the student, but also enabled her to think about it as a role enactment (Sandler 1976), of wanting to get rid of him because he is too much. The image permitted the emergence of her hard-to-bear emotional experience. The student's familiarity with image making meant that she intuitively understood that it could both express and contain what was, perhaps, felt to be unutterable in words.

Within supervision, students may use the image-making process consciously to imitate the art-making process used by a patient in the therapy session in order to facilitate a more conscious and deeper understanding of the patient's communication and experience. For example, a student brought material from a session with a 7-year-old boy to supervision.

Sessions with this child were filled with frenetic activity resulting in a chaotic feeling that the student found difficult to make sense of. She decided to use her image-making process to mirror his activities with the art materials as she had recorded them in her process notes. The result was that she realised how absorbing the process was, how powerful it was and it then made her feel more connected to him. The student's final mirror image was like a puddle of water both in its shape and its ability to reflect its surroundings in the wet paint. When she had completed her image, she had needed to go to the lavatory. Before leaving the room she had moved her image to the supervisor's feet. Later during the discussion she explained how important it had been for her to leave the image in the supervisor's care, as it had not felt safe to leave it elsewhere in the room.

During the discussion time, the student shared with the group her experience of what had happened in the session with the child and what happened to her in the supervision session. The child's image had begun as a face with staring eyes. According to the child there had then been a storm, which had obliterated the face and then a volcano that obliterated the storm. As he spoke he over-painted. The over-painting had hidden the different stages of its evolution. The child had then asked her to cut around the resulting shape and was very particular as to how and where she cut.

Mirroring his activities through concrete actions enabled the student to make a conscious identification with her patient's experience in his sessions. The student's physical experience through this enactment put her in touch with the child's emotional experience. The child's doing things so quickly in the sessions had prevented her from making any connection with them, but having slowed them down in the supervision process she had been able to connect to his feelings.

The need for evacuation, which the student expressed in going to the lavatory, was linked through the discussion in the supervision group on how this boy had no experience of a person who could help him mediate his primitive feelings. His hyperactivity was seen as a defence against linking and engaging in relating. Similarly the obliterating of one powerful image after another in the layering, described above, was a series of attacks on linking (Bion 1967) that left the child feeling very anxious and frightened. The sense of needing to be safely held was expressed by the student in her leaving her completed image next to the supervisor for safekeeping.

The process of image making had revealed to her the child's experience of powerful feelings that emerged when trying to engage with another person. Contact with another person precipitated overwhelming feelings, which in the absence of an experience of containment could only be dealt with by obliteration. She had experienced this as a series of attacks in the session. With greater understanding of his process she was better enabled to find a way of working with him.

Transferences in the supervision group can appear in the form of images made by students when trying to explore their work with their patients. The supervisor's recognition of this and responding to it can act as a model to the students of how to deal with transference with their patients. For example, a student working with children in a women's refuge painted an abstract picture with the words 'Fuck off' written in large letters across it. She was trying to explore her difficulties with aggressive feelings in her group, which had been expressed by the children's swearing. In the supervision group another student pointed out that, had this happened in one of her groups, she would have understood this as a direct communication of strong feelings towards her. The supervisor then took this up with the group by saying 'What if someone here wants to tell me to fuck off?' and proceeded to talk about how difficult it can be to manage those kinds of aggressive feelings. By the supervisor bringing the possibility of aggression straight into the supervision group, it was modelled to the students that he could survive a hostile attack and that aggressive feelings could be managed in the therapeutic setting.

## Discussion

Earlier we referred to the intimate knowledge of the therapist's mind that was lost during the development of supervision when the supervisor was no longer the therapist's analyst. What became clear to us through the above examples is that there was an increase in the level of intimacy and trust when image making was used in the groups. This enabled better communication of the therapist's experience.

It is a familiar experience for art therapists to hear anxieties expressed about how using the art materials would cause everything in the art therapy room to go out of control. To begin with, this anxiety about boundaries, expressed as a fear that supervision would be experienced as therapy, was also experienced by students and supervisors in the groups.

However, we found that the image making increased both conscious and unconscious communications in the form of enactments. The enactments were expressed both by the art making and the concrete presence of the art objects. Instead of the image making causing the groups to lose the focus of supervision, and become therapy, we found that the work of supervision was enhanced and deepened because more information about the clinical work was made available.

The point is that using the art materials involves actions that may be understood as enactments. With hindsight and reflection about the enactment, things that are otherwise inexpressible can emerge and become known. The enactment results in an image that is made for the purposes of deepening the therapist's understanding of the patient. This means that the image provides meaningful links and information that would otherwise be unavailable for exploration in supervision. There are three elements to consider when using art making within supervision: the making, involving the use of materials; the content, which may refer to both individual concerns and group dynamics; and the product, including how we then look at and think about it.

When the engagement and interplay between materials and the unconscious are sufficiently deep, an embodied image may arise. An embodied image has the potential to contain and convey meaning that is not expressible in words. Schaverien, in writing about the embodied image, points out that 'in the process of its creation, feeling becomes live in the present and so the psychological state of the artist/client is transformed' (Schaverien 2000: 59). So in a sense the making of the image in supervision can, in varying degrees, facilitate transformation, enabling more thinking, which can then be used to inform clinical work.

When we are looking at the image we can think about different levels of looking. This may be looking at the patient's intrapsychic world, or the intersubjective relationship between patient and therapist, or the patient, therapist and supervisor. In the context of group supervision this may involve looking at group dynamics. The process of how we look at images is important. How do we allow the meaning that is contained in the visual image to form into thoughts in our mind? This requires the ability to engage in visual thinking. Visual thinking allows us to imaginatively enter into a more playful space. Art therapists have an affinity with finding the metaphors inherent in images through their artistic awareness. The metaphor enables links to be made and meaning to be discovered in the supervisory material.

When trying to understand the images, we take the process of their making into account. Although students are in a group, the images are made in isolation. Making an image involves an internal dialogue between what is out there (the art materials and the image) and their internal processes. This is both conscious and unconscious. Another important aspect is the immediacy of the image, which relates to aesthetics and the concreteness of the art materials. Maclagan (2001) defines aesthetic experience in terms of it being an embodied way of exploring the range of meanings that can be conveyed by a painting's material (aesthetic) properties. He says that the aesthetic experience is situated between the subjective and objective and he emphasises the bi-directionality operating within the field that viewing the picture creates. The field also has an inter-subjective aspect that concerns the communications, both conscious and unconscious, passing between patient and therapist. This bi-directionality on an inter-subjective level is what is actualised and brought alive by the supervisees making the images in the room with us.

There are also factors that exert a pull away from the supervisory task when image making is introduced. Boundaries can be challenged or eroded and one of the supervisor's tasks is to be mindfully aware of this. There is also the seductive nature of the art process and aesthetic qualities of the image that can result in losing the focus on the patient. What is important is the *thinking* that goes into trying to understand what the image is doing and how it is being used by the supervisee in the group. Images may, for example, be used defensively. This may be in an evacuative way or in ways that prevent thinking or to protect the supervisee from threats to self-esteem and exposure of vulnerability.

Image making as part of the supervision process can enhance the work by acting as a container for anxieties and the inexpressible. It can function as a metaphor for both individual and group processes and as a metaphor to reveal more of the patient's internal landscape. The unconscious group matrix can be visually represented by the relationship between images when they are placed on the floor.

## Conclusion

Supervision is a complex multi-layered process that occurs within a relationship, the aim of which is to support and enable the therapeutic work. Supervisor and supervisee participate together in a process, which includes thinking about and creative imagining around the supervisee's communication of an emotional experience originating in their clinical work. The necessary identifications inherent in the emotional experiences of the therapeutic encounter may disturb the therapist's own well-being. Supervisory interventions such as support, normalising and containing help to foster a safe learning environment and to cope with these disturbances. This enables recovery from the countertransference. Within supervision, raw clinical material is transformed into thoughts that can be used in the service of enriching therapeutic work with the patient. Group processes, including the unconscious group matrix, can, through parallel process, reflect the dynamics of the clinical material. Within an academic context there is a constant need to balance academic learning requirements with the supervisory purpose of the group.

When considering the history of art therapy supervision, art therapists have been supervised not only by art therapists but by practitioners from a range of other related fields. The patient's image has been used as a source of information in various ways, but the use of image making by art therapists in the service of improving their clinical work is rare. We found that the engagement with the materials, together with the resulting image, produced information that could be used to deepen the level of exploration of the supervisory material, providing greater access to the therapist's unconscious mind.

The difference between image making in a supervision group and an experiential art-making group may not seem very great. What differentiates it is the focus of the understanding of all the communications in the group in terms of the clinical work. The image has been made in the context of supervision; the transformed unconscious of the student can then be taken back and used in the service of the therapy.

The experience described in this chapter has been within the context of the training institution but could be seen to be addressing important issues relevant to art therapy supervision elsewhere. As Rees says, 'It seems sad that the power of image-making processes harnessed so effectively in therapeutic situations are not more regularly exploited as part of the art therapy supervisory scenario' (Rees 1998: 237). It seems so logical to use the tools of our profession in the supervisory process in order to deepen our understanding of our clinical work.

## Acknowledgements

We would like to thank the students for their contributions, our colleagues in the department and our families for their support.

## References

Bion, W. R. (1962) *Learning From Experience*, London: Heinmann.
Bion W. R. (1967) *Second Thoughts*, London: Heinmann.
Brown, C., Meyerowitz-Katz, J. and Ryde, J. (2003) 'Thinking with image making in supervision', *Inscape*, 8 (2): 71–78.
Casement, P. (1985) *On Learning from the Patient*, London: Routledge.
Casement, P. (1990) *Further Learning from the Patient: The Analytic Space and Process*, London: Tavistock, Routledge.
Dudley, J., Gilroy, A. and Skaife, S. (1998) 'Learning from experience in introductory art therapy groups', in S. Skaife and V. Huet (eds), *Art Therapy Groups: Between Pictures and Words*, London: Routledge, p. 201.
Edwards, D. (1993) 'Learning about feelings: the role of supervision in art therapy training', *The Arts in Psychotherapy*, 20: 213–222.
Ehrenzweig, A. (1967) *The Hidden Order of Art*, London: Paladin.
Foulkes, S. H. (1975) *Group Analytic Psychotherapy*, London: Gordon and Breach.
Gordon, R. (1992) 'Supervision', in *The Practice of Supervision: Some Contributions*, London: Conference of the British Association of Psychotherapists, pp. 2–6.
Henzell, J. (1997) 'The image's supervision', in G. Shipton (ed.), *Supervision of Psychotherapy and Counselling: Making a Place to Think*, Buckingham: Open University Press, pp. 74–77.
Hinshelwood, R. D. (1989) *A Dictionary of Kleinian Thought*, London: Free Association Books.
Jacobs, D., David, P. and Meyer, D. J. (1995) *The Supervisory Encounter: A Guide for Teachers of Psychodynamic Psychotherapy and Psychoanalysis*, New Haven: Yale University Press.
Maclagan, D. (1995) 'Fantasy and the aesthetic: have they become the uninvited guests at art therapy's feast?', *The Arts in Psychotherapy*, 22 (3): 217–221.

Maclagan, D. (1997) 'Fantasy, play and the image in supervision', in G. Shipton (ed.), *Supervision of Psychotherapy and Counselling: Making a Place to Think*, Buckingham: Open University Press, p. 68.

Maclagan, D. (2001) *Psychological Aesthetics: Painting, Feeling and Making Sense*, London: Jessica Kingsley.

Rees, M. (1998) *Drawing on Difference: Art Therapy with People who have Learning Difficulties*, London: Routledge.

Sandler, J. (1976) 'Countertransference and role responsiveness', *International Review of Psychoanalysis*, *3*: 43–47.

Schaverien, J. (2000) 'The triangular relationship and the aesthetic counter-transference in analytical art therapy', in A. Gilroy and G. McNeilly (eds), *The Changing Shape of Art Therapy: New Developments in Theory and Practice*, London: Jessica Kingsley, p. 59.

Schur, Y. (1998) 'The personal artistic process of the art therapist as a basis for supervision', *International Journal of Art Therapy*, *4*: 32–36.

Searles, H. F. (1955) 'The informational value of the supervisors emotional experiences', in *Collected Papers on Schizophrenia and Related Subjects*, London: Maresfield Library (1986 edition), pp. 157–176.

Shipton, G. (1997) *Supervision of Psychotherapy and Counselling: Making a Place to Think*, Buckingham: Open University Press.

Yalom, I. D. (1970) *The Theory and Practice of Group Psychotherapy*, New York: Basic Books.

Winnicott, D. W. (1971) *Playing and Reality*, London, Tavistock Publications.

# Part III

# Purposes and challenges in supervision and research

# Chapter 11

# Agency and attention
## Purposes of supervision

*Chris Wood*

## Introduction

In a paper entitled 'In the aftermath of violence' about counsellors working in post-war Kosovo I found this:

> The counsellors are often stopped on the street and in the shops, with people wanting advice, to talk or cry. Unavoidably they are part of the community, and yet their roles caste them somewhat outside, into an expert position. Surrounded by tremendous suffering, initially, the staff decided that the centres needed to be open all the time . . . as the impact of the work became increasingly overwhelming, this could not be sustained. It was a struggle to recognise that caring for others over such a sustained period of time required caring for oneself as a counsellor . . . Supervision was established, because of resource issues it was largely peer based although this has caused strain and a supervisor has been appointed . . .
>
> (Altschuler, Agnoli, Halitaj and Jasiqi 2002: 286)

This makes some of the purposes of clinical supervision starkly apparent. We need help from supervision to sustain our capacity to think, to give attention and yet not be overwhelmed by the plight of our clients. When supervision is working it seems to help us as practitioners sustain a sense of our agency. It can also remind us of the benefits of standing back a little in order to pay attention in ways that can be different from the times we are actually with clients. In supervision it is possible to ponder and free associate.

I discuss how I think that art psychotherapy supervision shares many of the features of other forms of supervision, and I interweave my discussion with ideas about aspects of supervisory practice that are particular or peculiar to art psychotherapy.

To describe supervision when it is flourishing is to describe a good working relationship, in which both supervisor and supervisee have something to learn and something to contribute. Its purpose is the care of both client and therapist. It can enable a therapist to be aware of how they take care of themselves and yet still retain a lively attention for the needs of their clients. These two aspects of the relationship are vital and often causally connected.

Throughout the profession's history British art therapists have been pragmatic about the theoretical models that inform their practice. This is something they share with most professionals. In the current climate in which health and social care service purchasers are being strongly influenced by research evidence, the development of the profession may well depend on such pragmatism. Currently the majority of art therapists use analytical perspectives (without thinking themselves to be analysts) for understanding many of the details of the therapeutic relationship and the less conscious aspects of human experience. I think that this is due to a number of factors that involve a longer discussion than is possible here. However, it is relevant that for centuries artists have intimated that there are areas of human experience that are mysterious and slip below the surface of conscious experience and analytical theories (unlike others underpinning therapeutic work) do theorise the unconscious.

Art therapy sits at the intersection of many different theoretical approaches and the resulting eclecticism can sometimes seem difficult to justify; but this very eclectic nature of the use of theory may mean that it is easier to find or produce relevant research evidence. In the present economic climate it seems beholden on supervisors in all professions to understand the political pressure on practitioners and help them find both the necessary pragmatism and coherence with which to defend their practice. However, the emotional weightiness of much therapeutic work in the public sector can mean that theory and research are not the dominant considerations.

## The circumstances of some lives

Matters in the public sector in this country are not as stark as those in post-war countries, but aspects of the work are grim because of the levels of poverty, deprivation and uncertainty that many therapists encounter in the lives of their clients. Public sector clients young and old are likely to have difficult lives in difficult circumstances. They are often struggling economically and psychologically. Sometimes it might be hard for therapists to believe that therapy can make a difference. I continue to believe that the work is helpful, but understand and have sometimes experienced similar failures of confidence when hearing about the sad conditions of the lives of some clients. When a supervisory relationship *works* it can help.

In supervision attention to the relationship between therapist and client is the fundamental, but it is important to remember that, in addition to deprivation in the lives of clients, pressure on resources in the public sector can interfere with the attention a therapist can give. This makes it harder for them to know that the quality of their attention for the client will be of substantial value. Another increasing pressure, certainly on therapy trainees, is the high cost of training in terms of fees, training therapy and travel to placements. Most students, even full time students, now have to work while training.

Repeatedly the people I am supervising speak about the circumstances of the work setting and of their clients' lives. The environment in which therapy takes place seems to me to be properly part of the focus of supervision. I know that this is not a universally held view and that a small number of proponents of an analytical perspective might not agree, thinking that to 'dwell' on 'reality factors' (Shipton 1997: 2) is a weakness. It seems to me rather that it is a weakness not to allow for the constant interplay between internal and external realities. However, I acknowledge that sometimes when the environment is difficult this has meant that a lot of supervision time has been taken up with institutional issues. When this has happened, after acknowledging the importance of the setting, I encourage the supervisee back to focusing on the *details* of a session. This change in focus can provide perspective on what is needed from the environment and it can contribute to the supervisee's understanding of how it is possible to contain the therapeutic work in the circumstances that exist.

## Thinking about what makes supervision flourish

The practice of supervision is the central method for maintaining thought in the work. It is working when the relationship feels safe enough to enable the supervisee to explore the emotional interchange between themselves and their client. A sense of safety is very important because it is not always easy to acknowledge the impact of transference and countertransference feelings. Whereas when supervision feels safe enough it seems possible to day-dream and mull-over what is seen in the artwork and what is felt in the relationship.

In Sweden training courses for clinical supervisors are possibly the most developed in the world. They have been tried and tested in practice and some research during a 30-year period. They combine analytical and pedagogic ideas. A summary of the aims of these supervision courses is helpful:

- to form a learning alliance with supervisees;
- to focus on mutual influential interaction between patient and supervisee as well as between supervisee and supervisor;
- to recognize the presence and effect of parallel processes;
- to increase the dexterous use of theory and technique and the capacity for self-reflection and evaluation;

- to encourage the interest for and experience with tentative and explicit formulations, about the ongoing analytic process, and to recognize transference and counter-transference reactions;
- to formulate educational diagnoses, attempting continuously to evaluate the supervisee's difficulties and problems, related both to the lack of knowledge and of skill and to a defensive warding off of information;
- to recognize the influence and impact of the supervisor's own idiosyncrasies and countertransference reactions on the supervisory process.

(Szecsödy 1997: 113–114)

The Swedish courses are designed to counter the idea that supervision skill is an automatic by-product of therapeutic experience. Such therapeutic skill needs to be coupled with an understanding of how people learn (i.e. to couple therapeutic skills with pedagogic understanding). Again this seems to point to the need to be able to navigate backwards and forwards between internal and external experience. Sometimes the assumption is made that it is possible to move from the role of experienced therapist to supervisor without making the changes necessary in order to assume a different role. This can lead to one of the pitfalls in which supervision seems more like therapy for the supervisee and not supervision. In contrast, when it is working well supervision can enable the supervisee to sustain their sense of agency (a sense of their capacity to act) within their therapeutic practice; this is likely to mirror the possibilities for the client's sense of agency within the therapeutic relationship.

Jonathan Pedder (1986) discusses some of the general principles of supervision. He describes a spectrum between education and psychotherapy and then considers how different forms of supervision are positioned (according to the needs of the supervisee). In this paper (1986) Pedder cites Fleming's description of three models of both teaching and supervision as the jug, the potter and the gardener. Pedder reminds us that we take supervisees from where they are and that most already have considerable background experience of working with people.

They are not empty vessels into whom we pour from a jug; not inert lumps of clay to be fashioned after our own image. We are facilitators; gardeners, accepting the plants that spring up in our gardens and doing what we can by pruning.

(Pedder 1986: 2)

The gardening model is helpful. Gardeners tend the soil, they weed, plant, water and watch things grow and then maybe they prune. They also learn from gardening and they take pleasure in it. All of this is play of the highest quality. Pedder paraphrases Winnicott (1971) and suggests that supervision takes place in the overlap of two areas of play: that of the therapist and the supervisor. He also suggests that the aim of supervision is the 'internalisation of some self-sustaining agency' (p. 4), again paraphrasing Winnicott, suggesting that the capacity to work alone as a therapist is based on the experience of 'being alone' in the presence of someone, i.e. the supervisor. This made me think back to one adult who did that for me as a child and of another who did that for me as a supervisor when I first began working as a therapist. In some ways these are simple memories (although they have deep histories) that help me think about the work of helping supervisees remember, or restore the husbandry with which to nurture their internal resources and their agency for the work. I think we all need some personal ways of making sense of what we are trying to do as a supervisor.

## Opening contracts

I am increasingly convinced that agreeing a contract at the outset can provide a helpful frame for supervision, because it can free the therapist from having to negotiate, at a later more complicated stage, what can be uncomfortable aspects of power and institutional dynamics. Complicated processes of attunement between the therapist and supervisor mean it is not easy to predict whether or not there will be a 'fit' between supervisor and supervisee until the supervisory process begins; this is something that can be acknowledged and allowed for in the opening contract. If any power imbalance can be honestly acknowledged this may lead to parallel understanding of how the therapist might empower their client. Once this opening contract in the form of focus and a timescale for the external aspects of supervisory work are agreed, it can facilitate the therapist on an internal level and enable them to keep thinking.

When a supervisee is in training there is less room for manoeuvre in the opening contract, because there is less likelihood of changing supervisor (as a result of staff availability on training courses and also a finite number of placement settings). This might mean that supervision arrangements on training courses are constrained by available structures and also by the power imbalance that arises from the requirement for assessment of the supervisee.

## Being streetwise

However, my impression is that when trainees first begin placements in the public sector they are often shocked by the extent of client-need that they encounter. This means that the power imbalance in their supervisory relationships is unlikely, at least initially, to be their predominant concern. In a paper entitled with an implicit question, *Between Collusion and*

*Control*, Gertrud Mander discusses some of the functions of supervision for a trainee therapist in uncompromising terms:

> If it wasn't for supervision, trainees might disintegrate, go mad, get lost in the maze of new impressions, or panic for lack of sufficient capacity to take in, process and assimilate all they are confronted with.
>
> (Mander 2002: 41)

She continues by suggesting that the interconnected trinity of personal therapy, supervision and clinical practice during the training is designed to enable a trainee to enter the profession having acquired a sense of equilibrium. I think of this as acquiring the capacity to steadily navigate backwards and forwards between internal and external experience. As time passes and a therapist gains experience, supervision is unlikely be the element needed to prevent them going 'mad', but it still provides a significant contribution to maintaining their psychological health. I think it does this by supporting the therapist's sense of their own agency and by helping the therapist maintain aspects of an analytical (or symbolic) attitude in containing .what may be painful and conflicted communication from the client. The psychological health of the therapist directly influences the quality of the containment they are able to provide for their clients. This last point is importantly in the interests of the client, who at the very least needs a therapist who is psychologically streetwise, able to take care of themselves and retain the capacity to think about what is projected on to them. Although not written in a manner that intended an exclusively psychological agenda, this last point is implicit in the standards of proficiency issued by the Health Professions Council, in which there is an injunction for therapists to monitor their own health (HPC 2003: SOP 1a7).

The idea of a psychologically streetwise therapist as someone able to retain thought in the face of powerful projections is relevant for all forms of psychotherapy and its supervision. Maybe it is particularly pertinent in those situated in the public sector, where many factors compete for attention and make it harder to think. In the past art therapy educators might well have supported ideas that came from treatment philosophies that were rightly concerned to avoid labelling: in these the therapist was urged to meet the client first before reading their notes. Now to give this advice would be seen as unwise or even folly, because the public sector is the recipient of some of the most troubled in our society. Although incidents are rare there have been tragic consequences for some therapists (from a range of professions, including the arts therapies) who met clients before reading notes in an attempt to be unencumbered by the perceptions of other staff and so they had not known of warnings (e.g. Prins 2002). This means that it is not only helpful but necessary for a therapist to know about *what is happening on the street*, who they are going to meet and who else in the multi-disciplinary team is available to the client and to them as the therapist. Consequently it is harder now for a therapist to have first impressions. They are likely to be in receipt of a range of other people's impressions before they meet the client, so one of the supervisor's tasks may be to help the therapist be aware of how what they already knew influenced the first meeting. This is rarely straight-forward and it is further complicated by the need for the supervisor and therapist alike to be alive to the responsibilities of child protection.

Art therapy or art psychotherapy sits *in between* psychotherapy and psychiatry, between an internal and an external focus, because of its position within public sector health and social care (Wood 2001b). The profession's historical lineage (in common with other mental health pro-fessions) reaches back to Pinel's removal of the chains from mental patients during the French Revolution. It passes through 'Moral Treatment' in the nineteenth century and Social Psychiatry in the twentieth, both demon-strably effective methods of treatment built on the belief that to treat patients with respect is beneficial (Warner 1985; Wood 2001). This import-antly reminds us of the need for respect within a supervisory relationship, because it is a tap root from which much else can grow. I find it surprising that sometimes as supervisors we lose sight of the simple understanding that when the supervisee feels respected they are more likely to feel they can maintain respect for their clients.

## Particular issues in art psychotherapy supervision

Within the art therapy profession, theory and practice have developed by joining ideas about the power of expression, social psychiatry and psycho-therapy (Wood 2001a, 2007). These ideas broadly represent the different forms of attention that art therapy supervisees need to link together (with differing degrees of emphasis) when thinking about their work with clients. Knowledge of historical lineage and of the later influence of psychoanalysis is significant to art therapy and its supervision because it throws light on discussions about when aesthetic, psychotherapeutic or social-psychiatric sensibilities are helpful in relationships with clients (Wood 2001a, 2005).

It seems to me that the profession has been strengthened by each period of its history and that the most effective practice occurs when there is an integration of what has been learnt in the different periods of its develop-ment. Because of the range of theories used in art therapy I think theor-etical integration is more feasible than synthesis: but this does not have to mean integration without some underlying coherence and linking of ideas. One area in which coherence and linking are now particularly important involves helping supervisees to carefully consider the relevance of available research to their practice. The profession is unlikely to survive in the public sector, unless the mounting requirement for evidence of effectiveness is acknowledged. Supervisors, if they respond appropriately, can help supervisees work with the inevitable anxiety this creates.

As already indicated a British art therapist is likely to have been educated by a range of theories. They will have a clear understanding of the therapeutic frame, a notion of the unconscious, of working in the transference and of theories about art: but surrounding these fundamentals is a wide theoretical field upon which they may draw. This includes the need to acknowledge the 'real' circumstances of client lives, although primarily they will be thinking about the relationship with the client or groups of clients and how the art-making sits within those relationships. Also the majority of courses are beginning to help students understand the issues concerning research evidence.

What they need of a supervisor, given that the majority of art therapists working in the NHS do not receive clinical supervision from another art therapist,[1] is someone who will consider the combination of elements in their work with benign regard and some understanding. What they do not need (they have this in common with all therapists) is an overly prescriptive approach, which will not help them develop their own sense of agency and style and may be experienced as persecutory. However, it is important that supervisors of art therapists are interested in the artwork and do not see it as a distraction from the therapeutic relationship.

At the beginning of the work with a client, the art therapist needs to think about how they introduce the possibility of making art. Enabling the client to use art making to tell their story requires an intuitive attention to what might help the client begin to link the external activity of art making with their inner experience. It could be helpful to ask the client about how they used to paint and draw as a child or how they used to play (Wood 1986). It may also be helpful to show the client some art materials or to show them the possible uses of a journal or scrapbook for writings, sketches, colours or collage. A small book carried around can be a personal collecting place for the raw material and inspiration for art making.

The therapist's verbatim note keeping of early sessions could be useful to their thinking with the supervisor about enabling the client to begin and to develop their art making. Verbatim notes might be used at intervals to ensure that accuracy and detail are part of the supervision. It may also be helpful if the supervisee makes some art as a form of reflexive or reflective practice: reflexive in the sense of thinking about the impact of the work upon the therapist and their influence in the therapeutic relationship; and reflecting (as in a mirror) in the sense of what takes place in therapy.

Partly because supervision time is limited, reflexive and reflective practice in the form of art making is usually done in parallel with the supervision session, and the artwork is taken to supervision but not made during the time of supervision itself. This parallel making of art as a form of reflexive or reflective practice also safeguards the boundaries of supervision: making art during supervision might tend towards supervision seeming like therapy. The supervisee's art making with their client in mind can facilitate a day-dreaming sort of reverie, which might enable them to think less logically about their client and maybe notice unconsidered aspects of what is happening in their therapeutic relationship. This can be a valuable source of insight, whether at the beginning or part-way through a relationship. Geraldine Johnson, an art therapist explaining the value of this to her own sense of containment in the work, said to me, 'sometimes making an image with the client in mind is sufficient' (Johnson 2005, personal communication; see Chapter 10 for a fuller discussion of this).

Looking at the artwork made by the client is a distinctive part of art therapy supervision. The different ways in which the profession's literature has commented on this part of its supervision are interesting.

## Combining attention for the art and the relationship in supervision

Attempts to polarise aspects of the profession's development by setting aesthetic sensibilities against those needed for understanding the therapeutic relationship seem to me to be unhelpful. John Henzell's paper 'Art as an ally in therapy' is an example of this tendency to polarise aspects of the work:

> No less than psychiatry, psychotherapy immerses itself in a clinical language and ambience . . . How extraordinary that such an originally, *a*-clinical activity as art therapy should now ape all this.
>
> (Henzell 1994: 75)

He cites what he sees as a rogue's gallery of offenders, Freud, Jung, Milner, Naumberg, Neumann, Schaverien and Winnicott.

> Now while the authors I have cited . . . have much to say that is germane to pictorial imagery in and out of art therapy and psycho-therapy, the pertinence of this is blunted by the all-encompassing nature of their psychodynamic focus.
>
> (Henzell 1994: 77)

There may well be a struggle for emphasis, with injunctions to ourselves not to let aesthetic sensibilities be lost to psychotherapeutic ones, or to avoid letting contextual knowledge dominate attention given to a client's internal world; but it is confusing to polarise aspects of the work and set them against one another. What we often need in practice and what we are generally doing in supervision is looking for ways of combining and inte-grating what we know, with the client in mind. Dave Edwards seems to be referring to this aspect of the work as it affects the supervision of trainee art therapists, but what he writes has general relevance:

> The struggle to integrate seemingly complex and contradictory theories, together with difficult or powerful emotional responses to patients, institutions or unresolved internal conflicts may be experienced as threatening to overwhelm the beginning art therapist.
>
> (Edwards 1993: 214)

I think John Henzell's papers (1994, 1997) *protest too much* in their efforts to describe client images as uniquely instructive. His account makes the function of the client image in supervision seem almost like that of a psychic telepath: with the artefact used like a piece of cloth from a crime scene. Whereas he sees written notes, or tape recordings as 'reports of absent events' (Henzell 1997: 71) and therefore distorted, he sees artwork made in a therapy session as uniquely intact. 'A painting, drawing or sculpture made in therapy . . . are part of the very tissue of the session; through them the event itself survives as a material object' (Henzell 1997: 71). He points to the real problems of memory distorting what happens in therapy sessions, but suggests that 'the image remains as the mute witness and embodiment of an intention' (Henzell 1997: 75). I find it hard to imagine how it is possible to understand artwork made by a client without knowing something of the relationship with them; just as I cannot imagine understanding a dream without some reference or relationship to the dreamer. I recognise that Henzell wants to present a polemic against what he sees as the profession's over-reliance upon psychotherapeutic under-standing of the therapeutic relationship at the expense of its understanding of the artefact, but I do not understand why it should be assumed that aesthetic sensibilities preclude those for the relationship. He makes a much more powerful explanation for the power of the image when he is not using his clear aesthetic sensibilities in the service of an argument with psychotherapy:

> The image is isomorphic with our experience because it refers so directly to it while defying any easy paraphrase in words – it must be painstakingly translated . . . the image in the form of drawings, paintings or sculpture, presents us with the explicit challenge to this translation of what may appear ineffable, but which so exemplifies our psychological life.
>
> (Henzell 1997: 77)

This makes the place of images or artefacts in supervision much clearer. They may be isomorphic with the experience of the client, but they still present a challenge to translation. I think that the therapeutic relationship is intrinsic to the translation and the work of supervision is to facilitate the translation.

## Day-dreaming and mulling things over

The art therapist David Maclagan makes the case for working with fantasy in supervision:

> It also gives a kind of permission for the supervisee's less rational responses to be admitted and find a home. This is not a mere letting-off of steam, though the safety-valve factor is important; it is a valuable source of information. The image or the associative pattern a person or a situation gives rise to doesn't just tell us about how we see them; it makes a more objective contribution.
>
> (Maclagan 1997: 67)

He quotes Guggenbühl-Craig:

> To encounter a person creatively means to weave fantasies around him, to circle around his potential. Various images arise about the person and the potential relationship to him. Such creative fantasies are often quite far removed from so-called reality; they are as unreal, and as true, as fairy tales or myths. They use imaginative images to grasp the reality of the other person.
>
> (Guggenbühl-Craig 1971: 45)

Much of what Maclagan writes about fantasy is reminiscent of Philip Mollon's discussion of thinking in supervision being helped by 'mulling things over' in a day-dreaming sort of way:

> There are some simple techniques for helping a supervisee shift into a more free-associative, right-brain mode of thinking; for example, inviting them to talk about their experience of the patient, their feelings in response to the patient's behaviour etc. Often this will dramatically shift a flat surface discourse into a richly affectively illuminating exploration. With some supervisors it is an ongoing task to counter the tendency to use supervision not as a space for thinking, but for unburdening – in Bion's terms, the use of the mind as an evacuative muscle rather than as an organ for thinking.
>
> (Mollon 1997: 31)

*Ironically if supervision becomes a place of flat surface reporting it does not even help with unburdening*, whereas working with or 'playing with' the interplay between the internal and the external is what seems to help. I personally think that the strong focus of analytical theories on ways of navigating this interplay provides another explanation of the attraction of British art therapy to analytical ideas. However, Maclagan makes a legitimate case for widening our understanding beyond what he sees as the confines of an analytical frame. I agree in thinking that with the difficulties some clients face there can be a need to be pragmatic and modify the therapeutic method. There are a number of client difficulties that respond to a modified or different therapeutic method. Mollon (1998), for example, asserts that psychoanalytic psychotherapy is not the appropriate method for working with people who are traumatised. Papadopoulos (2002) suggests that 'therapeutic care' informed by psychotherapeutic insights but not therapy might be the most appropriate form of work for some refugees. Similarly psychotherapeutic work with people who have experienced psychotic episodes needs to be adapted. Brief-work models and cognitive approaches might be the most appropriate for some clients in some circumstances. These considerations about the most helpful approach to a client's difficulties are relevant to supervision with all therapists. Such modifications do not remove the central need in supervision with art therapists to find ways of linking ideas about the form of the relationship with those about any art made.

Schaverien's book *The Revealing Image* (1991) is concerned with a detailed exploration of the ways in which artefacts made in therapy sit within the therapeutic relationship. One passage in particular acts like a cipher for showing this in relation to supervision:

> I have noted that when I wish to discuss a picture which has been made by a client with a colleague or a supervisor, I sometimes find that my interest in the picture is not always understood by the other. My colleague does not always perceive the picture as I do. I may see the picture as extremely 'good' in some way, but my colleague sees the picture as merely a 'not very good picture'. Sometimes it may be faint marks on paper in which the lack of artistic ability is evident, and yet I see something else; the picture is animated for me by the context of the relationship in which it was made.
>
> (Schaverien 1992: 152)

This explains the potency of the relationship in therapy. In her opening line to a paper concerning active imagination Schaverien writes: 'Active imagination, like transference mobilizes the psyche' (2005: 127). This underlines how powerfully the spark of life in therapy originates within the therapeutic relationship. Much international research shows that the therapeutic bond or alliance, no matter what form of therapy being used, is closely related to a positive outcome (e.g. meta-review by Horvarth and Symonds 1991). Schaverien's work has been concerned throughout to find ways of theorising and enmeshing any art made within the therapeutic relationship. I think she manages to do this in a manner that does not polarise the aesthetic or the relationship and this careful weighing is the kind of attention needed.

## Conclusion

In this chapter I have been making the case for supervision, which facilitates the different forms of attention that have emerged from a profession's history. In art therapy I think this involves doing whatever possible to help the supervisee in their linking of ideas about art making, the relationship and the circumstances of the client's life.

In her student paper on supervision the art therapist Kristen Bolton included a series of images by the painter Salvador Dali. The painting 'Couple with their heads full of clouds' (1936) suggests a helpful way of visually conceiving the supervisory relationship. It acts like visual poetry in suggesting the mutually internal nature of much work in supervision. The painting also seems to imply the echoes in supervision relationships of those in therapy.

When an image is brought to supervision it seems to be helpful to encourage a time of quiet attention in looking at the image before speaking. It is also important to recall and hold in mind the client's demeanour, the feeling of their interaction and the circumstances of their lives. The words from a song 'second that emotion' have floated into my head and I think that this is because the phrase partly describes what we are about in supervision: we are cultivating thoughtful attention, which is something like *aesthetic criticism with feeling* for both the art and the relationship.

## Note

1   The trade union then known as 'Manufacturing, Science and Finance' (MSF) and now known as 'Amicus' reported in 1990 that only 29.3% of art therapists working in the NHS had supervision with an art therapist and unfortunately from what I hear from colleagues, in my regional group and nationally, this situation has not much changed in the intervening period.

## References

Altschuler, J., Agnoli, M., Halitaj, M. and Jasiqi, I. (2002) 'In the aftermath of violence', in R. Papadopoulos (ed.), *Therapeutic Care for Refugees and Asylum Seekers: No Place Like Home*, Tavistock Clinic Series, London: Karnac Books, pp. 271–291.

Edwards, D. (1993) 'Learning about feelings: the role of supervision in art therapy training', *The Arts in Psychotherapy*, 20: 213–222.

Guggenbühl-Craig, A. (1971) *Power in the Helping Professions*, Dallas, TX: Spring Publications.

Health Professions Council (2003) *Standards of Proficiency: Arts Therapies*, 034/ SOP/AS/A5 July 2003. www.hpc-uk.org

Henzell, J. (1994) 'Art as an ally in therapy', in J. Laing and P. Byrne (eds), *Starting from Scratch: Proceedings of the first Scottish International Art Therapy Conference*, Edinburgh: Edinburgh Press, pp. 73–83.

Henzell, J. (1997) 'The image's supervision', in G. Shipton (ed.), *Supervision of Psychotherapy and Counselling: Making a Place to Think*, Buckingham: Open University Press, pp. 71–78.

Horvarth, A. O. and Symonds, B. D. (1991) 'Relation between working alliance and outcome in psychotherapy: a meta-analysis', *Journal of Consulting and Clinical Psychology*, *38*: 139–149.

Maclagan, D. (1997) 'Fantasy, play and the image in supervision', in G. Shipton (ed.), *Supervision of Psychotherapy and Counselling: Making a Place to Think*, Buckingham: Open University Press, pp. 61–70.

Mander, G. (2002) 'Between control and collusion', in C. Driver and E. Martin (eds), *Supervision Psychotherapy: Psychoanalytic and Psychodynamic Perspectives*, London: Sage, pp. 40–50.

Mollon, P. (1997) 'Supervision as a space for thinking', in G. Shipton (ed.), *Supervision of Psychotherapy and Counselling: Making a Place to Think*, Buckingham: Open University Press, pp. 24–34.

Mollon, P. (1998) *Remembering Trauma: A Psychotherapist's Guide to Memory and Illusion*, London: Wiley (reprinted in 2002 by Whurr publishers).

Papadopoulos, R. (2002) *Therapeutic Care for Refugees and Asylum Seekers: No Place Like Home*, London: Karnac Books.

Pedder, J. (1986) 'Reflections on the theory and practice of supervision', *Psychoanalytic Psychotherapy*, *2* (1): 1–12.

Prins, H. (2002) 'Risk assessment: still a risky business', *The British Journal of Forensic Practice*, *4* (1): 3–8.

Schaverien, J. (1991) *The Revealing Image: Analytical Art Psychotherapy in Theory and Practice*, London: Routledge.

Schaverien, J. (2005) 'Art, dreams and active imagination: a post-Jungian approach to transference and the image', *Journal of Analytical Psychology*, *50*: 127–153.

Shipton, G. (1997) 'Introduction', in G. Shipton (ed.), *Supervision of Psychotherapy and Counselling: Making a Place to Think*, Buckingham: Open University Press, pp. 1–7.

Szecsödy, I. (1997) 'Is learning possible in supervision?', in B. Martindale, M. Morner, M. E. C. Rodriguez and J.-P. Vidit (eds), *Supervision and its Vicissitudes*, London: Karnac Books, pp. 101-116.

Warner, R. (1985) *Recovery from Schizophrenia: Psychiatry and Political Economy*, London: Routledge.

Winnicott, D. (1971) *Playing and Reality*, London: Tavistock.

Wood, C. (1986) 'Milk white panic: what do we do to people when we ask them to paint and draw?', *Inscape, Winter*: 2–8.

Wood, C. (2001a) 'Art, psychotherapy and psychosis: the nature and the politics of art therapy', Unpublished PhD thesis, held in the library of University of Sheffield.

Wood, C. (2001b) 'The significance of studios', *Inscape*, 5 (2): 41–53.

Wood, C. (2007) 'The evolution of art therapy in relation to psychosis and poverty', in A. Gilroy (ed.), *Art Therapy, Research and Evidence-based Practice*, Vol. 2, London: Sage Publications.

Chapter 12

# Working with ambivalence in the clinical supervision of art therapists

*Katherine Killick*

## Background

I have been supervising the clinical practice of art therapists since 1986, when I began to manage the art therapy service at what was then Hill End Hospital in St Albans. My clinical work within that adult psychiatric service is described in various papers and chapters in books (Killick 1991, 1993, 1996, 2000; Killick and Greenwood 1995; Killick and Schaverien 1997). I had established and developed my interest in art therapy as an approach to psychosis by the time I began to employ the understanding that I had gained in a supervisory capacity. My own experience of psychoanalytic supervision has been ongoing since 1980. This has been an integral part of my clinical work as an art therapist, and continues to be so in my work as an analyst.

Throughout this chapter I will be writing about supervision that is psychoanalytic in nature. I use this term in the general sense currently employed by the British Psychoanalytic Council, which includes the disciplines of psychoanalysis, psychoanalytic psychotherapy, Jungian analysis and analytical psychotherapy. Psychoanalytic supervision has been crucial in enabling me to think about the issues involved in working with regressed states of mind. My clinical approach, both to patients and to supervisees, has been further informed by my training and experience as a Jungian analyst with the Society of Analytical Psychology (SAP). This training has enabled me to become increasingly conscious of, and confident in, the psychoanalytic approach to clinical material that I had previously followed intuitively as an art therapist, both to patients and to supervisees. I remain particularly interested in regressed states of mind, and in the varying meanings of concretised transactions within the analytical relationship, both with patients and with supervisees. In this chapter I am concerned with the particular issue of ambivalence when it manifests as a defence against creative regression in supervision. The confidentiality issues involved in publishing material relevant to this issue are complex. I have decided to limit my presentation of clinical material to an example from my own experience as a supervisee, and to present the issue, as I have encountered it in my role as a supervisor, in generalised terms.

I commented in one paper that I wrote about working with psychotic anxieties and defences in art therapy (1996, reprinted 1997): 'In my experience of both working in these areas and working with students and supervisees, the therapist's faith in the process can be subtly eroded by countertransference feelings of despair and futility'. Unconscious despair is a kind of force field that exerts a similarly warping effect on supervision, defensively aiming to minimise its effectiveness in helping the patient into the dreaded states of relatedness and dependence. This paper is an attempt to understand the ambivalence, and underlying despair, that I find myself processing with some art therapists seeking supervision with me. Remaining of lasting interest to me are those supervisory relationships in which ambivalence can be understood within the context of the patient's transference to the therapist, because it is in this context that the containing function of supervision has meaning. The work of Harold Searles in particular, drawn from his experiences of working with profound ambivalence in patients, both as an analyst and as a supervisor, has helped to illuminate my efforts to understand.

## The nature of psychoanalytic supervision

Supervision is an integral part of training and working as a psychotherapist within each of the schools of psychotherapy, psychoanalysis and analytical psychology that meet the criteria of the British Psychoanalytic Council. The theory and practice of art therapy are deeply rooted in the theory and practice of psychotherapy, and the principles of training and developing as an art therapist are related to those in the wider context of psychotherapy. The wider context of the theory and practice of psychoanalytic supervision has been elaborated in the collections of papers edited by Martindale *et al.* (1997), Wiener *et al.* (2003) and Driver and Martin (2005).

At its most creative, the supervisory relationship functions along the lines described in a recent paper by Ogden (2005), as '. . . an experience in which the supervisor attempts to help the supervisee dream the elements of his experience with the patient that the analyst has previously been only partially able to dream . . . or has been almost entirely unable to dream . . .'. Acknowledging his stance to be within the tradition of Bion, Ogden describes dreaming as 'the unconscious psychological work that the individual does (both while asleep and in waking life) with his lived emotional experience'. Bion (1970) has described the attitude to emotional experience that fosters work of this kind. He writes 'The success of psycho-analysis depends on the maintenance of a psycho-analytic point of view; the point of view is the psycho-analytic vertex; the psycho-analytic vertex is O'. Bion's 'O' denotes '. . . that which is the ultimate reality represented by terms such as ultimate reality, absolute truth, the godhead, the infinite, the thing-in-itself'. He describes the attitude which maintains this point of view as one of 'faith': '. . . that there is an ultimate reality and truth – the unknown, unknowable, "formless infinite"'.

Yorke (2005) expands Bion's thinking in relation to supervision. He writes: 'The psychic dimension is irrational and access to it in supervision requires skills with intuitive and irrational methods of working. It is this aspect of supervision – that is, the irrational aspects of the experience with the supervisee – which are the "royal road" to the exhibition of O as the supervisory object. Its unknowable truth, and ultimate reality, is not accessible merely in the reconstruction'. He gives a lively and detailed account of one example of the way that this happened within a supervision session. The supervisee's fantasy of an egg mayonnaise sandwich within her session with the patient, which was reported to the supervisor, was informed, in the supervisor's mind, by the supervisor's fleeting memory of a dog being made to drink coffee. His understanding of the link between the two enabled him to work with the supervisee's reported fantasy in a way that enabled the supervisory dyad to access a deeper understanding of addictive elements within the patient's material.

It is generally accepted that emotional experiences occurring within the supervisor–therapist dyad resonate with those occurring within the patient–therapist dyad, and inform the supervisory process, as in Yorke's example. Searles (1955) describes this resonance as 'the reflection process' and it is commonly referred to as 'parallel process'. However, not all experiences within supervision can be attributed to the patient. Grinberg (1997) reminds us that psychological components in the supervisee and in the supervisor can contribute as well, and the supervisor's task is to try to sort out which experiences belong in which context, and to respond appropriately.

## Theoretical approach to art therapy supervision

My colleague Joy Schaverien has followed a similar path to mine, having trained both as an art therapist and as a SAP analyst. Her book *The Revealing Image* (1992) was and continues to be a seminal work in relation to the theory of art therapy practice. In this work, Schaverien presents us with a coherent and systematic way of thinking about the meaning of images and the way they are related to within an analytical relationship in art therapy. She elaborates the process of 'analytical differentiation' that is central to the work of any psychoanalytic relationship, and identifies the particular nature of this process when making art objects, relating to art objects and disposing of art objects are part of the frame of the relationship. In art therapy supervision, supervisory attention is also engaged in the process of 'analytical differentiation' in relation to the field of image making and concrete transactions concerning images. This takes place both within the reported experience of the supervisee and within the supervisory session. Schaverien's model helps us to expand our understanding of the context of Ogden's 'dreaming' in relation to the art therapy setting.

Schaverien (1992) differentiates between 'the life in' and 'the life of' the picture in art therapy. She identifies five stages in the process of differentiation, which I paraphrase as follows:

1  *Identification* – the state immediately after the picture is made in which 'the phenomenon is bared': '. . . a dawning of consciousness which is not susceptible to conceptual, and therefore, verbal analysis'.
2  *Familiarisation* – the picture is viewed, experienced as separate and the artist begins to understand its 'immanent articulation'.
3  *Acknowledgement* – the artist begins to consciously acknowledge the implications of the picture. Discussion with the therapist and verbal interpretation can contribute to the process.
4  *Assimilation* – the artist contemplates the picture and assimilates the material that has become conscious.
5  *Disposal* – decisions are made about what happens to the image empowered by the previous stages.

Supervision comes into play in relation to the life *of* the picture, in that pictures are often concretely transported to the supervision session, and most obviously informs the stages of 'acknowledgement' and 'disposal' in Schaverien's model. The therapist's approach to the patient's art in therapy is influenced by the supervisor's approach to the patient's image in supervision. The 'dreaming' that can occur between therapist and supervisor informs the 'dreaming' of therapist with patient. The supervisor's process is informed by the life *in* the picture, given that the actual object is in the room during the supervision.

Writing of the life *in* the picture, Schaverien differentiates between 'embodied' and 'diagrammatic' images. The diagrammatic image '. . . is controlled in its execution, and it is often figurative and specific . . . an *illustration* or a *description* of a feeling . . .'. The embodied image embodies affect, transcending '. . . what is consciously known . . . (it) develops in unexpected ways and usually takes a form which could not have been predicted and so it may surprise even its maker'. This distinction refers to the patient's relation to the images, and I now expand it to include the way that the therapist relates to the patient's images in supervision. What is striking to me is how often the art therapist in supervision needs active support in valuing the life *in* the picture, particularly when working with an ambivalent patient. Images that evidently (to the supervisor) hold 'embodied' meaning for the patient, and therefore the potential of the 'talisman' and the 'scapegoat transference', can be presented and related to in a 'diagrammatic' way in supervision.

The art therapist's training requires intensive experience of engaging with personal art making. The modes of thinking, experiencing and relating that are engaged in making art are precisely those that constitute Ogden's 'dreaming'. Accordingly, one might expect the art therapist to be well prepared to adopt Bion's attitude of 'faith' in relation to the unspeakable. Yet, in my experience, many art therapists in supervision have great difficulty engaging these levels of their psyche in their clinical work. While often claiming to be particularly well attuned to these aspects of reality, the art therapist may often be acting out a defence against being more fully immersed in them. Theory, images and patients' histories can be presented as if they are concrete 'facts' requiring a concrete, factual response from the supervisor, rather than material that contributes to deepening awareness of the 'dream' of the patient, which can come alive in supervision. Accordingly the life *in* the picture in the supervision session can be disregarded.

My work with those art therapist supervisees often involves establishing links between their attitude to their clinical work and the capacity for reverie that they have experienced as artists. This capacity has often been abandoned in the service of a requirement to 'know'. While this may relate to the way the patient's psychotic defences foreclose on terrifying reality, it may also relate to the art therapist's experience of his or her training, and the degree to which this fostered the integration of the art therapist's 'artist' self. The artist–dreamer in the supervisee is often inaccessible in supervision because this aspect of the supervisee has been abandoned, and exists in a state of unconscious despair. Accordingly I am sure that some of my ex-supervisees have left feeling that they 'couldn't get it right' with me, while maintaining the belief that they could. My attempts to invite them into a different way of relating to this despair have often failed. This difference involves recognising that the feeling of not being able to get it right with me is predicated on the belief that it is possible to get it right, that rightness is a delusion of oneness, that this delusion defends against the psychic pain of separation experienced at every developmental stage and that this is likely to be resonant with the patient's ambivalence.

## Ambivalence in supervision

Writing of the supervision of therapists traversing areas of profound ambivalence and despair in relations with patients whose individuation process has failed in infancy, Searles (1962) suggests that progress both in supervision and in therapy emerges as 'pleasurable, pre-ambivalent symbiosis'. In this state, fondness, playfulness and contentedness constitute a medium for individuation. In Jungian terms, this can be thought of as an archetypal transference, in which an environment conducive to the de-integration of archetypal potentials is established. This becomes possible when the despairing polarity of ambivalence has been contained within the supervision and within the therapy. Searles compares the dependence then possible within the patient–therapist relation to the happily suckling infant/ happily nursing mother dyad, and that within the therapist–supervisor relation to the nursing mother/father dyad. The example of supervision described by Yorke seems to me to have this pre-ambivalent quality. The supervisee was both able to be conscious of her fantasy of the egg mayonnaise sandwich and to include it in her reporting of the material. This is a very different state of affairs to the one where the art therapist brings images to supervision but does not relate to them in an embodied way.

Searles' discussion of problems in the supervision of psychotherapists who are training as psychoanalysts has informed my thinking about the nature and meaning of ambivalence in the supervision of art therapists. He writes '. . . he will tend to attribute his own best capacities to me, sit in more or less open-mouthed awe at my oracular formulations, mechanically try to apply my ideas and techniques to his work with the patient, without having made them genuinely his own, and thereby demonstrate, through the patient's adverse responses, that my views are asinine'. He proposes that the motivation for this behaviour is rooted in the supervisee's need to individuate as an analyst. He continues: 'We need to see how vulnerable he is to feeling caught between the patient's intense criticism on the one hand and the supervisor's disapproval on the other . . . his beleaguered areas of healthy self-esteem very much need our support and encouragement'. The beleaguered position described by Searles is particularly precarious when the therapist is processing the primitive despair characteristic of the psychic reality of infantile abandonment in the countertransference. Searles describes this as 'ambivalent symbiosis' in which the supervisee's intense and covert competitiveness sabotages the supervisor's help, while at the same time intense dependency, characteristic of the unintegrated infant in the patient, is clearly apparent. In my experience, maintaining an embodied connection with the patient's process via the images in the supervisory session maintains the potential for pre-ambivalent symbiosis, both within the supervision and within the therapy being supervised.

I have established that the optimum attitude to clinical material emerging in supervision is one of reverie aligned with faith in 'O', and that this attitude to the 'irrational' is the necessary precondition for creative work in supervision. Ogden (2005) differentiates between 'interrupted dreams' and 'undreamt dreams'. The latter are those that feature centrally in the situation that I am exploring. Bion's (1967) description of 'attacks on linking' has informed my understanding of a defensive process that can maintain the art in art therapy supervision as an 'undreamt dream'. Bion describes a '. . . state of mind in which the patient's psyche contains an internal object which is opposed to, and destructive of, all links whatsoever . . . emotion is hated; it is felt to be too powerful to be contained by the immature psyche, it is felt to link objects and it gives reality to objects which are not self and therefore inimical to primary narcissism'. This internal object is '. . . a breast that refused to introject, harbour, and so modify the baneful force of emotion . . .'. It is felt '. . . to intensify . . . the emotions against which it initiates the attacks . . . the links surviving are perverse, cruel, and sterile'. When supervising art therapists, I have noticed that a pattern often emerges in which the supervisee unconsciously requires the supervisor to participate in denying the particular significance of the very elements that characterise art therapy as a specific discipline.

Obviously there are reasonably straightforward situations in which the supervisee, having approached me for supervision, simply does not get on with me for some reason, on the basis of actual experience of me and of my way of working. What is of interest to me in the context of this chapter is a more impersonal state of affairs, one example of which is that I am approached to confirm that I will not/cannot offer supervision. The most extreme version of this state of affairs is my experience of art therapists contacting me concerning supervision, telling me that I have been recommended to them and, in the same breath, that I no longer offer art therapy supervision. This is not presented as a question. It is very hard to know what to say in response to such material, and I tend to clarify that they are looking for art therapy supervision and that I am a BAAT registered supervisor. In a similar style, I am then informed that I probably do not supervise work with the particular client group with whom they are working. I reply stating whatever experience I have had in supervising art therapists working with that client group. The therapist then presents another problem, such as geographical location, time or money. Even if these practical concerns can be addressed constructively, and we proceed to arrange an initial meeting, such a conversation often concludes with an answerphone message from the person concerned, notifying me that I obviously do not want to work with him or her, and cancelling the appointment. Or the person cannot find me geographically, proving that I am inaccessible, so never arrives for the session. Or, having arrived for the session at the wrong time, tells me that my way of handling this intrusion is inappropriate, whether I accommodate it or maintain the boundaries agreed. These are among many examples that come to mind. The point is that I can be of no help and the conversation concludes.

Despite the apparently futile nature of this activity, something – or someone – has prompted the therapist to contact me and engage in this activity with me, so it is serving some purpose within some context. The therapist may have been told to approach me by an authority figure, such as his or her employer, or therapist. If so, the meaning of this activity could be that the parents/mother/breast are felt to be offering something bad/ useless and the therapist's denigrating behaviour towards me acts out a defence against a fear of these feelings emerging in the relation with the idealised parent. Similarly, if a peer, or a friend, is in therapy or supervision with me, or has been, the activity in the context of that 'sibling' relationship might establish that the good object possessed by the envied sibling is in fact useless, thereby evacuating the pain of envy. Alternatively, the bad object persecuting the envied sibling is proven bad, and a state of fusion with the envied sibling gets rid of separateness, and therefore feelings of rivalry, envy, and so on. In the extreme scenario that I have sketched, I can only speculate about the meaning of being used in this way. In any event, the state of despair that can be inferred from this behaviour is not available for understanding in supervision within the context of a relation with a patient.

Less extreme, but equally intractable, examples emerge with some super-visees who establish more ongoing relations with me. I may be engaged in lengthy discussions about their clinical setting, in which pressure is exerted on me to denigrate other professionals, the patient's parents, the NHS, and so on, at the expense of looking at the patient's artwork. I am then asked, in the penultimate moments of the session, whether I have any interest in seeing the patient's artwork. Alternatively I am flooded by reams of art-work, lectured about 'Jungian' interpretations of the 'symbolic' content of the images, and then asked, again in the penultimate moments, what I think. My efforts to help the supervisee to attend to the patient's images, or to contextual issues, during the preceding 49 minutes of the session have apparently been experienced as persecutory attacks, and have simply resulted in a shift from one form of defensive behaviour to another. The supervisee apparently feels that I have not been saying what I think, or indeed have not been thinking at all. The uselessness of any contribution that I might make is confirmed by ensuring that I have no time in which to speak.

Another recurring pattern is that the supervisee brings masses of images to the session, which are laid out in front of me. The supervisee watches me intently. Any comment I make on the images is treated as if I am apparently relating to the body of images as a kind of psychological MRI scan. Inevitably the supervisee's knowledge of the patient far exceeds mine, and the session begins to have the feel of a guessing game, which nullifies 'dreaming' because it is based on an assumption that what is going on in the patient can be 'known'. Any comments I make on this, and invitations to reflect on the links between what is going on in our session and what might be going on between therapist and patient, are apparently experi-enced by the supervisee as persecutory attacks. Or the supervisee brings a folder of images, puts it down somewhere in my room and then proceeds to read copious notes about the process of several sessions. The images are not spontaneously made available to 'dreaming'. They are in the room as a kind of 'token gesture' inviting me to devalue them. If I comment on the presence of the images, wondering what their presence outside the realm of conscious awareness means, the supervisee behaves as if it were a requirement to 'do' something. In the situations where defences pre-dominate, the potential meaning embodied in the art remains unavailable to conscious awareness. Mindless doing, whether this is the doing of placing images in front of me or the doing of reading out notes, is presented as a substitute for the work of dreaming, and is rigidly maintained. Emotional experiencing apparently has to stay outside the realm of reverie. Verbal thought is dissociated from the averbal forms of thinking presented in the artwork, and the split establishes a domain in which a phantasy of omniscience maintains the delusion of power and control in relation to archetypal reality.

I think these generalised examples illustrate the gist of the situation that I am exploring here. In many cases, the defensive process that has been cheating the supervisee of the possibility of being nurtured by my under-standing is evacuated into me and is therefore unavailable to dreaming. My attempt to help the supervisee to recognise this, to begin to wonder about the extreme anxiety that must necessitate this degree of control and about links to the patient's material fails, in that it is experienced as another persecutory attack. This presents a state of affairs in which the impossibility of containment, which is part of despair, both predominates and remains unconscious. The feeling of helplessness and hopelessness is evacuated into me because the therapist cannot bear to experience this aspect of his or her own countertransference. However, when the supervisee can tolerate the feelings involved in accepting my understanding, this state of affairs may proceed into a creative experience of 'dreaming' the underlying nightmare, and understanding its context.

## Supervisory containment

Recognition of the existence and meaning of defences in supervision resonates with the 'parallel process' in the analytic relationship. My own experience of the deeply unconscious nature of the influence of the container/contained relation in analytical supervision serves to illustrate this. I was working with a patient with a borderline personality organisation on a four-times-weekly basis, and taking the material to weekly supervision with a senior analyst. The patient's relation to reality was deeply ambivalent and she employed radical defences against the psychotic anxieties that per-petually threatened to overwhelm her. In particular her defensive organisa-tion was characterised by the intrusive form of projective identification described by Meltzer et al. (1986). She brought numerous objects, including drawings, to her sessions and these were initially employed as a means of evacuating her experience, as were her use of words, gestures, and so on. As analysis proceeded, the experience that was being evacuated gradually became more available to conscious experience. This was the experience of being numb, paralysed and deadened.

The way in which the patient's deadness became available to 'dreaming' in the supervisory relationship was through my experience of finding it impossible to function psychologically in some sessions. At these times I was in a mindless state in which I was neither asleep nor awake, and in which the patient would sit watching me, stroking the arm of her chair (she would not use the couch) and smiling with a palpable degree of sadistic pleasure at my predicament. My associations, when I was capable of associating, were to serial killers who 'kill for company'. I was unable to write up these sessions and incapable of remembering their process. Quite unconsciously, I took different sessions to supervision, and my supervisor maintained a warm, consistent focus on the psychotic process in the material and the role of my patient's schizoid defences. Eventually I realised that my mindless states were relevant and meaningful, and that I had unconsciously attributed them to my own inadequacy. I realised that I had been feeling unconsciously guilty about being a 'bad analyst' and fearing that my supervisor would abandon me if I revealed my failings in supervision. Before that point, I was in a state of delusional countertransference, at one with the patient's mindlessness. Having become more conscious of my own ambivalence and the anxiety that it protected me from, I was able to 'risk' including the material in supervision.

This experience revealed the deeply unconscious aspects of supervision to me. In resonance with this, the way my patient used projective identification shifted from being predominantly evacuative to more communicative in nature. Work on analysing the patient's murdered/murderous infantile states could proceed, along with the gradual 'thawing out' of her deadened self, which she had projected into me. The 'undreamt dream' – which was a nightmare of early abandonment experiences – became more available to dreaming in supervision. I was, and still am, deeply impressed by the nature of the experience of the container/contained relation, in the sense described by Bion (1963, 1970) that transcends cause and effect. I think that the experience of containment in both settings gradually enabled the nightmare to become available to dreaming in both settings. This experienced enhanced my understanding of the role of supervision as containment.

Schaverien's (1992) discussion of the potential containing role of art as 'scapegoat' for the patient in art therapy can be extended to include its role in art therapy supervision. She writes '. . . analytical art psychotherapy offers a distinct way of developing a conscious attitude and so owning the split-off elements of the psyche through their disposal in the picture'. I have discussed in detail elsewhere how this can be facilitated in art therapy with patients in psychotic states (Killick 1991, 1993, 1996, 2000). The concrete presence and persistence of the images as objects in time and space is significant in fostering the potential shift from 'intrusive' projective identification to projective identification as communication (Meltzer *et al.* 1986). Similarly the presence of the potential communication embodied in the image maintains the potential for 'dreaming' to come alive in the supervision session regardless of the deadening effect of the defences that I have described. The images that are being related to in a 'diagrammatic' way by the unconsciously anxious art therapist in supervision can be enlivened if the supervisor attends to the 'embodied' elements of experience within them.

When supervising art therapists who are not in an embodied relation to the art made by their patients, I try to keep alive in my mind the possible experience of the patient as an artist, wondering how the making of the particular image felt, as an embodied experience, to the patient. This maintains the material that is embodied in the image within the field of the supervision session, even if nothing is actually said about it to the supervisee. Following similar principles to those that I developed in my work with ambivalent patients in art therapy, I try to encourage the supervisee to focus on the patient's process as revealed in the way the image was made. This feels like following the trail of an animal – the abandoned aspects of the therapist–artist, and the infant–patient. The supervisee often seems impatient to 'get on with supervision' while, feeling rather stupid, I maintain a lively interested focus on the image: 'so where did he start . . . oh with that line . . . then that, etc'. In a transformative supervision, the supervisee begins to look at and reflect on the image, and inevitably this engages the material that had been undreamt, discarded and located in the retreat of despair. The potential nature and meaning of the art in art therapy comes alive and inspires both of us to sincerely struggle with the awesome task of understanding, without hope of success, but well enough to be of some assistance to the patient.

## Conclusion

In art therapy, and in art therapy supervision, the potential for 'pleasurable, pre-ambivalent symbiosis' is enhanced by the presence of the patient's artwork. Schaverien's (1992, 1995) work establishes an analytic attitude to pictures made in therapy, enabling the affective life that is embodied in images to live and grow within the protected space of the relation with the therapist. More recently, Case (2005) has contributed the specific considerations involved in working with profound levels of defence in child patients. Both authors reveal the enlivening effect that the presence of images can have, once therapist and patient are able to relate to the life in the image. The same is true of supervision. When the art is not allowed to speak for itself, in the generalised scenarios that I described earlier, the therapist is acting out defences against the anxiety that the analytic, archetypal 'infant' material that is embodied in the images is uncontainable, and therefore cannot form part of the individuation process. When the therapist's unconscious despair merges with that of the patient, this cannot be exposed to the mind/mother/supervisor because she is unconsciously 'known' to be incapable of relating to pre-verbal thinking, of processing pre-verbal states and of fostering individuation in the supervisee. In my experience, the therapist's capacity to tolerate and relate to his or her own ambivalence within the supervisory relationship will determine the degree to which supervision can be 'allowed' to serve a containing purpose. This capacity is fostered, or not, by the training of the therapist, and most significantly by the relation between the training and the artist in the art therapist.

## References

Bion, W. R. (1963) *Elements of Psychoanalysis*, London: Heinemann.

Bion, W. R. (1967) *Second Thoughts*, London: Heinemann.

Bion, W. R. (1970) *Attention and Interpretation*, London: Heinemann.

Case, C. (2005) *Imagining Animals: Art, Psychotherapy and Primitive States of Mind*, London: Routledge.

Driver, C. and Martin, E. (2005) *Supervision and the Analytic Attitude*, London: Whurr.

Grinberg, L. (1997) 'On transference and countertransference and the technique of supervision', in B. Martindale, M. Morner, M. E. C. Rodriguez and J.-P. Vidit (eds), *Supervision and its Vicissitudes*, London: Karnac.

Killick, K. (1991) 'The practice of art therapy with patients in acute psychotic states', *Inscape, Winter*: 2–6.

Killick, K. (1993) 'Working with psychotic processes in art therapy', *Psychoanalytic Psychotherapy*, 7 (1): 25–38.

Killick, K. (1996) 'Unintegration and containment in acute psychosis', *British Journal of Psychotherapy*, 13 (2): 232–242.

Killick, K. (2000) 'The art room as container in analytical art psychotherapy with patients in psychotic states', in A. Gilroy and G. McNeilly (eds), *The Changing Shape of Art Therapy*, London: Jessica Kingsley, pp. 99–114.

Killick, K. and Greenwood, H. (1995) 'Research in art therapy with people who have psychotic illnesses', in A. Gilroy and C. Lee (eds), *Art and Music: Therapy and Research*, London: Routledge, pp. 101–116.

Killick, K. and Schaverien, J. (1997) *Art, Psychotherapy and Psychosis*, London: Routledge.

Martindale, B., Morner, M., Rodriguez, M. E. C. and Vidit, J.-P. (1997) *Supervision and its Vicissitudes*, London: Karnac.

Meltzer, D., Milana, G., Maiello, S. and Petrelli, D. (1986) 'The conceptual distinction between projective identification (Klein) and container-contained (Bion)', in *Studies in Extended Metapsychology: Clinical Applications of Bion's Ideas*, Perthshire, Scotland: Clunie Press.

Ogden, T. H. (2005) 'On psychoanalytic supervision', *International Journal of Psychoanalysis*, 86: 1265–1280.

Schaverien, J. (1992) *The Revealing Image: Analytical Art Psychotherapy in Theory and Practice*, London: Routledge.

Schaverien, J. (1995) *Desire and the Female Therapist: Engendered Gazes in Psychotherapy and AA Therapy*, London: Routledge.

Searles, H. F. (1955) 'The informational value of the supervisor's emotional experiences', in *Collected Papers on Schizophrenia and Related Subjects* (1986 reprint), London: Maresfield Library, pp. 157–176.

Searles, H. F. (1962) 'Problems of psycho-analytic supervision', in *Collected Papers on Schizophrenia and Related Subjects* (1986 reprint), London: Maresfield Library, pp. 584–604.

Wiener, J., Mizen, R. and Duckham, J. (2003) *Supervising and Being Supervised: A Practice in Search of a Theory*, London: Palgrave/Macmillan.

Yorke, V. (2005) 'Bion's "vertex" as a supervisory object', in C. Driver and E. Martin (eds), *Supervision and the Analytic Attitude*, London: Whurr, pp. 34–49.

# Chapter 13

# In pursuit of an object

## The supervision of art therapy research

*Andrea Gilroy*

## Introduction

This chapter's focus is the supervision of art therapy research in higher education. This is where the majority of my experience as a research supervisor over the last fifteen years has been: in post-art therapy training, taught masters programmes (i.e. MResearch, MA Hons, MPhil) and doctoral studies. In all these I have felt fortunate to be the supervisor and have been enormously stimulated by the projects themselves and by the processes of research supervision. I consider it to be one of the most pleasurable and important aspects of my work and hope that what I have offered to supervisees has been helpful and supportive whilst also being rigorous and constructively critical.

This chapter begins with a description of the formal context of research supervision in universities. (I use the terms 'supervisee' and 'student' interchangeably throughout.) I consider the motivation that drives art therapists to undertake research and the importance of finding the right supervisor. I explore learning, teaching and assessment and discuss containment in the supervisory relationship. The chapter is informed throughout by responses to a brief, informal questionnaire on research supervision that I sent to ex and current supervisees. I thank them all for their thoughtful, frank and generous responses, for giving me permission to quote them and for all that they have taught me about research supervision.

## Setting the scene

In recent years the Quality Assurance Agency (QAA, the organisation that monitors education in universities) and the research councils that fund doctoral studies (e.g. the Arts & Humanities Research Council (AHRC) and the Economic and Social Research Council (ESRC)) have addressed the quality of educational provision for postgraduate research and reviewed student progress and success. The QAA's National Qualifications Framework (2001) defined the learning outcomes required at various levels of education and situated different kinds of engagement with research within them. Masters degrees for example are awarded to students who can demonstrate their critical awareness of research at the forefront of their discipline and show their understanding of how research and enquiry creates knowledge; doctorates require that students create original research and acquire a detailed understanding of research techniques (p. 12). Thus masters students work at the edges of existing knowledge whilst doctoral students generate new knowledge. In my experience Masters-level art therapy trainees do indeed acquire an understanding of how research informs clinical practice, but experienced practitioners on post-training Masters-level programmes often generate new knowledge. Their theses cannot achieve the detail and originality of doctoral work or lead to an in-depth understanding of research methods, but nonetheless they often make a contribution to art therapy's evidence base (e.g. Mahony 1994; Wood 2002). They can also generate an abiding interest in research that propels art therapists into further learning and new projects.

Research supervision at all levels is a complex, multi-layered process, a craft that, until recently, has been learnt largely through doing. This apprenticeship model is based in experiences gained 'on the job', drawing on the 'internal supervisor' created through good and bad experiences of supervision. However, the quality of postgraduate research provision has, in the last decade, been a cause for concern because of the low completion rates of MPhil/PhDs and the explicit association between universities' research ratings, funding and research student enrolments and successful completions. Formal training for supervisors is now required, either before or as one begins to supervise research students (QAA 2004) and doctoral graduates are required to become competent, professional researchers. The learning outcomes and assessment criteria have been defined and the roles and responsibilities of research supervisors delineated in direct relation to policy about postgraduate research (QAA 2001).

It is immediately apparent that the language and formal, policy-related parameters of research supervision are different from those of clinical supervision. There are, however, some commonalities of intent: generally speaking, supervision aims to enable learning in a space set apart where a conversation occurs about something that is partly in the room. A key difference is that research supervision is (usually) finite and marked by the successful completion of a piece of academic work. Thus, from the outset, the focus of research supervision is on what happens at the end, on the production of an object.

Debate about research supervision explores the extent to which students should focus on scholarship attached to their individual project or on becoming generically skilled researchers, and whether these skills can be taught or are learnt experientially. This is paralleled in the discourse of clinical supervision in discussion of the extent to which therapeutic strategies and techniques should be addressed, but it differs in its focus on clients, relationships and conscious and unconscious processes in clinical work (e.g. Driver and Martin 2002; Wiener *et al.* 2003). Research supervision is also about people and processes, and authors acknowledge that learning and research involve emotion and relationship, especially with regard to students' successes and problems (Delamont *et al.* 1997, 2000; Phillips and Pugh 2005), but the higher education literature usually considers these in terms of 'personalities', the supervisor's 'style' and the supervisee's learning needs, not in terms of a dynamic process.

In the questionnaires I asked supervisees what they thought were the similarities and differences between research and clinical supervision. The general view was that there were more similarities than might at first appear. Both ensure that integrity, professionalism and ethical practice are maintained. In clinical supervision this relates '. . . to principles of practice . . . In research supervision the student has to abide by their stated methodology and to the parameters of the study' (J). Both involve a side-by-side approach and the person of the supervisee '. . . being in there with it – all mixed up – often emotionally. Successful supervision creates a space where "I" can see the "me"' (A). Both require critical reflection, the containment of anxiety and the instillation of confidence. Both involve careful listening that allows the supervisee to develop their ideas:

> In both it is important to create the atmosphere where the supervisee can experience her own expertise, to be uninhibited enough to explore what is not known so that it can become known. (L)

Differences were to do with purpose and focus. Guidance was more direct in research supervision. Here the focus is on the supervisee's interests, on *their* 'autobiographical project' (A) rather than the client's, and attention is given to developing theory and knowledge that contributes to wider understandings outside the intimate intersubjectivities of therapy:

> . . . what is important in research supervision is the development or furtherance of thought in a different way to clinical need. This often happens through pointing to the literature, exploring meaning and relating it to wider concerns than the day to day work of clinical supervision. It is perhaps less intimate than clinical supervision, where the dynamic between patient and therapist is strongly felt . . . explicit theory is less important in clinical supervision where meaning and insight can be found without necessarily naming the theory, but in research supervision, the theory is central. (L)

One supervisee commented interestingly on the differences between clinical and research supervision in clinically-based research:

> The clinical supervisor will have helped the research student make sense of the material at the time of working; the research supervisor will be working within a wider context which may eventually add to a broader understanding. (I)

Another summarised the differences thus:

> In research supervision the primary focus is the project, which is clearly set out and understood by both supervisee and supervisor from the start. Although a project may change the reasons for the change are explicitly noted and endorsed . . . and are not understood in terms of the supervisee's or subject's unconscious. However, supervisors might reflect on and address a supervisee's bias in relation to the research, which is interesting – it isn't taken back to the supervisee's unconscious, but understood within the framework and background of the topic being investigated. The methodology of research therefore can be replicated and the findings be thought of as reliable – unlike the uniqueness of a therapeutic encounter in a clinical setting. (G)

But herein lies a paradox: on one hand 'clinical supervision makes me feel much more vulnerable' (N), 'It [research supervision] should not be so personal or involve a touch of transference that needs unravelling' (I) but, as this person went on to say: 'Study is emotional as well as just plain learning. Especially when you're reaching out into the unknown' (I). Research supervision, like clinical supervision, has to contain the supervisee. It also has to contain the emotions that suffuse learning alongside the feelings that arise from doing a project that is often dear to the supervisee's heart.

## Motivation and 'the quest'

Delamont *et al.* (2000) suggest that doctoral students embark on research because they have a 'quest' to pursue a subject they love. This is '. . . an emotional and intellectual quest for personal fulfilment' (p. 49), albeit one accompanied by wanting a vocational and professional qualification. Art therapy research supervisees described just such a mix of motivations. Some related directly to working life, e.g. a desire for new skills to enhance career development or a need to counteract isolation and alienation from debilitating work, or some simply wanted time out to think. Several said that they wished to learn about research in order to counteract threats to art therapy services, one remarking that their service had seemed:

> . . . well-defended against any cuts or 'rationalisation' . . . However the powers that were at that time judged the department not to be able to demonstrate that we were clinically effective. The measure was proved by the gold standard – RCTs. . . . [the programme] provide[d] me with further knowledge and expertise in research methods so I could articulate and therefore better defend our profession. (E)

Others spoke of being attracted to research because the process seemed to suit their personality – be it obsessional, curious or philosophical – and of an enjoyment of its inherent creativity:

> I like the process of putting things together and creating new things. I like rigour and coherence. . . . I also like the feeling of being immersed in something. Possibly it reminds me of painting, or of some other merged state when all things outside seem secondary. (J)

But almost everyone spoke of a 'quest', of wanting to pursue 'burning issues and ideas in my head' (E). These often arose from clinical work that, as one person said:

> . . . really bugged me . . . the phenomenon I was experiencing didn't seem to be documented anywhere. I read and read everything I could lay my hands on . . . but still couldn't find the one thing I wanted . . . that is why I started on my own research. (F)

A mixture of pragmatism and altruism motivated supervisees to begin research, but the questionnaires showed that the primary driver for these art therapists was a passionate wish to think, explore and understand more about a primary, often longstanding preoccupation.

## Responsible recruitment

The phrase 'responsible recruitment' is one that has stayed in my mind from a short course on the supervision of MPhil/PhD students. It refers to the supervisor's initial assessment of the prospective supervisee's ability – practically, psychologically and intellectually – to sustain a lengthy period of independent, rigorous study and eventually be awarded a research degree. Supervisors have to ensure that candidates have a viable project that has been thought through, although not in a rigid, predetermined way that closes the research down before it has begun. Initial communication between potential supervisee and supervisor is often about an application to a university, or a research proposal, a funding application or a scholarship. This allows an evaluation of the strengths and weaknesses of the prospective supervisory pair: the potential supervisee's ability to articulate and design a manageable research project, to write, and be open to supervision, and of the skills and knowledge of the supervisor and their capacity for listening and responding appropriately.

'Responsible recruitment' therefore also refers to the research student recruiting the right supervisor to their project, this being, as several authors have observed, crucial to its eventual success (Delamont *et al.* 1997, 2000; Philips and Pugh 2005). Research supervisors are often approached on the basis of their expertise and publications, this, as one supervisee observed, being '. . . essential in terms of being able to point you in the right direction' (H). Supervisees' choice (when they have one) can be constrained by supervisors' accessibility and availability; it can also be complicated and enriched by, at doctoral level, having more than one supervisor. There are usually two, i.e. a first and second or associate/reserve supervisor (as per QAA guidelines, 2004) and sometimes a panel, the purpose being to build supervisory teams and research groups of competent, professional researchers. This can bring an exciting inter-disciplinarity to art therapy research. For example, supervisees', and my, theoretical horizons are currently being widened through co-supervision with colleagues from art history, education, psychoanalytic studies, psychology and visual art.

Art therapy is often a second, sometimes third career. Embarking on a period of research-based study involves change, a new layer of professional socialisation and the development of another aspect of identity that can result in career development, a new job or even joining a new professional group, a process that Delamont *et al.* (2000) describe as 'joining the academy' (of researchers). Art therapists usually begin research after several, often many, years of clinical experience; such maturity means that the disciplined, independent work that is key to research is not usually a problem. Critical reflection and neutrality will also be nothing new, but there is a cultural shift to be negotiated from the reflective process of ongoing clinical supervision to the structured, planned and product-oriented process of research supervision.

## Beginning

Getting off to a good start in research supervision involves much that is familiar to art therapists in terms of establishing the boundaries of time, place and expectations, but as they embark on research supervisees need to learn new skills and gain particular kinds of knowledge. These are usually taught, certainly at doctoral level, through generic, often multi-disciplinary courses that include qualitative and quantitative research methods, research ethics and various transferable skills such as the use of IT (e.g. the latest data analysis and bibliographic software) and presentation skills (for teaching and conference presentation). This can seem irrelevant to the individual imperative of designing and implementing real, live art therapy research, but the supervisee needs to gain a wide-ranging knowledge of research in order to make an informed choice about how best to investigate their research question. This learning can be overwhelming and confusing when the possibilities seem endless, but it can be exciting too; here the supervisor assists the supervisee in making appropriate methodological choices. The supervisee may also need advice about reading – '. . . being given an idea of where to look for what' (H) – not only on the topic itself but also 'contrastive' reading (that situates the research question in a wider, critical context) and analytical reading (that theorises: Delamont *et al.* 1997). A number of supervisees remarked on how useful this had been and how important it therefore was that the supervisor was widely read. In these early days of a project supervisees also learn how reading builds the foundations of research, namely how:

> . . . to question what has been written . . . [research supervision] helps you to judge good and indifferent writing and helps you to question dodgy ideas – it gives you the confidence through your own research to make judgements and appreciate other people's work. (F)

They learn too that this can be a lively and engaging process. One person for example remarked that a lecture on literature reviews:

> . . . really taught me something I didn't know before about playing with the material and being creative with it. This taught me that academic writing was creative all the way through. (N)

The research supervisor may also give practical assistance to their supervisees, e.g. contacting the 'gatekeepers' for fieldwork and assisting with applications to ethics committees.

Hawkins and Shohet (1989) suggest that clinical supervisors need a 'helicopter ability' that maintains an overall view but can move in to explore detail. This metaphor is helpful in thinking about research supervision too. From the outset the research supervisor has in mind the project's, and the eventual text's, overall coherence. A significant focus right from the start is therefore the establishment of a viable structure for the whole project, and for the eventual thesis, through a plan of work that can be achieved in the time available, setting '. . . small achievable goals rather than being swamped by the enormity of the whole thing' (D). Supervisors move between giving practical help and advice that helps supervisees to discover how they work best, and encouraging them to begin writing almost as soon as the project begins, two golden rules being 'write early and often' and 'don't get it right, get it written' (Phillips and Pugh 2005). Here the supervisor's experience of research and writing is critical, for example: knowing that what one thinks often emerges through the act of writing; that a large project or piece of writing builds over time through numerous smaller pieces; and that different aspects of the research process take different amounts of time. At the same time the research supervisor has to keep an eye on a university's regulations and/or the requirements of a funding body and ensure that the supervisee is familiar with all of these.

These pragmatic aspects of research supervision focus on what Szecsody (1990) terms the 'dumb spots', referring to the supervisee's lack of knowledge and information, in this context of research and its methods and processes. Early on in the supervisory process learning about research per se is accompanied by a dismantling of the supervisee's research proposal, a process where 'blind spots' may be identified, i.e. where the supervisee's defences may influence their work. Everything has to be interrogated in terms of the researcher's beliefs and biases and the project's underlying assumptions, theoretical foundations and proposed methods. The task is to open up and explore the whole topic and to refine a research question that will be addressed in a particular way. These early stages of the research process can be both disconcerting and liberating, and can take a surprisingly long time. This is time well spent. The very nature of the research needs to be rigorously interrogated and discovered anew in supervision as an increasing understanding of the field, and of research and its methods, informs what the project is to be. Here the supervisee must feel sufficiently contained to be able to leave the security of their imagined project and explore every aspect of the field before articulating a precise research question and delineating the parameters of their research.

## Containment

McGlashan (2003) likens the clinical supervisor/supervisee relationship to that of mother and child and suggests that the contained frame of supervision enables the supervisee to think the unthinkable that might otherwise be intolerable, unexpected or frightening so that the hardly-known thought is transformed into something that can be thought about. A similar process occurs in research supervision. One supervisee said that learning about research had been '. . . a bit like Bion's idea of infants with thoughts without the means to think them . . . the course and the relationships encountered provided a kind of Alpha function' (B). During the early stages of research the supervisee's ideas may not form a coherent narrative and so the supervisor's task is to help the supervisee articulate them within a research framework. This has an anxiety-reducing, containing function, the significance of which came through clearly in the questionnaires: of 'orchestrating thoughts and then helping me in distilling them without losing the excitement' (E); '. . . helping me tease out what I am really interested in. I always felt I could enthuse and enthuse you and you seemed to do a bit of mirroring' (I). Others commented similarly:

> I think the supervision time was crucial to me. During this time I learned that I could speak freely, without fear of feeling stupid. I could speak of my clinical practice without feelings of shame which meant I could develop the ability to think freely. In that thinking what was useful was the development of ideas. If I came with a fragmented and unformed idea, by talking I found it began to find shape which I could then take away and develop. (L)

It is important that the supervisor listens, thinks and responds to the material the supervisee presents in an attentive way, being careful to not shape material prematurely and remaining open while the project is still being formed, while it is becoming itself.

Wharton (2003), describing the establishment of supervisory boundaries in clinical supervision, pays attention to the physical location of the session and says that the room should be quiet, private, comfortable and stimulating. Several supervisees commented on the 'warmth and friendly comfort' (L) of my office that also seemed to have a containing function:

> There was a wonderful view out of your window onto the garden . . . You had interesting books lying about on your desk space and bookshelves which could be picked up and looked at. (C)

Consistency was important too, almost everyone remarking on the importance of the research supervisor being 'reliably there in the supervision' (C) and being interested: 'Having someone interested and supportive of your project, actually feeling their enthusiasm!' (B). What was important was that supervisees had someone who 'was looking out for me, was interested personally in what I had to say, and wanted to encourage the best out of me' (H). A relationship that has these containing functions has transferential material within it, its extent and significance varying in research supervision from 'It's like returning home to base when I feel out of touch' (I) to 'The transference relationship . . . was . . . vital to my progress and self confidence . . . central to my success . . . [the] holding of me and the project was so, so important' (A). This shifts and develops as the research proceeds.

## Learning, teaching and assessment

Mander (2002) describes how good teaching and productive learning does not occur through 'imposition from above' but rather happens as a 'flash of insight' arrived at through a mixture of discussion, exploration and transmission of enthusiasm for a subject. Delamont *et al.* (1997) add that one of the most important functions of a research supervisor is to enthuse their supervisee. The importance of this came through clearly in the feedback questionnaires. It seemed that enthusiasm had been conveyed in two ways: through supervision where the supervisor had 'conveyed the excitement of discovering something for herself that had not been done before' (F), of '. . . excitedly talking about the detective nature of research, and how impossible it is to know at the beginning what you will find by the end' (L); and through lectures and seminars – from the research supervisor, other researchers and ex-supervisees – who described their personal research journeys. These had conveyed a deep and abiding interest in a topic that '. . . seemed to sanction a relationship with the subject/something personal which I had previously supposed, incorrectly, was absent in research' (G). One had used photography in a way that captured a supervisee's imagination: 'It was compassionate and wonderful and elegant, the images spoke although the patients could not, it was moving and inspiring in its attention to the image' (C), while another had conveyed the free-floating but focused immersion in a subject that characterises research: '. . . we got a sense of delving into things in a broad way and the throwing up of material and texts which crystallized the research' (C), and yet another had demonstrated the way the researcher had posed a huge research question and '. . . then had to shrink it down and make it much smaller . . . she fined it down . . . and then let her mind wander . . . [and] . . . found all these fascinating ideas . . . and so off she went' (C). Supervisees valued sessions that made research accessible, that '. . . brought research alive and made the whole process of research seem exciting and desirable to do' (F). They also valued presentations where the researcher had been 'frank about floundering around' (C) and described the pitfalls as well as the triumphs of their researches.

Mander (2002) and Stewart (2002) usefully explore different teaching and supervision 'styles'. They describe supervisors who are over-enthusiastic and swamp their supervisee or who impart too much knowledge through a concrete set of instructions. Equally detrimental is a laissez-faire attitude from a supervisor who praises everything in order to avoid conflict and judgement. Delamont *et al.* (1997) speak similarly about the importance of the research supervisor on one hand supporting a student's confidence but on the other being clear when things are not going well. Collecting and analysing data, for example, does not always proceed smoothly and the supervisor may have to intervene and help the supervisee abandon a research design or method that simply is not working. They suggest that learning about research entails 'acts of faith' (p. 75) on the part of the supervisee: that research is possible; that it will lead to new and interesting findings; and that it will make a contribution to knowledge. It also entails trust in the supervisor's experience and judgement. It is up to the supervisor to sustain a supervisee's belief in their research. This too came across in the questionnaires, supervisees speaking of the importance of the supervisor being 'calmly encouraging and able to contain the anxieties' (C) and 'a . . . not spoken and probably unconscious communication that I was capable' (L).

However, supervisors are not infallible. Crick (1992) discusses how bad supervision can result in the supervisee taking on their supervisor's views and experiencing these as a burden. This came painfully to light in the questionnaire responses. A few supervisees described occasions when they had felt obliged to explore methods or ideas because I had suggested them. One remarked that an off-the-mark suggestion from me had made her 'feel dull and lose interest' (I). Another said:

> I felt I was being pushed into an area that was incomprehensible and unhelpful. . . . I found it hard to understand and frightening. I felt I was in a straightjacket that stopped all movement and I struggled with myself over my desire to please (therefore obediently carried out what I experienced as your recommendations) and my inability to make it work. (L)

What seemed to have happened, in these cases, was that I had not been sufficiently attuned to supervisees' developing research 'styles' or to their emergent vision of their theses. One supervisee wondered in the questionnaire if our miscommunication had been related to the university's requirements. Indeed they had. Such situations had evoked in me a concern either about methodological rigour or adequate description of the field, these being explicitly related in my mind to the final object and its eventual readers, the examiners. The research supervisor's responsibility is in direct relationship to their continuing assessment of their supervisee's work, and to its eventual examination. Whilst there is no 'right' way to do research, learning outcomes have to be met and theses have to be 'defended' according to assessment criteria associated with the appropriate level of study. Both supervisee and supervisor want a satisfactory object to be produced and an MA, MPhil or PhD to be awarded!

However, Phillips and Pugh (2005) and Delamont *et al.* (1997, 2000) say that the supervisor should not become preoccupied by assessment but remain open-minded so that the potentially intrusive and inhibiting effects of the examination and the power relationship in supervision can be diminished. There must be sufficient trust for the supervisee to think freely and to disagree with their supervisor so that neither their learning nor their research is impeded. Research supervisors must also ensure that a balance is maintained between praise and criticism of supervisees' work. The supervisor must, for example, be clear when they think the work is not reaching the required standard or is going in the wrong direction. She or he must also be careful to differentiate between criticism of a chapter of a thesis and their estimation of the supervisee's overall ability. Their intention should always be to communicate their confidence that the supervisee will succeed and be able to achieve the required standards of research and scholarship.

Learning, teaching and assessment can, however, evoke transferential material that has to be acknowledged and, if appropriate, addressed. Supervision, as Wharton (2003) notes, evokes ambivalence, and unconscious processes come into play. Supervisees come with high expectations of support and containment, but some associations may be with surveillance and control. The implicit academic framework of research supervision can evoke memories from school, undergraduate or postgraduate education. One supervisee, for example, wrote about her difficulties in breaking old working habits and not giving me drafts of her thesis to read. She recalled how we had spoken about this and remembered that I said to her 'let me do my job'; at the time she did not know how and so the pattern continued. She said, however, that 'It *was* very helpful when (you) asked me "Is it because I'm me?", that is not the "cosy mummy" tutor from the initial training programme but someone in a position of authority who seemed . . . unreachable, more formal, more of the "headmistress"'. She added: 'In retrospect it would have been helpful to explore . . . this past experience [way back to school times] of feeling compelled to produce the finished article and not ask for help' (F).

## Keeping going

A key aspect of the relationship between research supervisor and their supervisee is that it changes. For example, once a research project is well underway the frequency of supervision may diminish and there may be periods of intensive fieldwork when supervisees are out of geographical reach and communication is by phone or email. Research supervision may not maintain a consistency of time and place: site, field and studio visits can be hugely important to the shared understanding that comes from supervision in the space where the research 'lives'. Supervision can also last well beyond the analytical hour, especially when meetings are less frequent, and can extend into more social times and places.

But research can be a solitary process. Several supervisees commented on the significance of the research supervisor's continuing support that was 'enthusiastic and interested. . . . Her encouragement to keep at it was vital' (F). This was especially important when supervisees were feeling low or were working at some geographical distance – '. . . you were very encouraging when I was feeling rather despondent . . . I greatly appreciated the interest because I was very isolated' (J) – or when the research was just taking time:

> . . . the encouragement/support provided over an extended period made a significant difference especially at low points on the research journey . . . it was . . . about not giving up on me. (K)

This highlights the importance of the supervisory relationship and, given that research does take time, indicates that other sources of support are necessary too. The QAA emphasises the importance of universities and supervisors offering facilities for postgraduate research students such as seminars and supervision groups. '. . . (H)aving a place to bring our shared anxieties and experiences about the work was edifying, containing and reassuring' (G), but Delamont et al. (1997) say that supervisors should also encourage research students to engage with 'motivational jolts', i.e. present their work at seminars and conferences and submit papers to journals, all of which enable supervisees to get feedback on their work. These, together with the alliances that develop in research groups between new and more experienced supervisees and post-doctoral researchers, induct the supervisee into the academic community, a process that is, Delamont et al. (2000) say, a powerful social mechanism for the generation of knowledge that is key to the intergenerational shaping of research skills and the development of a strong disciplinary culture.

In art therapy, the disciplinary culture of art making and group work invites an engagement with art at some point in the research process. I asked those supervisees who had taken part in studio-based research groups – usually occurring over a few days – whether these had informed their research. Respondents reported that they had '. . . helped clarify . . . helped shift my focus and get more directly to the meat of the issue' (D). For some they had been pivotal:

> Now we're talking! This has been very important. I might not realise it at the
> time but profound research understanding has flowed from this particular
> well. . . . The most complex and exasperating questions, thoughts and blocks
> have responded well to the wordless approach. (A)

Others, however, thought initially that introducing art making into a
research group was, although welcome, '. . . a bit indulgent – shouldn't I
just be sitting at home writing'. However, the '. . . more playful element in
the art-making is helpful' (O), as this person then went on to describe:

> The first time we used the art materials I found myself wandering off in my
> thinking . . . which was not unconnected to the research . . . but it led me to
> wonder how I was managing the emotional charge that the (work-related)
> problems were creating. In an entirely verbal discussion I don't think I would
> have allowed myself to wander off in what was, in the end a fruitful way. . . . I
> approached my thesis more directly and . . . began to think about the
> relationship between words and images and marks. . . . Maybe this is why
> using the art materials . . . could be really important because the dialectic
> between words and images is central to art therapy. (O)

Art-making in a supervisory context can thus mirror the discipline, and
often the research topic and research process, in useful and interesting
ways. Another spoke of deliberately exploring this:

> I decided to make visual symbols of the different binaries in parts of the
> research. I found that I was making symbols that didn't have any obvious
> reference though to the text. . . . Later I realised that the reason for this had
> been an unconscious play on pairs, pears which are yellow like lemons. I had
> slid pears into lemons without realizing. . . . There's something about the art
> being anarchic and only approachable on another level. Making the pairs did
> make me think of using binaries as the structuring agent of the project. (N)

How the art-making process informs the research process and how it is
subsequently spoken about is, however, not without difficulty because
conversation can revert to what was termed 'art therapy mode'.
Dissatisfaction with this may reflect the group's (and the discipline's)
learning and research about how art therapists situate and think about their

own art practice, but, as one respondent said, the use of art materials in a research group '. . . brought us together as a community – it has helped us to share the anxieties and the struggles, and getting a sense of how each other of us operates helps the verbal discussions immensely' (O).

There usually comes a time in the middle of the research process when the supervisee has amassed a pile of data; this is welcome (a sign of progress) but daunting (there is work to do). This is when the supervisory pair become truly engrossed as findings emerge and new and exciting discoveries are made. Here one of the supervisor's tasks is to help the supervisee with 'Staying on the ball – identify(ing) themes and connections' (E); another is to help the supervisee distinguish between important findings and other, less significant material that can be discarded, and yet other results that point to what might come next. The supervisor helps the supervisee concentrate on the essentials and see the overall shape of their emerging thesis, but s/he also has to ensure that the supervisee does not reach premature conclusions, miss unexpected findings or get caught in reactivity to the research. This can be particularly important when the research and/or writing about it '. . . carries the same dynamic as the case or theoretical area describes – the research supervisor needs insight into these things' (I).

Indeed she does. One supervisee was deep in the process of analysing a mass of visual and verbal data and, in supervision, seemed to have it all sewn up. I recall feeling rather exasperated and thinking that something important was missing. I challenged the analysis and suggested that there might be other, less immediately obvious findings and that the supervisee should re-visit the data with a more open mind. 'E' disappeared. Every now and then I would email and ask how things were going but there was no response. Time was ticking on and the date for submission of the thesis was approaching. I sent another, urgent message, and this time he telephoned me. He said, and reiterated in the questionnaire, that he had been 'devastated' when I had said in response to his data analysis: 'So what – we know this – what is new?'. I was horrified. How could I have said such a thing? My exasperation had been all too evident and had shaken E (and me) considerably, but he did revisit the material, as he described:

It caused me to go into myself and not want to carry on. When I tried to go back to the work I found a tremendous emotional and mental block – exhaustion. Although this was difficult at the time it did make me step back and look at myself and my work and how I was perceived, the work and myself. This in fact was my main learning and it was key to the whole project. The research became about critical reflection . . . you can only come to conclusions when you have had the feeling inside yourself and observed it. (E)

What seemed to have happened was that the supervisee had, subconsciously, looked for findings in the data that would address difficult workplace issues. This understandable sub-text, his 'blind spot', had clouded his vision and made it hard to see powerful material in the data about disempowerment. This had been enacted in the research, and then re-enacted in supervision.

Another supervisee had some unexpected and potentially tricky findings that were not directly related to her research question. It seemed to me that she was either unaware of their potential significance or was avoiding them because she feared they might be too hot to handle. She said:

> . . . I reported an outcome . . . in passing . . . which I had not recognised as significant or worthy of note and you helped me to see it as a valid finding in its own right although not the focus of the research . . . it opened up a new set of interesting questions, which was exciting and stimulating. I didn't know research was so alive! (G)

Learning like this cannot happen entirely through didactic methods. As Delamont *et al.* (1997, 2000) say, research is more like a craft that develops through experiential learning, project management and writing. Learning about research is social and occurs through enculturation into the traditions of research that come largely through supervision, e.g. about how peer review works, how research is situated in a context, how to balance this with data, findings, analysis and interpretation, and how to construct a thesis or research report. It also occurs through what Phillips and Pugh (2005) and Delamont *et al.* (1997, 2000) describe as supervisees seeing their supervisor 'at work', that is witnessing their supervisor's ongoing research activity through their teaching and publications. This continues in research supervision through conversations about areas of shared interest and research that have within them 'moments of intellectual connectedness' (L), of 'profound connectedness. . . . We do spark often and creativity flows in quite an unexpected way . . . new thoughts and synchronicities' (A). As interests converge there may be opportunities for joint presentations and papers, but areas of potential overlap need to be addressed sensitively so that neither is constrained by the research activity of the other. The supervisory relationship may thus develop into a truly collegial, working relationship and eventual friendship that lasts beyond the finite boundaries of a research project.

## Reaching the end

There comes a point when a supervisee has completed the data analysis and attention focuses entirely on producing drafts of chapters and, eventually, the whole thesis. Almost everyone commented in the questionnaires on the importance of prompt, detailed and practical feedback on drafts of written work that helped them to organise and edit their writing. This was cited as one of the most confidence-building things a supervisor could do: '. . . the most helpful thing in general terms was the giving of structure – and my certainty as a result, that I was going about the task in a good enough way' (I); '. . . this was an eye opener because it was actually direct, practical help, which helped my confidence enormously' (N). But by the time supervisees are writing-up a whole and final draft of their thesis they will have developed their own style and should be able to evaluate their own work; they will have become their own expert and the supervisor's interventions will consequently diminish. This is the point the research supervisor has worked towards from the start. At the beginning of research supervision the relationship between supervisor and supervisee is asymmetrical – one has more knowledge and experience of research than the other – but this changes as dependency diminishes and the supervisee's knowledge about their research exceeds the supervisor's.

As writing-up nears completion the supervisor and supervisee think together about who might be appropriate examiners. Examiners do not undertake work at either Master or doctoral levels because of financial reward but because it is interesting and supports the development of a discipline. A likely connection to the supervisee's topic is one guiding factor in approaching possible examiners of doctoral theses, as is sympathy to the basic assumptions and methodology of the thesis. The examination process includes a viva, i.e. an oral examination about the project. Delamont *et al.* (1997) say that supervisors can and should help to reduce their supervisee's anxiety by demystifying the process and reducing any likelihood of referral by ensuring that the supervisee has been properly obsessional and presented an impeccable thesis, and that s/he is well-prepared, e.g. through role-playing mock vivas. What should supervisees be prepared for? Tinkler and Jackson (2004) and Delamont *et al.* (2000) say that examiners judge a doctoral thesis according to a number of criteria: it should have a well-defined topic and research question; a thorough review of the literature; show the competent use of appropriate research methods; clear presentation of data; a proper relation to existing knowledge and use of theory; and offer a clear and coherent research 'storyline' that runs through the thesis. Ensuring that all these have been achieved is the primary task of the supervisory pair.

## Conclusion

I recall a supervisee whose anxiety at the beginning of her research caused her to go through everything in huge detail and to need frequent reassurance that all was well. When she eventually did a pilot interview there seemed to be difficulty with one question in particular and so we re-worded the question and re-jigged the interview schedule, only to discover in the interviews that her respondents faltered at exactly the same question. G's anxiety about her research design rose exponentially, but it became clear in supervision that responses to the problem question pointed to an important finding that was directly related to her primary research question. Her sudden realisation that process material like this was data – that what her respondents were unable to say was as interesting as what they did say – was very pleasing for us both.

It is hugely satisfying for both supervisee and supervisor to travel through the research process: to begin with a vague idea, then refine a research question, design, implement and conduct a project, and then to write it up and eventually produce the longed-for, final object. The containment of the person and their project throughout the whole process is critical. As one respondent said: 'Without this particular kind of containment I don't think I could possibly have completed' (C). Why? Because learning about and 'doing' research is an intensely personal process that can change how one views and operates in the world. 'Research', as one supervisee said, '. . . has become a landscape through which I'm travelling' (A). It is a fascinating process and a real privilege to be travelling alongside.

## References

Crick, P. (1992) 'Good supervision: on the experience of being supervised', *Psychoanalytic Psychotherapy*, 5 (3): 235–245.

Delamont, S., Atkinson, P. and Parry, O. (1997) *Supervising the PhD: A Guide to Success*, Buckingham: Open University Press.

Delamont, S., Atkinson, P. and Parry, O. (2000) *The Doctoral Experience: Success and Failure in Graduate School*, London: Falmer Press.

Driver, C. and Martin, E. (2002) *Supervising Psychotherapy: Psychoanalytic and Psychodynamic Perspectives*, London: Sage Publications.

Hawkins, P. and Shohet, R. (1989) *Supervision in the Helping Professions*, Milton Keynes: Open University Press.

McGlashan, R. (2003) 'The individuating supervisor', in J. Wiener, R. Mizen and J. Duckham (eds), *Supervising and Being Supervised: A Practice in Search of a Theory*, Basingstoke: Palgrave/Macmillan, pp. 19–33.

Mahony, J. (1994) 'Perceptions of art therapy and its absence in alcohol services', *Inscape*, 1: 15–18.

Mander, G. (2002) 'Supervision: between control and collusion', in C. Driver and E. Martin (eds), *Supervising Psychotherapy: Psychoanalytic and Psychodynamic Perspectives*, London: Sage Publications, pp. 38–50.

Phillips, E. and Pugh, D. (2005) *How to Get a PhD: A Handbook for Students and their Supervisors* (4th edn), Maidenhead: Open University Press.

Quality Assurance Agency (2001) *National Qualifications Framework*, Gloucester: QAA.

Quality Assurance Agency (2004) *Code of Practice for Research Degree Programmes*, Gloucester: QAA.

Stewart, J. (2002) 'The interface between teaching and supervision', in C. Driver and E. Martin (eds), *Supervising Psychotherapy: Psychoanalytic and Psychodynamic Perspectives*, London: Sage Publications, pp. 64–83.

Szecsody, I. (1990) 'Supervision: a didactic or mutative situation', *Psychoanalytic Psychoptherapy*, *4* (3): 245–264.

Tinkler, P. and Jackson, C. (2004) *The Doctoral Examination Process: A Handbook for Students, Examiners and Supervisors*, Buckingham: Open University Press.

Wiener, J., Mizen, R. and Duckham, J. (2003) *Supervising and Being Supervised: A Practice in Search of a Theory*, Basingstoke: Palgrave/Macmillan.

Wharton, B. (2003) 'Supervision in analytic training', in J. Wiener, R. Mizen and J. Duckham (eds), *Supervising and Being Supervised: A Practice in Search of a Theory*, Basingstoke: Palgrave/Macmillan, pp. 82–99.

Wood, M. (2002) 'Researching art therapy practice with people suffering from AIDs-related dementia', *Arts in Psychotherapy*, *29*: 207–219.

# Index